INSIGHTS INTO ROMANS

THE TWO PILLARS OF FAITH IN CHRISTIANITY

GAYLORD I. BOWMAN

authorHOUSE®

AuthorHouse™
1663 Liberty Drive
Bloomington, IN 47403
www.authorhouse.com
Phone: 833-262-8899

Published by AuthorHouse 10/12/2020

ISBN: 978-1-7283-7027-9 (sc)
ISBN: 978-1-7283-7025-5 (hc)
ISBN: 978-1-7283-7026-2 (e)

Library of Congress Control Number: 2020915658

Print information available on the last page.

Dedication

Some time ago I attended a dramatic presentation
directed by one of my granddaughters at her church.

In particular, I remember a statement
made by one of the characters.

He said, "You really cannot understand the meaning or depth
of love until you have looked upon the face of God."

Romans is a book about God's love for us
when we really don't deserve it.

This book is dedicated to all those willing to look upon the face
of God and discover the meaning and depth of God's love for us.

Contents

Introduction

Because of the importance of the doctrines defined in Romans, many commentaries have been written about it. Unfortunately, many have been written by Bible scholars desirous of demonstrating their personal scholarship and as a result present a dissertation that often requires the reader to be familiar with obscure theological terms. Greek was the language of the original manuscripts and therefore an understanding of the language is invaluable. However, you can become so involved in the nuances of the Greek language that the true message of Romans becomes lost.

The Bible is written to be understood by everyone, layman as well as the theological scholar. After over thirty-five years as a missionary in another culture, I am deeply conscious of the need to communicate in a way that can be understood by everyone. In this book, I have attempted to present the material in a way that will provide a clear understanding of the message of Romans. For this reason, some may find its presentation too simplistic. While you may view it as lacking in profound theological dissertations, I hope you will, instead, discover the essential message of Romans. My prayer is that many of you may find a new appreciation of what is one of the greatest books in the Bible on Christian doctrine.

Romans was intended by Paul to be a clear doctrinal statement of the message of Jesus Christ as it apples to the individual believer. The book of Romans identifies many important foundational doctrines of Christianity. It is as we learn these great evangelical truths and apply them to our lives, that we are truly "born again." When Paul wrote this letter, the gospel message had been preached for over a quarter-century in hundreds of towns and villages.

It was written at a time when there were hundreds, perhaps thousands, of people still living who had walked with, talked with, or personally heard Jesus Christ. There is probably no other book in the Bible whose authenticity has been more widely accepted by those who had personally lived or experienced its message as taught by Christ. Because of the accuracy of its message, it soon became the accepted go-to source for many of the foundational truths of Christianity.

Many commentaries and students of Romans miss an important principle of Paul's understanding of Christianity. They understand the message of Romans to be that a simple declaration to "believe on the Lord Jesus Christ" is all that is necessary to become a Christian. The New Testament tells us that when Jesus came into contact with men possessed of demons, the demons themselves often loudly acknowledged that Jesus was the Son of God, and they said it with fear and trembling. However, their acknowledgement of the deity of Jesus did not mean they were saved by this proclamation.

While Paul understood the necessity of a personal faith that accepted Jesus Christ as the Son of God, he also recognized the need for that faith to be evidential. Paul puts it this way in Romans1:16-17,: *"For I am not ashamed of the gospel, for it is the power of God for salvation to everyone who believes, to the Jew first and also to the Greek. For in it the righteousness of God is revealed from faith to faith; as it is written, 'But the righteous man shall live by faith.'"* Notice the two objectives of faith that Paul identifies. In verse 16, he says our salvation comes from our faith to believe in the power of God; in verse 17, he says our faith is revealed as we live a righteous life. Many "Christians" profess a belief in Christ, but fail to show evidence of that faith in their lives.

In Romans, Paul will show that through Jesus Christ God's grace provides for our eternal salvation. He will also say that this faith must be accompanied by evidence in the life of the believer, if indeed it is a genuine faith. We are justified by faith, and we are also sanctified by faith. These are the twin pillars of a complete Christian.

It is my sincere hope that as you read and study this book, God will cause its message to move in your life in a new, vital, and exciting way. May you see the face of God's love in this book, and may you be moved to act upon this revelation in your life.

Setting the Scene

Let's take time to look at some of the ingredients that make this book so important for us to study. To better understand Romans we must try and put ourselves in the author's shoes. If we understand his motivations and the situation around him, it will help us understand what he is trying to accomplish in his writing. In this section, I will share something about the author—those he was writing to, and what he was trying to accomplish when he wrote the book of Romans.

The Author:

Paul is identified as the author of this epistle in its very first verse. Therefore let's look at some of the things that shaped Paul's life and made him the man of God that he was.

He was born in the city of Tarsus, the capital of Cilicia, in what is now southern Turkey. At the time he was born, this city was second only to the cities of Athens and Alexandria in its importance as a center of education. Both his parents were Jewish and also Roman citizens, which was rare at that time. However, his parents were proud of their Jewish heritage and gave their son the Hebrew name of Saul and were careful to see that he was raised according to the Jewish traditions of that time. This meant that as a young boy (five to thirteen years of age), he was expected to study the Torah (the Jewish scriptures) and also learn the value of working at the family trade. In Saul's case, he received training as a tentmaker, probably because the goats, which were the main source of the hair required to make the rough cloth used for the tents, flourished in this area, making this a common trade in that community.

Saul apparently was a good student of the Torah, and at thirteen undoubtedly had his *"bar mitzvah."* After thirteen, young men who showed special promise in their studies of the Torah were encouraged to continue onto rabbinical studies. In Saul's case, he continued his rabbinical studies in Jerusalem, being taught, as he testifies, at the feet of Gamaliel (Acts 22:3: *"I am a Jew, born in Tarsus of Cilicia, but brought up in this city, educated under Gamaliel, strictly according to the law of our fathers..."*). Gamaliel was a highly regarded teacher of the Law, and was also the grandson of the famous rabbi Hillel. Saul's studies under Gamaliel were concentrated on gaining an extensive knowledge of the Torah and Jewish law. Saul apparently excelled in this as he eventually became a Pharisee, noted for his zealous defense of the Jewish tradition. According to Acts 26:10, he even appeared to be a voting member of the Sanhedrin, the governing body of Judaism, though he was still considered a young man.

It was while Saul was at the height of his zeal of Judaism that Jesus Christ met him on the road to Damascus. Think of how Saul must have felt when he heard the voice of Jesus Christ coming from heaven, telling him that his attacks against the Christians were personal attacks against Himself, the Messiah, the Son of God. Remember at this time Saul thought of Jesus as a enemy of Judaism. This dramatic meeting with Christ, accompanied by Christ's offer of forgiveness, irrevocably changed Saul's life and his name. As a result of his personal experience with the "grace" of Jesus Christ, he was to transfer the same zeal in his new ministry that he had exhibited previously in his defense of the Jewish Law and its traditions.

After his Damascus road experience, Paul spent three years in the wilderness. Up to now, Saul had been living and studying in Israel using his Hebrew name. From here on we will use his Latin name, Paul, as his ministry was now to the world, not just Israel.

Upon his return to Jerusalem, Jewish Christians treated him with suspicion, as they remembered his past actions in persecuting them. As a result, he soon returned to his home city of Tarsus and took up his trade of tent making. A few years later, he was approached by a Christian named Barnabas, asking for help in leading a ministry in the city of Antioch. Paul quickly agreed, and with his new zeal to preach the gospel of Christ's grace, he soon found himself commissioned to set out on a journey to spread the gospel to the pagan world around him. His first missionary journey was to last five years, after which he was asked to return to Jerusalem to give a report on his activities and to explain his actions in emphasizing a ministry to the Gentiles. There he again shared his experience on the road to Damascus, and how Jesus had told him he was to be His chosen minister to the Gentiles. After receiving the blessings and encouragement of the church in Jerusalem, he immediately set out on his second missionary journey. This one was to last about four years. After a short rest, he then set off on his third (and last?) missionary journey, which was to last for five more years.

It was on his third missionary journey, while staying in Corinth, probably during the winter of 57 A.D., that Paul wrote Romans. When Paul wrote this epistle, he had not yet been to Rome and felt the need to introduce himself and his ministry and to explain his motives in writing to them. He must have decided that the best way to do this was to share the principal doctrines of the gospel as he had come to understand them. At the same time, Paul wanted to give them notice of an impending visit, and his desire for their prayers and support for a planned missionary journey to Spain.

Many apparently opposing qualities made up Paul's fitness for his life's work. His own life was a unique blend of three principal cultural and social influences. He lived the first twelve years of his life in one of the centers of Greek culture and literature. From birth, he also enjoyed all the privileges that were associated with Roman citizenship.

Finally, born of Jewish parents, he had been thoroughly educated in Judaism and a strict adherence of the Mosaic Law. He was Hebrew in heart and mind, yet had been exposed to the philosophies of the Greek culture, while at the same time experiencing the privileges and advantages of a freeborn Roman citizen.

Here was a man, called Saul among the Jews and Paul among the Gentiles, who as the "Apostle of the Gentiles," was to become known throughout the Christian world. He was a man with a brilliant intellect, an iron will, a compassionate heart, and a man who was at the same time ardent, energetic, uncompromising, and severe. But it was his sudden and miraculous conversion and call by Christ that was to leave the greatest mark on his life and leave him with a special appreciation of the meaning of God's grace and forgiveness. By the time he wrote this epistle, Paul had experienced the many trials mentioned in 2 Corinthians 11. Yet he was a man who unquestionably lived a life of complete dedication and love for Jesus Christ.

The Recipients of the Letter: the Church in Rome

Probably no single individual man was responsible for founding the church in Rome. In a sense, you could say Peter may have had an important hand in it. In Peter's audience on Pentecost were devout men who were sojourners from Rome, both Jews and proselytes (see Acts 2:10). It would have been surprising if some of these converts to Christianity did not make their way back to Rome. It was undoubtedly these Jews and proselytes who had witnessed the miracle of Pentecost and had returned to their homes in Rome that were responsible for started the church in Rome. In the beginning, these "lay" people were primarily Jews, or Gentiles who had previously been converted to Judaism.

The church in Rome experienced a strong Jewish influence as a result. This was to change as the Jews were eventually forced by the authorities to leave the capital at different times. In the meantime, Gentile Christians from Judea, Asia Minor, and Greece found their way to Rome and the church. Previously the Jews had insisted that many of the traditional privileges and customs of Judaism be incorporated into the fledgling Christian church. With the growing number of Gentile Christians now joining the church in Rome, its demographics became increasingly Gentile who, being free from the cultural and religious prejudices of the Jews, were open to the message of the gospel. These different elements of the early church were often in conflict and had a divisive effect on the church. This same evolution was being repeated throughout the world as the Christian church began assuming its eventual unique identity. In his letter Paul was to address these issues.

Rome was the capital of what was, at that time, one of the greatest empires in the world. Nobody was more conscious of that than those who lived in Rome. There was no doubt in their minds that they were the *privileged* of the *privileged*. As a result, those from outlying areas were considered their social inferiors. After all, Rome had all the greatest men, the latest philosophies, the latest in plays and entertainment, including a variety of sports, and all the best religions. In other words they were the "crème de la crème."

This same mentality is associated today with many residents of capital cities the world over. In the United States, those living in Washington D.C. like to think that the world moves around what happens in their city. New Yorkers consider themselves as true cosmopolitans; Bostonians consider themselves special because of their historical heritage; and the Angelinos, the brash, uncouth, yet dynamic people of Los Angeles, consider themselves the center of a changing world. If you were to look at the newspapers from each of these areas, you can sense different writing styles for each area. Paul, knowing the people to whom he was writing, wrote in a style that would appeal to them; therefore, we will find that the Book of Romans has a distinctive flavor all its own when compared with Paul's other writings.

Helpful Hints on Understanding the Book of Romans

Corinth is likely the place where Paul wrote this epistle, since Phoebe of nearby Cenchrea was apparently entrusted with carrying the letter to the church in Rome (see Romans 16:1-2). The epistle was written just as Paul was about to set out on what was to be his last journey back to Jerusalem.

This book was not written in the informal style of Paul's other epistles, but as a formal, logical presentation of his message, a style designed to be appreciated by the "superior Romans." Whatever the philosophical beliefs and intellectual capacity of the believers in Rome, Paul paid them the compliment of believing they would understand what he wrote. The Jews needed instruction with respect to God's promises to Israel and their part in the fulfillment of Christianity. For the Gentiles, basic Christian doctrines needed to be clarified, and they needed advice on practical matters involving the Christian lifestyle and its effect on those around them.

The Greek and Roman world of Paul's day was filled with people who believed they had no future. According to Greek and Roman philosophy, at the moment of death, there was no future hope for the body or the soul. As a result, Paul mentions the subject of hope in Romans more than in any other New Testament book.

We will discover that this book's foundational subject is "Justification by Faith." We will also discover that a key element in Romans is "righteousness." Where can it be found, and how can we be assured of receiving it?

A recurring theme in Romans is salvation; a salvation presented in terms of the righteousness of God, which when received by the individual in faith will be evidenced in a new life for the believer (see Romans 1:16-17). Paul will show that both the Jews and Gentiles are in need of the same salvation, and that they must be united, freed of national prejudices and traditions, as a living example for believers of all nations. He will show that the gospel as the power of God unto salvation is meaningless apart from the individual's awareness of sin, condemnation, misery, death, and a desire to live a righteous life.

The first eight chapters expound the basic doctrines of the gospel as understood by Paul. The next three chapters are national and answer questions regarding the special relationship of the gospel to the Jews. The remaining chapters are practical, as they show how we are to apply the doctrines of the gospel to our individual conduct. In the end, Romans is intended as a complete expression of the Apostle Paul's doctrines as they apply to Christianity. Martin Luther, hundreds of years later, was to call it "The Masterpiece of the New Testament."

Chapter 1

Introductions

Introduction:

Paul had three purposes in writing this chapter:

- To introduce himself, his ministry, and his motivation in writing to the Romans.
- To introduce the gospel that he preaches.
- To show that no one is exempt from their need of the gospel.

Paul introduces himself, his ministry, and his motivation for writing in verse 1 and verses 5 through 15. This is the longest introduction of any Pauline epistle. The reason is that he had never previously visited this city, nor had a part in the founding of the church in Rome. Therefore, Paul uses these introductory verses to identify his authority as an apostle, to congratulate them on their testimony among the brethren, and to notify them of his intention to visit Rome soon.

Paul introduces the gospel that he preaches in verses 2 through 4 and in verses 16 and 17. In verses 2 through 4, he identifies the gospel as something God had promised in times past to the Jews. In verses 16 and 17, he identifies the gospel as believing in Jesus Christ and then living a life in conformance with that belief.

Paul begins with the presentation of the doctrine of justification by faith in verses 18 through 32. These verses are designed to show that all men are subject to condemnation by a just God.

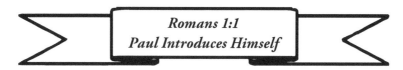

Romans 1:1
Paul Introduces Himself

Verse 1: Paul, a bond-servant of Christ Jesus, called as an apostle, set apart for the gospel of God,

Paul immediately identifies himself as the author of this epistle. Then identifies his credentials as a messenger of God.

He begins by identifying himself as *"a bond-servant."* A more accurate translation might be "bond-slave." Among the Jews, if a person had encumbered himself with debts he couldn't pay, his creditors could auction them off as a slave. The price the highest bidder paid was then divided among the creditors. The person thus auctioned off must serve six years as a slave. After serving six years he was eligible to be freed, however if he decided he wanted to continue as a slave in that household, and if his master was agreeable, the owner would then bore a hole through the lobe of the slave's right ear with an awl. This identified them as a "bond-slave" to that master for the rest of their life. Therefore, in ancient Israel, to call someone God's "a bond-servant" was a declaration of his irrevocable and voluntary commitment to serving God as long as they lived.

Second, Paul declares himself as *"an apostle."* An apostle means "one who is sent." Notice he uses the adjective "called." To Paul, his being an apostle was because Jesus had specifically chosen him to be His witness. Acts 9:15 indicates that Jesus thought so too when he instructed Ananias as to what to say to Paul - (*"But the Lord said to him, 'Go, for he is a chosen instrument of Mine,..'"*). Paul based his claim on the fact that he had received his commission directly from Christ Himself.

To be accepted as an apostle in those days, it was necessary to have seen Christ and to have personal knowledge of His life and doctrines, and the person's commission had to have been confirmed by the signs accompanying his labors. In 1 Corinthians 9:1 Paul says, *"Am I not free? Am I not an apostle? Have I not seen Jesus our Lord? ..."* and later in 2 Corinthians 12:12, *"the signs of a true apostle were performed among you with all perseverance, by signs and wonders and miracles."*

Third, Paul says he was *"set apart for the gospel of God."* "Set apart for," indicates that its proclamation was to be his primary task. Paul considered himself separated *for* something, not *from* something. Paul was convinced that his compulsion to proclaim the gospel was from God Himself. Thus Paul identifies his spiritual credentials to the people in Rome.

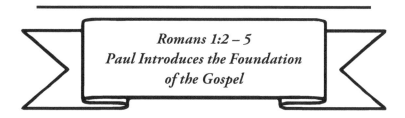

Romans 1:2 – 5
Paul Introduces the Foundation
of the Gospel

Verse 2 which He promised beforehand through His prophets in the holy Scriptures,

Paul now focuses on the origin of the gospel he preaches. He begins by declaring that the gospel he preaches was specifically promised by God in *"the holy Scriptures."* To Paul the gospel that he preaches was the fulfillment of God's promises made to the Jews and through the prophets in the Old Testament. The gospel was not a contradiction of Judaism, but rather represents its completion and fulfillment.

Verse 3 concerning His Son, who was born of a descendant of David according to the flesh,

Paul reminds his readers that Old Testament prophecy predicted that the Messiah would come from the genealogy of David. To fulfill God's promise regarding His Son's human ancestry, it was necessary to limit His descent from David to His human nature, so we find the added explanation *"according to the flesh."* What Mary mothered was a natural body for God to indwell. John 1:14 says, *"And the Word became flesh, and dwelt among us, and we beheld His glory, glory as of the only begotten from the Father, full of grace and truth."* Paul is informing his readers that the gospel he preaches is about the Son of God, the Messiah who was promised in the Scriptures, and that this Son was a flesh-and-blood descendent of David.

Verse 4 *who was declared the Son of God with power by the resurrection from the dead, according to the Spirit of holiness, Jesus Christ our Lord,*

It is helpful to understand that the Greek word translated as "declared" could also be translated "defined" or "demonstrated." Paul now goes on to tell his readers that the person he preaches about demonstrated his authenticity as the Son of God by showing His ability to conquer death. Resurrection did not make Jesus the Son of God; it simply was the seal of God as to the authenticity of His declaration that He was the Son of God. Paul's purpose here is to show the *Deity* of Jesus Christ, who had occupied a human form.

Verse 5 *through whom we have received grace and apostleship to bring about the obedience of faith among all the Gentiles, for His name's sake,*

This verse summarizes a threefold progression in Paul's calling:

- "**grace**" - by which he was saved;
- "**apostleship**" - his being set apart to be Christ's witness;
- *"to bring about the obedience of faith among all the Gentiles"*

One of the clearest definitions of grace is that it is "God's undeserved favor on mankind." Paul acknowledges that it was because of Christ's grace he received his calling as an apostle.

Next we see that the message is intended to bring about mankind's obedience to God through their declaration of faith.

Finally, he emphasizes his special commission as an apostle to the Gentiles. The Greek word "Ethnos" translated "Gentiles," literally means "a race," "a nation." Therefore, his work was meant for all mankind.

Notice the four special features in the above verses regarding the gospel that Paul preaches. First, in verse 2 we see that his message is in accordance with the Scriptures.

Second, in verses 3 and 4, we see that the message is about God's Son, whose identity was authenticated by His resurrection. Third, in verse 5 we see that the gospel is for everyone. Fourth, in verse 5 it was meant to bring about the obedience of all mankind to God. Truly, here is the gospel of Jesus Christ in a nutshell.

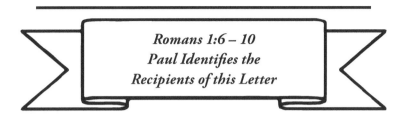

Romans 1:6 – 10
Paul Identifies the
Recipients of this Letter

Verse 6 among whom you also are the called of Jesus Christ;

One thing we often forget about Paul is that he could be very diplomatic when the occasion required. In these next verses Paul compliments the recipients of this letter and identifies with them. In our day, we would say he "attempts to establish a rapport with them." Notice how Paul includes those in Rome: *"you also are the called,"* as possessing the same calling that he has received. He begins by noting that they became believers because of the effectual calling of Christ.

Verse 7 to all who are beloved of God in Rome, called as saints: Grace to you and peace from God our Father and the Lord Jesus Christ.

Notice how Paul manages to describe the source of their salvation, their physical location, and their special relationship with Jesus Christ.

First, Paul identifies his readers as "***beloved of God in Rome.***" Second, they are saints by virtue of having been "***called***" by God.

He concludes with a benediction. Grace and peace come from the conviction that that the Lord loves us, lives in us, and protects us.

Verse 8 First, I thank my God through Jesus Christ for you all, because your faith is being proclaimed throughout the whole world.

Three things are of interest in this verse. First, for Paul, God was not a philosophical abstraction, but a personal friend. He was *my* God. Second, his prayers for them are "through" Jesus Christ, acknowledging that Jesus

Christ is our intercessor before God. Third, he congratulates them for having a faith that is known throughout the world. Now that's quite a testimony. What an encouragement this had to be to those in Rome!

Verse 9 For God, whom I serve in my spirit in the preaching of the gospel of His Son, is my witness as to how unceasingly I make mention of you,

Verse 10 always in my prayers making request, if perhaps now at last by the will of God I succeed in coming to you.

Now Paul moves on to assuring the church in Rome of his personal concern for them. Paul appeals to God as his witness that he constantly prays for them and desires to visit them.

Paul begins his doctrinal instruction by clarifying that the gospel he preaches is ***"the gospel of His Son."*** Notice how in verse one he called it ***"the gospel of God."*** It was only after he had shown how the gospel of God had been fulfilled in His Son in the previous verses that he now identifies that the gospel is that of His Son.

In verse ten, Paul wants them to understand that his prayers for them have been ***"unceasing"*** and specific. This is one of the keys to a successful prayer life, the willingness to make our prayers specific. Finally, Paul acknowledges that his prayers were always subject to ***"the will of God."*** Paul's prayers were frequent, specific, and mindful of God's will.

Romans 1:11 – 15
Paul Declares His
Purpose in Writing to Them

Verse 11 For I long to see you in order that I may impart some spiritual gift to you, that you may be established;

Now Paul identifies the reasons behind his desire to visit them. Because Paul loved to teach the Word of God, it created within him a longing to visit them *"in order that I may impart some spiritual gift to you."* Paul always wanted to share the gospel in such a way that it would provide a better understanding of Jesus Christ. In Rome, Paul wanted to do this that they might have a stronger spiritual foundation.

Verse 12 *that is, that I may be encouraged together with you while among you, each of us by the other's faith, both yours and mine.*

Paul is careful to place himself on the same level as the Roman believers by stating that his presence in Rome will result in a *mutual* encouragement. In truth, at no time can any minister stand before others and teach and preach the Word of God without being just as encouraged and established in the faith as the listeners may be. An equality of fellowship is produced in the sharing of a "common faith."

Verse 13 *And I do not want you to be unaware, brethren, that often I have planned to come to you and have been prevented thus far in order that I might obtain some fruit among you also, even as among the rest of the Gentiles.*

The Romans had probably expected a visit from him earlier, so he explains that he had been delayed from visiting them earlier, because he had felt God leading him in other directions.

Paul shares that he wants to visit them: *"that I might obtain some fruit among you also."* This quest for spiritual fruit was the objective in all of Paul's activities. What was this fruit that he expected to obtain? It was witnessing personal growth in spiritual knowledge and in the sharing of a mutual love in service of the Lord. To Paul, this was the desired result in his ministry.

Finally, Paul is deeply conscious that he had a special calling as "the apostle to the Gentiles." He goes on to say that he expects the same fruit in them that he has experienced in his ministry to the Gentiles.

Verse 14 *I am under obligation both to Greeks and to barbarians, both to the wise and to the foolish.*

In this verse, we see the first of Paul's "I am" statements. Here it is ***"I am under obligation."*** Paul felt an obligation to God to preach to both Greeks and barbarians; that is, to both the learned and unlearned, and to those who were civilized and those who weren't. Paul wanted to make it clear that the gospel was open to everyone without distinctions of nationality or cultural development. The inclusion of ***"to the wise and to the foolish"*** was intended to identify individuals' reactions to their acceptance to his message of the gospel. It seems many churches today are willing to compromise the gospel message so as not to offend the "foolish" of the world?

Paul's strong feelings may have risen from feeling that he had personally experienced God's grace and forgiveness, even after a life dedicated to persecuting Christians.

Verse 15 Thus, for my part, I am eager to preach the gospel to you also who are in Rome.

Here we see the second of Paul's "I am" statements: ***"I am eager."*** This statement is an admission of Paul's personal desire to preach to the church in Rome. The preaching that Paul is talking about is the proclamation of the gospel to those who are already believers, with a view to a deepening of their understanding of God and a strengthening of their faith. Notice that there is an intimation that whether he does so or not, rests not with him, but with God.

One of the lessons we might learn from Paul is that even if one has the intellectual and formal preparation for preaching, but is lacking in zeal, he cannot hope for much success.

Some Observations on Verses 1-15

These first fifteen verses are an example of Paul's diplomacy when confronting other believers. He begins by establishing his credentials as an apostle. He points out that the gospel he preaches is not new, but was prophesized in the Scriptures (i.e., the Old Testament). Paul goes on to compliment his readers on their faithfulness to God.

Paul expresses his desire to visit them and gives three things he hopes to accomplish with a visit: 1) that he might help them grow spiritually; 2) that the Romans might be an encouragement to him; and 3) that he might experience spiritual fruit among them.

Paul closes with how he feels obligated to God to preach the gospel to everybody whatever their situation.

For Paul, his being an "ex-persecutor" of Jesus Christ undoubtedly left him especially desirous of working to please Christ in return for the forgiveness that he had received. Success to Paul was in the faithful proclamation of the gospel. The results were in the hands of a forgiving Savior.

Paul's example should remind each believer of their sacred obligation to proclaim the gospel to all men, because of the debt we owe to a Savior who forgave us while we still were sinners. If Paul was never able to get over the act of grace by Jesus Christ in forgiving him, how can we?

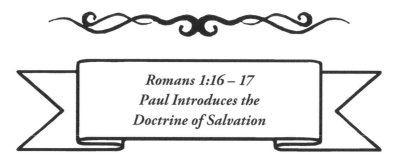

Romans 1:16 – 17
Paul Introduces the
Doctrine of Salvation

Verse 16** **For I am not ashamed of the gospel, for it is the power of God for salvation to everyone who believes, to the Jew first and also to the Greek.

This verse begins with the third of Paul's "I am's": ***"For I am not ashamed of the gospel."*** Because he hadn't shared the gospel in Rome, he apparently felt that some might have felt his was due to timidity or fear that the gospel might seem impotent and ineffectual in that great capital city. Paul wanted to make it clear that he was not ashamed to preach Christ anywhere, and identifies four reasons why he was not ashamed of the gospel.

A. Because of what it is: "*for it is the power of God*" Interestingly the word "power" in Greek is "Dunamis," the same word we use to derive the word "dynamite." The power of the gospel transformed Paul's life, and he would never forget it. Paul had witnessed God's power changing lives everywhere he preached.

B. Because of what it does: "*for salvation*"
Salvation's basic meaning is that we have been saved (past tense) from that which would or could cause us harm or even death. You could say salvation means "deliverance" from harm. To Paul, the gospel is responsible for bringing about the deliverance of mankind from God's condemnation and death and to offer eternal life instead.

C. Because of whom it's for: "*to everyone*"
To the Jew first, and then to the Greek, was the divinely planned historical order of the presentation of the gospel. The problem was the Jews misunderstood the significance of their calling. They believed it was corporate, and that to be born a "Jew" was to be assured of God's good favor. When the Jews refused to accept Jesus Christ as God's Son, it was then that God moved the disciples and the apostles to proclaim the gospel to the Gentiles. However, it was always God's intent that the gospel was intended for everyone.

D. Because of its simplicity: "*who believes*"
Salvation has no reality, validity, or meaning apart from a personal declared belief in God. The acceptance of Jesus Christ is always a personal matter.

Verse 17 For in it the righteousness of God is revealed from faith to faith; as it is written, "But the righteous man shall live by faith."

Here Paul identifies how one's declaration of faith must be evidential in our lives.

A. "*For in it the righteousness of God is revealed.*" For something to be revealed it must be seen by others to confirm its existence. God allowed the sacrifice of His Son for man's sins in order that man might appear righteous before God. God's righteousness is revealed by this provision of salvation in spite of mankind's sinful nature.

B. *"From faith to faith"*: Here is one of the most important doctrines concerning man's salvation. It is how faith in the gospel and God's righteousness is revealed in man. The requirement of the first faith can be seen in the previous verse when Paul notes that the first requirement for salvation is to believe. Believe what? Paul shows us in verses two through four, that it is the belief that Jesus Christ is the Son of God and was sent by God to earth in the form of a man. The second faith governs the believer's continuing existence as a child of God when it says *"But the righteous man shall live by faith."* Faith that says it believes, but does not accompany that belief by action in support of that belief, is incomplete. Christian faith is like two columns that hold up the front of a building. If you remove either one, the front of the building will collapse. It takes both columns – belief and action - to support the building. For Paul it is the evidence of a changed life that demonstrates the validity of our declaration of faith that we believe.

Some Observations on Verses 16-17

These two verses are two of the most important verses in the New Testament.. Many theologians would have you to understand Paul taught that to believe that Jesus is God's Son was all we needed to be saved. These two verses point out that Paul felt that such declaration of faith was not enough. The validity of a faith to believe must be evidenced in a changed life. In this, Paul is in complete agreement with Jesus and James, Jesus' brother.

In John 15:1-11, Jesus compares God, His Father, with a caretaker of a vineyard. He, Jesus, was the vine, and the believers were the branches. Jesus notes that the branches that produced no fruit were worthy, only of being destroyed by fire. However, if the branches produced fruit, it was evidence that they were obtaining their life from the vine. In James 2:14-26, James notes that our deeds are evidence of our faith, and that if no deeds are evident, our faith is dead. Paul says in verse 17 here, that God is revealed in our "faith to faith." The first faith is to believe in Jesus. The second faith is the faith to live a righteous life. Without both, we are incomplete. A declaration of faith without accompanying deeds is a mere intellectual assent to the probable truth of the matter, without the inner conviction of it. It is like telling everyone that a particular switch will turn on the lights, yet you avoid flipping that switch to turn on the lights. Your declaration is not accompanied by the i conviction of the truth of the matter. What do others think when they don't see evidence of Christ in your life, in-spite of your declarations of fidelity to Him?

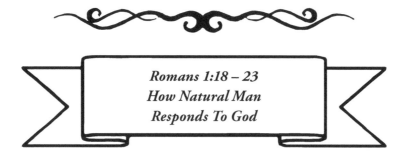

Romans 1:18 – 23
How Natural Man
Responds To God

Verse 18** **For the wrath of God is revealed from heaven against all ungodliness and unrighteousness of men, who suppress the truth in unrighteousness,

Notice how the presentation of God's character changes from the previous verse. In verse 17, the righteousness of God is revealed, and in this verse, the wrath of God is revealed. Both righteousness and wrath are legitimate parts of God's character. The difference is the gospel. The gospel provides a way for sinful man to make himself righteous before God, thereby avoiding the just wrath of God.

In many ways, this verse summarizes of the rest of this chapter. The preaching of the gospel is at the same time the revelation of the righteousness of God in dealing with men, and also the revelation of God's wrath against the sinful nature of man. Our objection to the idea of the wrath of God is shaped by human experience, which says wrath is evidence of an emotional loss of control. However, God's wrath is not an emotion, but rather a holy reaction to that which is in rebellion against Him. Ephesians 5:6: *"Let no one deceive you with empty words, for because of these things the wrath of God comes upon the sons of disobedience."*

The object of God's wrath is the result of ungodliness and unrighteousness of man. The first identifies an irreverence of the nature of God; the second, an irreverence of His ordinances, His law. Both represent attitudes of rebellion against God. Since man recognizes that certain acts must result in punishment from a just God, man prefers to *"suppress the truth in unrighteousness."* In other words, man chooses to ignore God's truth by attempting to ignore His existence. Herein lies the foundation of the theory of evolution and humanism.

Verse 19 *because that which is known about God is evident within them; for God made it evident to them.*

The existence of God is inescapably revealed within all men. When creation is rationally viewed, its very order shows the necessity of a Creator. The nature of mankind inherently wants to feel that they are not mere transient accidents, but that life has a meaning and purpose. Man's struggle to make life meaningful can only be successful when he acknowledges the existence of a Creator God, much like a child is most at peace when he knows there is someone who cares for him and gives him a sense of direction and purpose.

Verse 20 *For since the creation of the world His invisible attributes, His eternal power and divine nature, have been clearly seen, being understood through what has been made, so that they are without excuse.*

Paul tells us that our inner awareness, which knows there is a God, also possesses an awareness of God's nature and attributes.

This verse identifies four characteristics of the revelation of nature in creation:

- *It has never changed since the creation of the world.* The word translated "world" is "kosmos" in Greek, which literally translates to "order." In other words, this can be translated "since the creation

13

of order." There are several unchanging physical laws that govern the natural world around us. Gravity, the speed of light, heat always flows from the warmer to the colder, every animate thing is dying (i.e., losing energy) these are just a few of the unchanging laws of nature. To accept any view but that of an intelligent Creator, we must deny the unchanging nature of those laws.

- *It is a reflection of God's power and divine nature.* Probably the first impression nature gives us is a feeling of personal insignificance. We cannot look over the countryside without feelings of awe at the complexity and attention to detail seen in the world around us. If we are being honest with ourselves we recognize that "Man could not have done it better." While observing the glories of nature, we cannot help but be aware of the evidence of the "order" of creation. Perfection is not an accident, but the result of a perfect Creator.

- **It can be clearly seen.** A person who looks at a masterpiece by Rembrandt may be said to be looking at the inward nature of Rembrandt, for the artist has expressed himself in his painting. So it is as man views nature; we are seeing the inward nature of the God of creation. We cannot sit by a campfire at night by a lake in the mountains, with a waterfall flowing into it at its opposite end, listen to the quiet sounds of life around us, and sing "How great though art," and not be impressed with the evidence of God's perfect creation.

- **It can be understood.** Revelation in creation does not stop with perception, but we cannot escape the conclusion that it can only be understood if there is a Creator. Psalms 19:1: *"The heavens are telling of the glory of God; And their expanse is declaring the work of His hands."* Job 12:7: *"But now ask the beasts, and let them teach you; And the birds of the heavens, and let them tell you."* Job 12:8: *"Or speak to the earth, and let it teach you; And let the fish of the sea declare to you."* Finally Job 12:9 says: *"Who among all these does not know That the hand of the Lord has done this…?"*

"So that they are without excuse." We have never discovered an ancient culture that was atheistic. It wasn't until worship came under the control of men that man became polytheistic. God will judge the heathen

by the light of what they perceive in nature, but what about you and me? How can we look at the perfection of a newborn baby and not see the perfection of God before us? The height of ignorance is to look at that baby and think that he is the result of some accidental evolution from primeval slime into a four-legged animal, then into an ape, and finally into this evidential perfection in front of us.

Verse 21 ***For even though they knew God, they did not honor Him as God, or give thanks; but they became futile in their speculations, and their foolish heart was darkened.***

Paul now identifies an important principle: religious knowledge, unless acted upon, will always lead to futile speculations. The mind of man has a religious vacuum; where there is the absence of God, there is always the presence of an alternative to God. All religious knowledge is based upon an image that man has formed of God in their minds. They would much prefer their god to be one of their own creation, rather than acknowledging a superior God for in this way they can ignore their accountability towards Him. The result is humanism, the worship of self, which denies the existence of God in spite of clear evidence to the contrary. The end result is the ultimate moving away from God and "*becoming futile in their speculations.*"

Verse 22 ***Professing to be wise, they became fools,***

The best definition I know of is that wisdom is "the ability to use the knowledge you possess in a way that will improve that which you contend with." When man refuses to acknowledge the existence of God and insists upon his own interpretation of the existence of things around him, he falls into the fatal error of the presupposition that there is no Creator. It is a fatal mistake philosophical enlightenment for spiritual illumination. The Greek word that is translated "became fools" is the same word we use to get the English word "moron," or someone who is incapable of learning or reasoning.

Those who refuse to accept God as the Creator are the authors of theories and mistaken beliefs, as popular as they are empty and absurd.

The more they boast of their wisdom, the more conspicuous becomes the incompetence of their thinking.

In the absence of God in our lives the inevitable result is the loss of the positive physical and moral values that God imparts. A good example of this can be found in our nation and schools today. As they separate themselves from God, they experience the loss of the individual moral responsibility that God imparts. The consequence is the increasing presence of violence in our nation and schools. It is then when they ask the foolish question: "Why is this happening?"

Verse 23 and exchanged the glory of the incorruptible God for an image in the form of corruptible man and of birds and four-footed animals and crawling creatures.

Man is more comfortable with a god of his own creation, because it places god on his own level and under his authority. The result is that "modern man" ends up worshiping himself or an object of his own creation.

Primitive man was generally monotheistic; idolatry was introduced later as individuals began to realize that when they controlled man's worship, they really controlled the worshippers themselves. When Aaron made a golden calf, he said he did not intend to lead the people to worship this image. He said in Exodus 32:5: *"Tomorrow is a feast to the Lord,"* insinuating that the calf was intended as an aid to devotion, but God saw it differently. They had exchanged the reality of God's presence for an image of their own making, instead of giving honor to the one who had brought them there.

Throughout the ages, man has paid homage to his own created images of God. Many of these images are nothing but copies of ***birds and four-footed animals and crawling creatures.*** Spiritual idolatry is the most striking characteristic of many developed nations of the modern world.

Some Observations on Verses 18- 23

God would not be a just and loving God if He did not react to man's evil. The rejection of God by man is inexcusable on the basis of ignorance.

The revelation of God in His work of creation is sufficient to render man inexcusable. Man's use of a tree to both make an idol, which he worships, and at the same time to use as fuel for a fire to warm himself would be laughable if it weren't so sad. The worshipping of an inanimate image of man's own creation is intended to give them feelings of superiority over that which they "worship."

The end result of rejecting the God of creation is the rejection of the truth that He reveals to man in creation. This, in turn, leads to moral irrelevance, which inevitable leads to the degeneration of mankind in society around them.

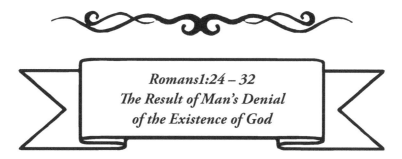

Romans 1:24 – 32
The Result of Man's Denial
of the Existence of God

In these verses we see a four-step process in the degeneration of those who deny the existence of God. Each of these steps will be marked by the phrase *"Therefore God gave them over."* This simply means God took His hands off and let man's willful rejection of Him produces its ugly results of the futility of a life without God. Paul is writing this epistle from Corinth, a city notorious for its sexual immorality, providing him with a living example of what happens when man rejects God, worships idols, and substitutes the morals of the world.

Verse 24 Therefore God gave them over in the lusts of their hearts to impurity, that their bodies might be dishonored among them.

Verse 25 For they exchanged the truth of God for a lie, and worshiped and served the creature rather than the Creator, who is blessed forever. Amen.

The *"giving themselves over"* presupposes the prior existence of these desires. The first step in the deterioration of man starts with their willingness to accept the dishonoring of the natural function of their bodies. Understand that man's perversion of his body can only be justified by his belief that there is no superior being to question his motives.

The second step in the deterioration of man is religious, **"…for they exchanged the truth of God for a lie."** Mythology and idolatry grew out of man's need to recognize some power in the universe greater than them, while refusing to give God the place of supremacy. Jeremiah 10:14: *"Every man is stupid, devoid of knowledge; Every goldsmith is put to shame by his idols; For his molten images are deceitful, And there is no breath in them.*

Verse 26 For this reason God gave them over to degrading passions; for their women exchanged the natural function for that which is unnatural,

Verse 27 and in the same way also the men abandoned the natural function of the woman and burned in their desire toward one another, men with men committing indecent acts and receiving in their own persons the due penalty of their error.

These two verses introduce the second **"God gave them over."** Here is the third step in the deterioration of man: physical degeneration. In turning from God, man naturally sinks into the sensual. Abnormal sexual lusts are often associated with idolatry, becoming a part of the service rendered to these false gods. The temple to Aphrodite (Venus) in Corinth had more than a thousand priestess prostitutes to serve her worshipers.

The perversion of sex is the unique contrivance of the human species. Paul refers to the degradation of the females first, since their corruption is proof that all virtue is lost. The apostle wanted to place a special emphasis on the male-with-male perversion; as of the two homosexual sins it was the most prevalent. Leviticus 18:22: *"You shall not lie with a male as one lies with a female; it is an abomination."* The folly of homosexuality is evident in its inability to reproduce the human species. Homosexuality is not an alternate lifestyle! Notice the promise of a physical penalty associated with this behavior. If truthfully practiced, its ultimate result will be the demise of mankind. *"And receiving in their own persons the due penalty of their error."* When we do away with God, we do away with all moral restraints, and man cannot avoid the physical consequences of his actions. Anyone who looks at the world today cannot fail to see the tragic physical results of individuals who have exchanged the truth of God for a lie.

Verse 28 *And just as they did not see fit to acknowledge God any longer, God gave them over to a depraved mind, to do those things which are not proper,*

Verse 29 *being filled with all unrighteousness, wickedness, greed, evil; full of envy, murder, strife, deceit, malice; they are gossips,*

Verse 30 *slanderers, haters of God, insolent, arrogant, boastful, inventors of evil, disobedient to parents,*

Verse 31 *without understanding, untrustworthy, unloving, unmerciful;*

In verses 28-31 we are introduced to the next step in man's degeneration; mental degeneration. ***God gave them over to a depraved mind.*** A depraved mind cannot be trusted to make good moral decisions. Morality becomes relative, and there is no absolute right or wrong. Originally the word translated as "depraved" was applied to metals that failed to pass the assayer's test. In other words, that which was presented as genuine was found to be false. The genuineness of man's mental attitude toward God determines his actions toward his fellow man.

Notice it says that man's natural desires begin to completely occupy their thinking, ***being filled with:***

- ***all unrighteousness:*** unrighteousness describes man's relation with God; in other words, they purposely defied God.
- ***Wickedness:*** deliberate, planned injustice toward their fellow man.
- ***Greed:*** the craving for more and a desire to fulfill those cravings, whatever the cost.

- *Evil:* doing things they consciously realize are wrong, but they don't care.

Next the verses go on to describe the results of the depraved mind in their actions towards others, as they are *full of:*

- *Envy:* the displeasure of seeing someone having something we begrudge him, accompanied by our desire to have it.
- *Murder:* an open disregard for the value of life, particularly those we feel stand in our way of getting our desires
- *Strife:* a quarrelsome disposition and its natural consequences
- *Deceit:* the deliberate deception of others through cunning and treachery
- *Malice:* the desire to disregard the feelings of others to obtain what we want.

In the end, we are faced with the external effects of a depraved mind, as **we *are* now**:

- *Gossips:* people who like to spread rumors about others
- *Slanderers:* people who minimize another's reputation by misrepresentation
- *haters of God:* people who are self-proclaimed atheists
- *insolent:* people who treat others with contempt
- *arrogant:* people who consider themselves superior to others
- *boastful:* people who are quick to let others know how important they are
- *inventors of evil:* people seeking new pleasures and sins
- *disobedient to parents:* people who have no love or respect for their parents
- *without understanding:* people who think they know it all, and in the process don't realize how little they do know
- *untrustworthy:* people who cannot be trusted
- *unloving:* people who feel love is a useless emotion
- *unmerciful:* people who feel any display of mercy is for the weak

Here is a verdict on our present-day society. No ultimate moral values can be retained by those who think of God as an anachronistic survivor of medieval superstition. Think of the present-day attitude that abounds in favor of abortion that completely justifies the killing of another human.

Verse 32 - *and, although they know the ordinance of God, that those who practice such things are worthy of death, they not only do the same, but also give hearty approval to those who practice them.*

The final step in the degeneration of man is the encouragement of others to practice the same sins they are involved in.

The most degraded men are not without the knowledge of God and of his righteous judgments. The fact that God's law is indelibly stamped upon man's consciousness means that he can never sin with a clear conscience. However, this knowledge does not prevent them from indulging the very sins that they know merit the judgment of God. The most damning condition of man is not the practice of sin, but the encouragement of others to practice the same sins. They are even worse sinners in the eyes of God than those who simply practice them. Sin grows exponentially when it meets with no disapproval from society and when there is even a subliminal permissive approval from society.

Some Observations on Verses 24-32

Note the three expressions: ***"God gave them over"*** - in verse 24, to immorality involved in cultic prostitution; in verse 26, to individual perverse sexual relations; and finally, in verse 28, to a depraved mind. There is a direct correlation between man's rejection of God and God's rejection of man. God's final ***"giving them up"*** shows that when God takes His hands off man the result is that not only does natural man sin, but he encourages others to follow his example. In many ways this is a commentary on our present-day society.

Final Thoughts on Chapter 1

We saw three characteristics of Paul in this chapter. First, we saw the diplomatic Paul. While introducing himself he was careful to congratulate his readers on their reputation for an excellent testimony of their faith in Christ. At the same time, he was careful to make them feel like equals. What he expected to do when he visited them he also expected them to do for him, which was encourage one another.

Next we see the evangelistic Paul. While Paul was desirous of visiting them, he also wanted them to clearly understand the gospel message he was anxious to share. It was a gospel whose roots were founded in the Jewish Scriptures, and yet a gospel that found its fulfillment in the person of Jesus Christ. It was a gospel that required the believer to accept Jesus Christ as the Son of God, yet it was a gospel that required this decision be reflected in a change in lifestyle as well. Proclamation without an accompanying substantiation is an empty well.

To reject the evidence of God in creation was to condemn oneself to total degeneration in the eyes of God, an action worthy of the wrath of a just God.

Paul closes with a summary of the development of the humanistic philosophy. We begin with the rejection of the existence of a Creator God (atheism); this results in the evolution of man without God (the theory of evolution) and allows man to say that he cannot help what he has become; this then results in moral relativity (there is no absolute right or wrong); with the end result being amorality (without morals - there are no restraints on the actions of man). Unfortunately I believe this is evident in our schools, our politics, and in the streets of our cities today, here in the United States.

Chapter 2

God's Principles for Judgment

Introduction:

Verses 21 to 32, from the previous chapter, close with the idea that when natural man rejects God he turns to sin, and encourages others to join in his sin. Here in verses 1-16, Paul will show that a righteous God has no choice but to judge individuals based on whether they believe in Him and accept His values, or choose not to believe in Him and accept the values of the world. Paul will identify four principles upon which God's judgment of mankind is based. These principles are not the basis for salvation, but the basis of God's judgment.

The apostle next points out in verses 17-29 that the Jews are not exempt from God's judgment, as they practice some of the very evils they condemn in others. Many of the Jews felt they were exempt from God's judgment based on:

- Their special covenant relation to God
- Their superior knowledge of God
- Their circumcision in obedience to God's command

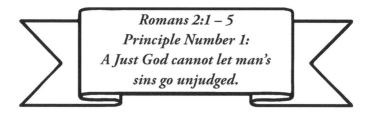

Romans 2:1 – 5
Principle Number 1:
A Just God cannot let man's
sins go unjudged.

Verse 1 Therefore you are without excuse, every man of you who passes judgment, for in that you judge another; you condemn yourself; for you who judge practice the same things.

Paul begins by expressing his conclusion before presenting his reasons for his conclusion. He goes on to say his conclusion includes everyone who passes judgment on another**.** The word *"judge"* carries the thought of judging with an adverse verdict. In judging others, we often use a value system that is the product of our own values. For example, "I found a stick as big as myself, and I divided it into six equal parts, calling each part a foot. That makes me six feet tall." We are guilty of this same reasoning when we judge according to our own measuring stick.

"For you who judge practice the same things." This thought is really a continuation of the last verse of the previous chapter where it states that sinners often encourage others to do what they are doing as a way of justifying our own actions. David was afflicted with this way of thinking. 2 Samuel 12:5-7: *"Then David's anger burned greatly against the man, and he said to Nathan, 'As the Lord lives, surely the man who has done this deserves to die. And he must make restitution for the lamb fourfold, because he did this thing and had no compassion.' Nathan then said to David, 'You are the man! Thus says the Lord God of Israel, "It is I who anointed you king over Israel and it is I who delivered you from the hand of Saul."'"* The same things we are quick to accuse others in the world of doing, we who think of ourselves as followers of Jesus Christ, are often doing the same but refuse to admit it.

Verse 2 - And we know that the judgment of God rightly falls upon those who practice such things.

Here then is the first principle of God's judgment: 'God rightly judges those who practice judging others.' The presumed exclusion by the Jews of escaping God's judgment was founded on the assumption that God will not judge them according to their deeds, but according to their national and ancestral relationship to Abraham. Unfortunately as it says in 1 Samuel 16:7: *"... God sees not as man sees, for man looks at the outward appearance, but the* LORD *looks at the heart."* Man cannot see the motivations of man; therefore, his judgment is prejudiced by his own set of values. God, on the other hand, sees the innermost motivations of man, therefore can pronounce a righteous judgment.

Verse 3 *And do you suppose this, O man, when you pass judgment upon those who practice such things and do the same yourself, that you will escape the judgment of God?*

Since man does not immediately experience God's judgments, he mistakenly thinks he has escaped them.

Here are four ways that we may avoid judgment when we break human laws:

- We escape discovery
- We escape the jurisdiction of the court (i.e., by time or distance)
- If caught, we obtain our release based on a legal technicality
- If caught and judged, we successfully escape from prison.

However, none of these avenues are open to man when a righteous God judges him. God's judgments reflect a complete awareness of the truth of the matter and the mercy of God does not provide for an indifference to sin.

Paul writes in 1 Corinthians 3:13, *"… each man's work shall be made manifest: for the day shall declare it, because it is revealed in fire; and the fire itself shall prove each man's work of what sort it is"*

Verse 4 *Or do you think lightly of the riches of His kindness and forbearance and patience, not knowing that the kindness of God leads you to repentance?*

While the forbearance and patience of God ought to bring men to their knees in thankfulness; instead, those who sin think the lack of God's immediate judgment on them exempts them from future judgment. Conversely the Jews imagined their receipt of God's blessings and promises, meant that they would not be judged as God judges others.

Man's feelings of self-righteousness in seemingly escaping God's judgment, ignores the fact that a just God must ultimately bring man's sin into accountability and judgment. The mercy of God in not immediately judging our sins should lead us to be thankful that we have a merciful God. This in-turn gives us an opportunity to repent and seek acceptance by God. However, the availability of receiving repentance and salvation from God is accompanied by a warning that the refusal to repent will ultimately man to the wrath of a just God.

Verse 5 But because of your stubbornness and unrepentant heart you are storing up wrath for yourself in the day of wrath and revelation of the righteous judgment of God,

Paul reiterates that though sinful man may not have felt the wrath of God, this does not mean that God's judgment has been suspended. In reality, their continued refusal to accept God's offer of acceptance merely means they are storing up their sins in God's record book for His final judgment. There is a future day when God will be revealed to all mankind, and at that time they will experience the wrath of a righteous God.

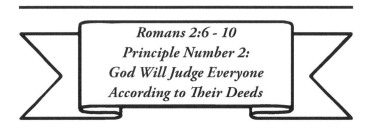

Romans 2:6 - 10
Principle Number 2:
God Will Judge Everyone
According to Their Deeds

Verse 6 who will render to every man according to his deeds:

Here we are introduced to the second principle regarding God's judgments: 'God will judge to each person according to their deeds.' Men's deeds reflect an index of their character; and provide the evidence by which

God judges them. Profession of a belief in God does not supersede the need for action in support of that belief. Three features of God's righteous judgment are indicated in this verse:

- Its certainty: ***Who will render***
- Its universality: ***To every man***
- Its criteria: ***According to his deeds***

2 Corinthians 5:10: *"For we must all appear before the judgment seat of Christ, that each one may be recompensed for his deeds in the body, according to what he has done, whether good or bad."* The wicked will be punished according to their works. The righteous will be rewarded according to their works. One's deeds are the visible evidence of the authenticity of our relationship with God.

Verse 7 *to those who by perseverance in doing good seek for glory and honor and immortality, eternal life;*

This verse identifies the first of two classes of individuals: those who persevere in doing good. This group of people practices good deeds, not only in the eyes of other people, but in the eyes of God as well. To them their good deeds are evidence of having a living relationship with God. Their good deeds are intended to honor God and insure an eternal life spent with Him. One of the questions Jesus may ask when we stand before Him could well be, "What have you done among men that brought honor and glory to Me?" Those who cannot answer this question in a positive way Matthew 25:46 says, *"And these will go away into eternal punishment, but the righteous into eternal life."*

Verse 8 *but to those who are selfishly ambitious and do not obey the truth, but obey unrighteousness, wrath and indignation.*

This verse identifies the second of the two classes of individuals: those who are filled with selfish ambition and persist in doing evil. In the eyes of God, these are in revolt against Him and they ***do not obey the truth.*** These are those who make light of the biblical doctrine of individual human responsibility. They are the "Me Generation," who go through life concerned only about what they can get out of it. In that future day of judgment they can only expect to feel the indignation and wrath of a righteous God.

Verse 9 *There will be tribulation and distress for every soul of man who does evil, of the Jew first and also of the Greek,*

Paul reiterates what will happen to this second group of people in an attempt to startle the Jews out of their self-deception that they were immune from God's judgment. The priority of the Jews being first in the receipt of God's final punishment runs contrary to their belief that God's punitive judgment was for the Gentiles only. However, Paul maintains that since the Jews were the first to receive God's mercy, before the Greeks or Gentiles, then it can be implied that this same order will also be taken into account in the final judgment. Luke 12:48 expresses this: *"From every one who has been given much, much will be required; and from the one who has been entrusted with much, all the more will be demanded."* Like many Christians, the Jews thought the possession of the knowledge of God and the receipt of His spiritual blessings was an insurance against divine retribution.

Verse 10 *but glory and honor and peace to every man who does good, to the Jew first and also to the Greek.*

Paul ends this section of verses by referring to the first group of individuals: those who persist in doing good. He points out that their "good" works of both the Jew and Greek will result in their glory, honor, and peace. Notice however, how Paul continues to express the thought that God's actions will take into account the Jews first.

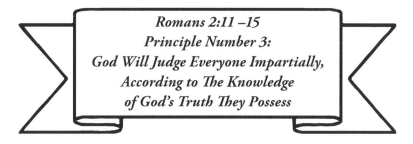

Romans 2:11 –15
Principle Number 3:
God Will Judge Everyone Impartially,
According to The Knowledge
of God's Truth They Possess

Verse 11 For there is no partiality with God.

Here is the third principle of judgment: God's judgment is impartial. In this, Paul is subtly reminding the Jews that *who* they are is not as important to God as their relationship with Him. Acts 10:34: *And opening his mouth, Peter said: "I most certainly understand now that God is not one to show partiality,"* Clearly it is not who ancestry is that is important to God at the final judgment. In this next verse we see why this is.

Verse 12 For all who have sinned without the Law will also perish without the Law; and all who have sinned under the Law will be judged by the Law;

Since than everyone has sinned than God must have a standard he uses in the final judgment of men. Here we have God's standard identified: God will judge everyone according to their knowledge of His law. Knowledge of what God desires of us always brings greater responsibility, and therefore if neglected, greater liability. Luke 12:48: *"And from everyone who has been given much, much shall be required: and to whom they entrusted much, of him they will ask all the more."* God understands that men may be placed in an environment that limits their ability to receive personal knowledge of His law. Therefore, those who sin without God's revelation being communicated to them, although they are to be judged, will be judged by a different standard than those who have received God's revelation and still sinned.

Verse 13 for not the hearers of the Law are just before God, but the doers of the Law will be justified.

Notice the previous verse did not say knowledge of the law ensures one's salvation, only that it affects God's standard whereby they will be judged.

Recognize that in Paul's time the Law was read in the presence of the people (manuscripts were rare and very valuable), and it was by their hearing of the law that their knowledge of it was obtained. In this, the Jews were privileged because they were regularly exposed to the reading of the Law. However, according to Paul, the righteous were not those who "*heard the Law*" but those who were "*doers of the Law.*" Here again, Paul is saying as he did in chapter one, that salvation comes to those who act upon the profession of faith.

This is the first occasion that the word "justified" is used in this epistle, and it refers to one's status in the sight of God. The problem is that to obtain that status in the eyes of God through the Law demands perfect obedience to the Law, and that is impossible. Now with God's provision of grace through Christ's death on the cross for our sins, those who accept Christ as their Savior, are now seen by God as justified because God now sees them through His Son who died for their sins. The believer is one who does the works of the Law out of gratitude for their salvation and in a desire to please God.

Verse 14 For when Gentiles who do not have the Law do instinctively the things of the Law, these, not having the Law, are a law to themselves,

Paul states that those who are without the written Law will be judged without reference to that Law, and that Law will judge those who live under the Law.

"*The things of the Law*" refers to those regulations stipulated in the Law. The believing Gentile in their desire to please God instinctively tries to live by the Law.

Verse 15 in that they show the work of the Law written in their hearts, their conscience bearing witness, and their thoughts alternately accusing or else defending them,

Bt their instinctive attempt to live according to the Law, the Gentiles confirm that they have the Law written on their hearts. Whenever they fail to follow the dictates of their conscience, they are confronted with the conscience's desire to bring their conduct into conformity with God's Law. The function of conscience in the Gentile is parallel to the function of the Law for the Jew.

It is important to note that Paul does not say "the" Law is written upon their hearts, but the work of the Law. In other words, knowing instinctively what pleases God and then doing it. The conscience of natural man may be blurred by sin, but the enlightened conscience is open to the workings of the Holy Spirit, which leads us to recognize the need to seek forgiveness when we sin and is proof that God's law is evident in our hearts.

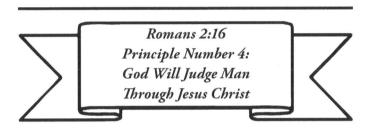

Romans 2:16
Principle Number 4:
God Will Judge Man
Through Jesus Christ

Verse 16 on the day when, according to my gospel, God will judge the secrets of men through Christ Jesus.

Here is the fourth and final principle by which God will judge mankind: God will judge mankind through Jesus Christ. The good news of the gospel involves what we are saved *to*, as well as what we are saved *from*. Grace does not dispense with judgment. However, the exciting thing for believers is that when God looks at them, He sees them through His Son who has already died for and forgiven their sins: therefore, in the eyes of God, they appear blameless and not deserving of punishment.

Some Observations on Verses 1-16

In these verses Paul identifies four principles a just God will use to judge mankind.

- **A Just God cannot let man's sins go unjudged.**

The very concept of a righteous judge demands that a person's violations of God's law cannot be ignored. To do so would make the judge unrighteous. Therefore, man must recognize that though God does not immediately judge him for his sins that this does not mean that he will not ultimately be judged for them. The very definition of righteous demands it.

- **God Will Judge Everyone According to Their Deeds**

This is what one would expect of a just and righteous God. However, the Jews found this hard to accept. They felt they were exempt from God's judgment as they were the first to be chosen by God with His offer of forgiveness and salvation.

- **God Will Judge Everyone Impartially, According to The Knowledge of His Truth They Possess**

This principle answers the question about how a just God can judge those who have never heard of Him just as severely as those who have full knowledge about Him and have denied Him. The answer is, He doesn't. Understand that the lack of one's knowledge of Him does not excuse their need for salvation. It only establishes that a just and righteous God will take that in consideration when He judges mankind.

- **God Will Judge Man Through Jesus Christ**

This means believers will appear justified and able to stand in God's presence, because God now sees them through His Son, who paid the price for their sins.

In these principles, Paul is addressing man's attitude toward God as our ultimate judge. Men like to think that since their acts of disobedience of God are not immediately punished, that God will never judge them. Paul reminds them that a just God cannot excuse disobedience, but must judge it. However, since God is righteous, He will judge mankind according to their knowledge of His plan of salvation for them. Paul reminds them that they cannot ignore their conscience because it is through their conscience that God warns them of what is right and what is not. Paul ends with the best part of all: God will judge us as we are seen through His Son, Jesus Christ who paid the penalty for our sins. For the unbeliever, this is no comfort at all. However, for the believer who has acknowledged who Jesus Christ is and has asked Him for forgiveness for their sins it is great news.

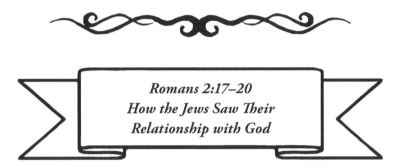

Romans 2:17–20
How the Jews Saw Their
Relationship with God

Verse 17 But if you bear the name "Jew," and rely upon the Law, and boast in God,

Verse 18 and know His will, and approve the things that are essential, being instructed out of the Law,

From through these verses through chapter 3:13, Paul is addressing himself directly to the Jews. He begins with what the Jews considered the foundation of their religion: their possession of the Law. They felt that because it was given to them by God and with their special knowledge of the Law, they were exempt from the judgments of God. In these two verses, Paul identifies five reasons the Jews felt they were exempted them from the judgments of God.

- They **bear the name "Jew,":** They considered this title designated them as the chosen people of God. It was their ancestral relationship to Abraham, who first received God's promises, that was the primary source of the false confidence of the Jews.
- They **rely upon the Law,:** They considered the Mosaic law as the foundation of both their civil and religious regulations and obligations.

- They ***boast in God:*** They boasted that he was *their* God, and that they were the sole beneficiaries of His favor and that all other nations were therefore pagans.
- They ***know His will,*** : Because of their study of the Law, they felt that they alone knew the will of God.
- They ***approve the things that are essential,:*** As a result of their being "instructed" in the law, the Jews supposed this made them able to discern the things that were important to God.

As Paul saw it, it was because of their perceived superior endowments that they bragged about their presumed favored position with God. Micah 3:11: *"Her leaders pronounce judgment for a bribe, Her priests instruct for a price, And her prophets divine for money. Yet they lean on the Lord saying, 'Is not the Lord in our midst? Calamity will not come upon us.'"*

Verse 19 and are confident that you yourself are a guide to the blind, a light to those who are in darkness,

Verse 20 a corrector of the foolish, a teacher of the immature, having in the Law the embodiment of knowledge and of the truth,

Paul goes on to explain how the Jews felt they were called for a special divine purpose. In these verses, he identifies four divine purposes for which they felt they were called.

- They were ***confident that you yourself are a guide to the blind:*** Notice he states that they "***are confident that you yourself are a guide,***" not that they *were* guides.
- Each Jew thought of themselves as ***a light to those who are in darkness,***
- Each Jew thought of themselves as ***a corrector of the foolish***
- Each Jew thought of themselves as ***a teacher of the immature,***

The Jews were committing a twofold error with their reliance on the law: (1) they felt that the mere possession of, and instruction in, the law gave them a security and superiority in their relationship with God; (2)

They felt that their special knowledge of the law gave them a superior mission that only they could fulfill.

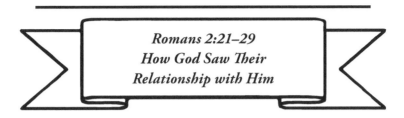

Romans 2:21–29
How God Saw Their
Relationship with Him

Verse 21 you, therefore, who teach another, do you not teach yourself? You who preach that one should not steal, do you steal?

Verse 22 You who say that one should not commit adultery, do you commit adultery? You who abhor idols, do you rob temples?

Verse 23 You who boast in the Law, through your breaking the Law, do you dishonor God?

Verse 24 For "the name of God is blasphemed among the Gentiles because of you," just as it is written.

In these first four verses, Paul draws attention to the inconsistencies of Jewish life by asking four rhetorical questions. These questions were designed to show that the Jews were committing the very sins they so loudly condemned in the heathen. Paul identifies five sins they were practicing that were the cause of their current rejection by God.

- *You, therefore, who teach another, do you not teach yourself?* In other words they were not practicing what they teach
- *You who preach that one should not steal, do you steal?* According to the prophet Malachi and Paul they were stealing from God
- *You who say that one should not commit adultery, do you commit adultery? You who abhor idols, do you rob temples?*
- *Through your breaking the Law, do you dishonor God?*

- *You are causing the name of God to be blaspheme among the Gentiles*

The Gentiles judged the character of a deity by the conduct of those who claimed to be its followers. The Jews' outward conduct gave a lie to their doctrine and profession that was dishonoring to God.

Paul is implying, "How can you say that you rely on God and His law, teach others the meaning of this law, preach that they should live in harmony with it, and yet you do not practice what you preach?" Today the name of Christ is often dishonored by the inconsistencies of which self-proclaimed Christians live, dishonoring God and His sanctuary.

> The gospel is written a chapter a day
> By deeds that you do and words that you say.
> Men read what you say, whether faithless or true.
> What is the gospel according to you?
> *(from "Through the Bible with J. Vernon McGee")*

Verse 25 For indeed circumcision is of value, if you practice the Law; but if you are a transgressor of the Law, your circumcision has become uncircumcision.

In the last five verses in this section, Paul warns the Jews that they have failed to recognize the true source of their salvation. Paul begins by saying that neither circumcision nor the possession of the law is sufficient to guarantee their salvation. Circumcision was the sign and seal of the covenant to Abraham; designed to identify God's chosen people. The Jews came to think of circumcision as a sign of the provision of their salvation by God.

Paul's taught that circumcision had no inherent efficacy beyond that of a sign and seal of a covenant that God would bless those who kept the covenant; those who transgressed the law, God would not bless but would judge them for their transgressions. Jeremiah 4:4: *"Circumcise yourselves to the Lord And remove the foreskins of your heart, Men of Judah and inhabitants of Jerusalem, Lest My wrath go forth like fire And burn with none to quench it, Because of the evil of your deeds."* Jeremiah 9:25: *"Behold, the days are* coming," declares the Lord, "that I will punish all who are circumcised and yet uncircumcised…"

For the believer today, the ceremony of baptism does not provide for salvation. It is to be a public declaration of identify with God. However, if the lifestyle of those baptized gives no evidence of God in their life, the ceremony has no significance before God and is in fact detrimental to that individual's testimony of faith in God.

Verse 26 *If therefore the uncircumcised man keeps the requirements of the Law, will not his uncircumcision be regarded as circumcision?*

If the breaking of the Law renders one as though he were uncircumcised, then the keeping of the Law should render one as though he were circumcised. 1 Corinthians 7:19: *"Circumcision is nothing, and uncircumcision is nothing, but what matters is the keeping of the commandments of God."*

Everything depends on obedience to God's laws, and circumcision can be the evidence of either justification or condemnation before God.

Verse 27 *And will not he who is physically uncircumcised, if he keeps the Law, will he not judge you who though having the letter of the Law and circumcision are a transgressor of the Law?*

A sign is a symbol of a reality, not the reality itself. Circumcision was intended to be an outward sign of the reality that one was living in obedience to God's law. However, there is no value in the outward and visible sign unless it is accompanied by the reality behind the sign.

The same is true with respect to all the traditional signs practiced by today's Church, such as water baptism, communion, etc. They have value and significance only when accompanied by evidence in the life of believers that they are living in obedience to God's commandments.

Verse 28 *For he is not a Jew who is one outwardly; neither is circumcision that which is outward in the flesh.*

The Jews were building their doctrines on the fact that their circumcision showed they were God's chosen people, and therefore had a guaranteed entry into eternity. The rabbis even believed that if a male child died before he was circumcised, circumcision must be performed on the dead child's body. However, Jesus reminded the rabbis in John 8:39: "*They answered and said to Him, 'Abraham is our father.' Jesus said to them, 'If you are Abraham's children, do the deeds of Abraham.'*"

Verse 29   *But he is a Jew who is one inwardly; and circumcision is that which is of the heart, by the Spirit, not by the letter; and his praise is not from men, but from God.*

Paul's meaning is clear: "For he is not a Jew who is one outwardly, but he is a Jew who is one inwardly." The circumcision of the heart is effected by the Spirit, and not by obedience to the prescriptions of the law. Religion, to be acceptable to God, must originate from the heart.

Some **Observations** *on Verses 17-29*

Paul notes thirteen things that the Jews felt set them apart:

(1) that they are men of praise;
(2) that they are men of thanksgiving;
(3) that their trust is in the Law;
(4) that their boast is in God;
(5) that they know God's will;
(6) that they approve the things that are excellent;
(7) that they are leaders of the blind;
(8) that they are a light for those who are in darkness;
(9) that they are instructors of the ignorant;
(10) that they are teachers of babes
(11) that they are men who direct others;
(12) that they are men who preach against theft, adultery, and idolatry;
(13) that, finally, they are men who glory in the commandments of God.

The problem was that they often did not practice them. The Jews felt that since God called them, they were not subject to the same judgments of God as the Gentiles. What happened is that they assumed God's forgiveness was independent of their obedience to His Law.

Final Thoughts on Chapter 2

Chapter one ended with the conclusion that the normal nature of man was to reject God and instead create his own god. In his rejection of God, natural man turned to a life of self-pleasures. To justify his sinful lifestyle, he encouraged others to do as he did.

Chapter two begins with Paul declaring that as a result of man's sinfulness, a just God must pronounce judgment on mankind. Paul states that God judges according to four principles:

- God's judgments are just because He judges based on man's heart and even defers immediate judgment to give them time to repent.
- God will judge everyone on the basis of their actions.
- God will judge everyone on the basis of their knowledge of God's will.
- God will judge mankind through His Son, Jesus Christ. Those who accept His Son, He will accept: those who reject His Son, He will reject.

Paul closes this chapter by declaring that the Jews were not exempt from God's judgment. Their very pride in the idea that they had been chosen by God was the seed that led to their downfall. This caused them to behave in a manner that contradicted what they knew God desired. They preached it and taught it, but they failed to live it. A just God, therefore, had no choice but to judge them by the same standards and principles He used on everyone who was not a Jew. They failed to understand that His giving them the Law was intended to make them more aware of their sinfulness, therefore more dependent on God's forgiveness. They failed to recognize that religious tradition does not replace a contrite heart before God. Salvation comes from our acceptance of who God's Son is and then in living to please Him, not in some religious ceremony or tradition.

Chapter 3

Mankind's Need for God's Provision

Introduction:

In this chapter, Paul introduces some objections raised by the Jews to their being subject to God's judgments. The basis of their objections was that if, in spite of their being sealed as members of a chosen race, they were still subject to the "wrath of God"; then there was no advantage of being a Jew, against being a Gentile, in a relationship with God. This they knew had to be false as why else who God had chosen them.

This same attitude exists among many believers today who feel their membership in a church is sufficient to guarantee their salvation. At the same time live lives in obvious disobedience to the practices commanded by God and the Church. In turn, there are others who are indifferent to the Church and yet exhibit more evangelical faith and fervor regarding the practices commanded by God and yet are considered heathens by the former group.

This chapter is divided into three sections:

- Verses 1-8 contain a brief statement and refutation of Jewish objections to Paul's declaration that they are subject to God's wrath just like all mankind.

- Verses 9-20 are a declaration that man's works, even if in conformance to the Law, will not result in their being justified before God, and this is supported by Scripture.
- Verses 21-31 are an explanation of God's provision, showing how man may be justified before Him.

Chapter 3:1 - 8
Objections Raised by the Jews

Verse 1 *Then what advantage has the Jew? Or what is the benefit of circumcision?*

Paul concluded chapter two with the statement that both Jews and Gentiles will be judged according to their works and by their knowledge of God's will. In this verse, we see the first of three objections raised by the Jews: What is the advantage of being a Jew if God sees them in the same way He sees the Gentiles? If Paul was right, then there really was no advantage of being a Jew and no profit in their circumcision and their being chosen by God as His people.

What the Jews failed to understand was that just because God had chosen them, He also made it clear that they were subject to His judgment when disobeying His commands. In Amos 3:2 it says *"You only have I chosen among all the families of the earth; Therefore I will punish you for all your iniquities."* We can see an example of this note how parents may discipline their children for their disobedience, while at the same time tolerating similar behavior in someone else's children, recognizing they are responsible to a different authority.

Verse 2 *Great in every respect. First of all, that they were entrusted with the oracles of God.*

Paul starts his answer their first objection by noting that they alone were entrusted with God's law. In Deuteronomy 4:8, God's says through Moses, *"Or what great nation is there that has statutes and judgments as righteous as this whole law which I am setting before you today?"* To the Jews than was accorded the unique privilege of all nations as being the custodians of the "***oracles of God***." The word "oracle" is used four times in the New Testament: Romans 3:2; Hebrews 5:12; 1 Peter 4:11, Acts 7:38 and is defined as "divine utterances. As used here, it is intended to include the written Law, God's verbal instructions to Moses, and the words of the prophets regarding the promises of God, literally the entire Old Testament. Since God entrusted His Word to the Jews, they must accept that they are also subject to the judgments pronounced in those words on those who are disobedient to them.

As members of the Christian Church, we enjoy the advantage of having God's entire Word. Therefore, we must also accept the responsibility that goes with that. Now that we know what God expects of us, we must also accept that we are subject to God's judgment when we disobey His Word.

Verse 3 What then? If some did not believe, their unbelief will not nullify the faithfulness of God, will it?

The "***some***" also implies that there were some who did believe. The "***unbelief***" of those who did not believe was based on their rejection of Jesus as the Messiah. God had entered into a solemn covenant with the Jews, promising them all the benefits of the Messiah's kingdom; however, the Jews failed to understand that if they were to expect to receive God's special blessings, they must also recognize the Messiah when God presented Him to them. Their objection then was 'Just because ***'some'*** of the Jews rejected God, surely that does not mean that God's covenant promise to them had been abandoned by God.

Verse 4 May it never be! Rather, let God be found true, though every man be found a liar, as it is written, "THAT THOU MIGHTEST BE JUSTIFIED IN THY WORDS, AND MIGHTEST PREVAIL WHEN THOU ART JUDGED."

In Greek, the strongest phrase to express an impossibility was, ***"May it never be!"*** Paul answers their second objection by reassuring the Jews that while "*some*" have been disobedient and defiant of God, God will remain faithful to His Word for those who were faithful to Him.

There is no breach of the promises of God involved in the condemnation of the unrepentant Jews. God is faithful to His promises; however, He is also faithful to His warnings of judgment. Psalms 51:4: "*Against Thee, Thee only, I have sinned, And done what is evil in Thy sight, So that Thou art justified when Thou dost speak, And blameless when Thou dost judge.*"

Verse 5 But if our unrighteousness demonstrates the righteousness of God, what shall we say? The God who inflicts wrath is not unrighteous, is He? (I am speaking in human terms.)

Paul now describes the third objection of the Jews. According to the logic of the Jews, if their unrighteousness reveals the faithfulness and grace of God, then how can they be condemned by a righteous God?

Paul's explanatory statement, "*I am speaking in human terms,*" is due to his having used the word "*unrighteous*" in connection with God. By asking these questions, he is using the human mode of interrogation and reasoning.

Verse 6 May it never be! For otherwise how will God judge the world?

Paul answers his rhetorical question by using the rabbinical method of answering a question, which is asking another question. Could God be a just God if the world could say that His actions were inconsistent with justice? Even an unbeliever undoubtedly feels that some people ought to be judged for their evil actions. The problem is that an unbeliever often feels that they should not be judged for their actions, but feel that it is only just that others are. A just God cannot judge the world using this principle.

Verse 7 But if through my lie the truth of God abounded to His glory, why am I also still being judged as a sinner?

The question raised in verse five is repeated. If my sinfulness allows the grace of God to abound, then how can I be judged as in rebellion against God? In other words, if the "privileges" of the Jew only serve to increase their responsibilities, then it would appear those benefits were a serious liability.

Verse 8 ***And why not say (as we are slanderously reported and as some affirm that we say), "Let us do evil that good may come"? Their condemnation is just.***

Some claimed that since Paul preached that we are saved by grace, he is in substance saying, "Go ahead and sin because ultimately your sin only allows God's grace to be displayed." By reducing the reasoning of the Jews this shocking immoral conclusion, Paul answers their objection. Any doctrine that conflicts with the principles of God's morality must be false, no matter how plausible the arguments in its favor. Therefore, anyone who claims this false doctrine, their condemnation is deserved as it would be contrary to the actions of a just God.

*Some **Observations** on Verses 1 - 8*

In chapter 2, Paul defined four principles whereby God judged all mankind. He concluded that chapter by showing that the Jews were not exempt from God's judgments because they had focused their devotion on the Law, rather than the Lawgiver, God. Paul recognized that the Jews assumed they had a special exemption from God's judgments because God had chosen them. In the above verses, Paul considers three objections the Jews used against their standing before God in judgment.

Their first objection was that if they were subject to the same judgment before God as the Gentiles, then what profit was there in their being God's chosen people? Paul answers by saying that God chose them to entrust them with His special provision for all mankind. They were chosen to be the example of what happened when a people obeyed and kept God's Word.

Their second objection was that if they were subject to God's judgment in spite of their being chosen by God, then this must mean that God was not keeping the promises God had made to their ancestors. Paul replies that God always keeps His promises.

Their third objection was that if their unbelief demonstrates God's faithfulness to His Word, how could He judge them for their sins when they were actually providing God an opportunity to prove His faithfulness? Paul reminds them that a just God can only judge righteously if He judges *all* mankind by their actions and deeds. If any man disobeys God's Word, he must expect that a just God will be forced to judge him for those actions.

Romans 3:9 – 18
Man Is by Nature Sinful

Verse 9 What then? Are we better than they? Not at all; for we have already charged that both Jews and Greeks are all under sin;

Here Paul reaches the conclusion that Jews who are sinners have no advantage over the Gentiles. The Gentiles sinned in spite of the evidences of a Creator God in nature and their natural conscience, while the Jews sinned in spite of their possession of God's Law.

The oracles of God, of which the Jews were the recipients, taught them what God expected of them, but their possession of this knowledge did not give them a superior standing with God in regard to individual sin.

Galatians 3:22: *"But the Scripture has shut up all men under sin, that the promise by faith in Jesus Christ might be given to those who believe."*

Verse 10 as it is written, "THERE IS NONE RIGHTEOUS, NOT EVEN ONE;

Here Paul reverts to the Scriptures to emphasize the absence of righteousness is the normal condition of man in God's eyes. Psalms 14:1-3; 53:1-4; *"The fool has said in his heart, There is no God, They are corrupt, and have committed abominable injustice; There is no one who does good,"* *"God has looked down from heaven upon the sons of men, To see if there is anyone who understands, Who seeks after God. Every one of them has turned* aside; together they have become corrupt; There is no one who does good, not even one. Have the workers of wickedness no knowledge, Who eat up My people as though they ate bread, And have not called upon God?"

Verse 11 THERE IS NONE WHO UNDERSTANDS, THERE IS NONE WHO SEEKS FOR GOD;

Man's search after righteousness must begin with his recognition that he is a sinner in the eyes of God. Because man fails to recognize his lost condition, he fails to understand his need for God; he does not even seek after God on his own.

Verse 12 : ALL HAVE TURNED ASIDE, TOGETHER THEY HAVE BECOME USELESS; THERE IS NONE WHO DOES GOOD, THERE IS NOT EVEN ONE."

Paul notes that when mankind turns away from God he descends into spiritual blindness. The spiritually blind cannot understand God's offer of forgiveness. This spiritual blindness also results in mankind's inability to do good in the eyes of God. In this total absence of goodness, man wanders through life purposeless, in a lost condition, and useless to God.

Verse 13 "THEIR THROAT IS AN OPEN GRAVE, WITH THEIR TONGUES THEY KEEP DECEIVING," "THE POISON OF ASPS IS UNDER THEIR LIPS";

The man who does not seek God deceives himself by declaring there is no God. Their verbal declaration that there is no God not only reflects their self-deceit, but poisons others against the existence of God..

Psalms 5:9: *"There is nothing reliable in what they say; Their inward part is destruction itself; Their throat is an open grave; They flatter with their tongue."* Psalms 140:3: *"They sharpen their tongues as a serpent; Poison of a viper is under their lips."*

Verse 14 "WHOSE MOUTH IS FULL OF CURSING AND BITTERNESS";

Unfortunately, what comes out of our mouth is often a reflection of our innermost character. Our speech is often used to criticize, curse, and complain. Murder doesn't always involve the death of the body. The destruction of another's reputation or character is just as surely an act of murder. Psalms 10:7: *"His mouth is full of curses and deceit and oppression; Under his tongue is mischief and wickedness."*

Verse 15 *"THEIR FEET ARE SWIFT TO SHED BLOOD,*

Notice the five distinct body parts identified in these verses: the first four are organs involved in speech, and the fifth is the feet. The feet are mentioned because they often transport us into our sins. Isaiah 59:7: *"Their feet run to evil, And they hasten to shed innocent blood; Their thoughts are thoughts of iniquity; Devastation and destruction are in their highways."*

Verse 16 *DESTRUCTION AND MISERY ARE IN THEIR PATHS,*

As a result of man's desire to sin, he often leaves destruction and misery behind him.

Verse 17 *AND THE PATH OF PEACE HAVE THEY NOT KNOWN."*

Paul tells us that our tendency toward sin often results in our feet taking us where we shouldn't be. Man's natural tendency is toward self-gratification, even if it comes at the expense of others. Since self-gratification is never satisfied man is never at peace with himself.

Verse 18 *"THERE IS NO FEAR OF GOD BEFORE THEIR EYES."*

Sinful man lives as if God does not exist. If he admits to the existence of a superior Being, then he must also admit that this Being has the ability to judge his actions that are contrary to the wishes of that Being. Sinful man may even admit to a theoretical belief in God's existence, but he will not admit to His being submissive to him. The lack of instant judgment by God on a man's sins reinforces man's idea that there is no reason to fear God, as clearly He doesn't exist. As King David says in Psalm 36:1:

"Transgression speaks to the ungodly within his heart; There is no fear of God before his eyes."

Some Observations on Verses 9 -18

Paul makes it clear that the natural actions of man are not peaceful in nature, but rather result in conflicts as he seeks to satisfy his own desires. Since man does not seem to receive instant punishment for his sins, he reasons that there clearly cannot be a superior Being or God. At the same time, he doesn't recognize that this failure to find God is of his own making. The result of man's spiritual blindness is that he becomes offensive and useless in the eyes of God. In the end, sinful man discovers that his life is purposeless and has no real meaning.

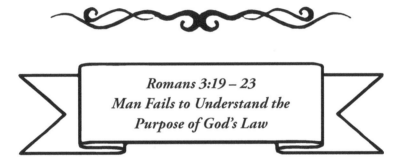

Romans 3:19 – 23
Man Fails to Understand the
Purpose of God's Law

Verse 19 Now we know that whatever the Law says, it speaks to those who are under the Law, that every mouth may be closed, and all the world may become accountable to God;

The regulations regarding how man was to conduct his life, as identified in the Old Testament was intended to provide the Jews with a standard of how to live to please God. In practice it was impossible to live in complete obedience to the Law. This verse evokes the image of the defendant in court who, when given the opportunity to speak in his own defense, refuses when he recognizes the overwhelming and irrefutable evidence against him.

One day, everybody will stand before God to answer for their actions, and will be given an opportunity to defend their failures. However, in the presence of God, their guilt will be so obvious that they will have nothing to say in their own defense.

Verse 20 *because by the works of the Law no flesh will be justified in His sight; for through the Law comes the knowledge of sin.*

The Law demands nothing less than moral and spiritual perfection, which no man in his own power can attain. This therefore, should create within man a sense of awareness of their sins. Since we cannot satisfy the demands of the Law, then our forgiveness must depend on a power other than our own. Galatians 2:16 says, *"…nevertheless knowing that a man is not justified by the works of the Law but through faith in Christ Jesus, even we have believed in Christ Jesus, that we may be justified by faith in Christ, and not by the works of the Law; since by the works of the Law shall no flesh be justified."*

Verse 21 *But now apart from the Law the righteousness of God has been manifested, being witnessed by the Law and the Prophets,*

Paul now develops the doctrine of justification. The implication is that if God is righteous, then it follows that He must have made a provision for our obtaining righteousness before Him, *"apart from the Law."* Here Paul is reminding his Jewish readers that the righteousness of God is clearly seen when you consider His giving of Moses' Law and by the words of the Prophets.

Verse 22 *even the righteousness of God through faith in Jesus Christ for all those who believe; for there is no distinction;*

With great emphasis, the apostle repeats the thought that God's righteousness is granted to *all* who put their faith in and become true believers in Jesus Christ. The object of our faith, then, is the important thing. Galatians 3:28 confirms this when it says, *"There is neither Jew nor*

Greek, there is neither slave nor free man, there is neither male nor female; for you are all one in Christ Jesus."

Verse 23 for all have sinned and fall short of the glory of God,

This verse views the sin of every man as a historical fact, ***"for all have sinned."*** Since all have sinned, no one can base his hope of acceptance by God on his own righteousness. It is not the quantity of sin in a person that separates him from God, it is the refusal to acknowledge that we cannot face God on our own merits.

Some Observations on Verses 19 - 23

These verses were intended to clear up some faulty thinking regarding the Law among the Jews. The Jews thought that obedience to the Law was an end unto itself; and totally covered their relationship with God. However, God intended the Law to be a signpost that pointed the way to a righteous relationship with Him. The Law showed that man's imperfect obedience of the Law, broke their personal relationship with a righteous God. The sacrifices they made for the forgiveness of their sins were only effective until they sinned again, which they could not avoid doing. The Law was intended to show that since they could not obtain a permanent forgiveness by God on their own merit, then is was clear that God needed to provide something for the permanent forgiveness of their sins. This something was the provision of His Son who was willing to die on the cross for our sins. However it still remained for man to exhibit an act of faith to accept God's provision. In effect, the provision of His Son Jesus Christ actually fulfilled the demands of the Law and completed it.

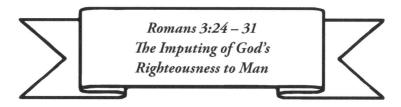

Romans 3:24 – 31
The Imputing of God's
Righteousness to Man

Verse 24 *being justified as a gift by His grace through the redemption which is in Christ Jesus;*

Justified is a once-for all declaration by God on behalf of the believing sinner, that as a result of their belief they can now stand in the presence of God justified (just-as-if-they-had-never-sinned). It is a gift from God, not something we earn through our personal endeavors. Ephesians 2:8 says, *"For by grace you have been saved through faith; and that not of yourselves, it is the gift of God."*

The word "redemption" in Greek is *"apolutrosis"* and is literally translated "a release obtained by the payment of a ransom." Redemption is derived from the Greek idea of purchasing a slave with the view of setting him free. In Ephesians 1:7 it says; *"In Him we have redemption through His blood, the forgiveness of our trespasses, according to the riches of His grace."* God justified man before Him when He allowed His Son Jesus Christ to pay the ransom for their sins on the cross.

Verse 25 *whom God displayed publicly as a propitiation in His blood through faith. This was to demonstrate His righteousness, because in the forbearance of God He passed over the sins previously committed;*

In Hebrews 9:5, the Greek word for mercy seat is *"hilasterios"* and is the same word translated as 'propitiation' in this verse. A "propitiation" is an act, or an accomplishment, or a gift that is intended to appease or satisfy God and obtain His mercy or blessings. In many ancient cultures, this idea eventually led to human sacrifices. They were trying to find the "gift" that would appease the gods and cause them to respond by giving good things to the people.

In the Old Testament, this same concept of redemption was applied to the "mercy seat" on the Ark of the Covenant in the Holy of Holies. It was where God's mercy could be asked for and received. In the Bible the word propitiation is only used to describe the sacrifice that Jesus Christ made on the cross. Jesus Christ acted as man's propitiation gift to God so that man could stand before God in righteousness and receive God's blessings. It was the shedding of Jesus' blood on the cross that satisfied God and resulted in the justification of man before God. 1 John 2:2; *"…and He Himself is the propitiation for our sins; and not for ours only, but also for those of the whole world,"* and 1 John 4:10: *"In this is love, not that we loved God, but that He loved us and sent His Son to be the propitiation for our sins."*

The question might be asked, "Why did God chose this method of payment for man's sins?" God could have used other less dramatic means to provide a sacrifice for the sins of man.

Perhaps by sacrificing the purest of animals, or maybe a million unblemished sheep, or even just by a statement of forgiveness that He had forgiven mankind of their sins. However, God allowed the sacrifice of that which was closest to Him to fulfill the regulation He had established in the Old Testament for a kinsman redeemer to pay the cost of redeeming property that had been lost. Remember that God owns the earth but lost His ability to roam freely over the earth when man first sinned. The earth then fell under the authority of Satan and needed to be redeemed so God could again roam freely over an earth free of the presence of sin. This redeemer per had to be the closest living relative of the original owner; able to pay the cost associated with the redemption; and willing to accept the responsibilities associated with the redemption. The cross was the ultimate demonstration of God's righteousness.

Up to the time when Christ died, God saved on credit; He did not visit men with wrath commensurate with their sins. However, this suspension of judgment was not equivalent to forgiveness. As it says in Acts 17:30, *"Therefore having overlooked the times of ignorance, God is now declaring to men that all everywhere should repent."*

Verse 26 *for the demonstration, I say, of His righteousness at the present time, that He might be just and the justifier of the one who has faith in Jesus.*

Paul reiterates that the justice of God is shown by his provision for the justification of sinners. The justification of man is not the result of a general faith in God, but rather in a faith directed towards Christ. Paul wants us to understand that this provision from God of His Son, Jesus Christ showed God's justice in providing the means for man to appear righteous in His sight in a way, where it was apparent that the works of man were inadequate.

Verse 27 Where then is boasting? It is excluded. By what kind of law? Of works? No, but by a law of faith.

Since there can be no question of anyone putting God in his debt through their works, then any boasting about works is simply a self-declaration of one's human achievements and is not evidence of faith. The law presents the principle of faith, but was never intended to be the object of faith.

The law of faith requires that man believe in Jesus Christ and His sacrifice at Calvary. It is also a faith that must be accompanied by actions on the part of man, not to secure man's salvation, but to demonstrate the sincerity of his faith by attempting to please God.

Verse 28 For we maintain that a man is justified by faith apart from works of the Law.

Justification by works is always determined to the perceived value of those works by the person seeking justification. The works of the Law are not works that the law produces, but works which the law demands. This verse is a reaffirmation of what has gone before.

My hope is built on nothing less
   Than Jesus' blood and righteousness;
      I dare not trust the sweetest frame,
         But wholly lean on Jesus name.
            On Christ the solid rock I stand;
               All other ground is sinking sand.
Author "Edward Mote" and his song "My Hope is Built on Nothing Less" ("public domain")

Verse 29 Or is God the God of Jews only? Is He not the God of Gentiles also? Yes, of Gentiles also,

Deuteronomy 6:4: *"Hear, O Israel! The Lord is our God, the Lord is one!"* This verse is the foundation of Jewish theology. If one takes the position that justification is by the Law, then it stands to reason that there must be two Gods -- one for the Jews, one for the Gentiles. If works in conformity with the Law are what salvation is based, then Gentiles living apart from the Law have no chance to be saved. However, if we acknowledge that there is only one God, then, we must also accept that there is only one-way of declaring men righteous for both Jews and Gentiles.

Verse 30 since indeed God who will justify the circumcised by faith and the uncircumcised through faith is one.

The Jews had been taught all their life that they were the sole recipients of God's special favor; therefore, the idea of a universal God fills them with conflicting emotions. They had forgotten that God had foretold them that their obedience to Him would be the means of blessing all mankind. Galatians 3:8: *"And the Scripture, foreseeing that God would justify the Gentiles by faith, preached the gospel beforehand to Abraham, saying, 'All the nations shall be blessed in you.'"*

Justification before God is by faith. For the Jew is the faith exhibited by acknowledging Jesus Christ as the Messiah. For the Gentle it is through their faith in acknowledging that Jesus Christ is God's son and acting upon that faith.

Verse 31 Do we then nullify the Law through faith? May it never be! On the contrary, we establish the Law.

The Law was never meant as a means of justification. It was given to convict man of sin. Jesus Christ fulfills the intent of the Law. Matthew 5:17: *"Do not think that I came to abolish the Law or the Prophets; I did not come to abolish, but to fulfill."* Faith in Christ establishes the practicality of obedience of the Law, while providing God with the means for man to appear righteous before Him.

Some Observations on Verses 24 - 31

Paul wants to make it clear that righteousness can only be imparted to man as a gift from God. Man must recognize that it is not something he can earn through any special effort on his part, but rather is received through accepting and acknowledging God's sacrificial gift, the sacrifice of His Son on the cross. This provision of God's forgiveness and mercy made the fulfillment of the Law possible.

Final Thoughts on Chapter 3

The Jews always felt that because of their special calling as a people by God, they were exempt from God's judgment on sin. After all, He had given them the Law and told them they would be blessed they obeyed it. When Paul said all men were sinners, they naturally objected. Paul looked at their objections and pointed out that the Law was not intended to provide for their righteousness, but rather to show them their need for God's forgiveness since they could not show perfect and complete obedience to the Law. Forgiveness by God had to come from Him. As prescribed by the law, God provided the perfect sacrifice needed for man's appearance of righteousness before Him. God gave His Son as a sacrifice for man's sins; now it was up to mankind to recognize and accept God's provision. The Jews needed to understand that this provision was for everybody. In God's eyes, all men have an equal need of His forgiveness and His offer of salvation through His Son, Jesus Christ.

Chapter 4

Justification by Faith

Introduction:

In the previous chapter, Paul defined the doctrine of justification by faith. Now he turns to the Old Testament to illustrate this doctrine. He begins by showing that Abraham was justified before God by his faith in the power of God. Therefore, it can be inferred that Abraham's faith is an example of the kind of faith necessary for the justification of all mankind. What follows is Paul's defense of the proposition that justification is by faith, not by works or heritage.

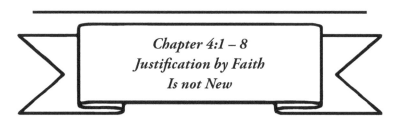

Chapter 4:1 – 8
Justification by Faith
Is not New

Verse 1 What then shall we say that Abraham, our forefather according to the flesh, has found?

Paul challenges the Jews to consider the basis of Abraham's relationship with God was based on.

Verse 2 For if Abraham was justified by works, he has something to boast about; but not before God.

According to the teaching of the rabbis, Abraham had earned God's favor through his actions. They held that it was for this reason that he was chosen to be the father of God's chosen people. This teaching ignored two important facts. One, Abraham's father earned his living making idols, and it was only after living seventy-five years around these idols that God sought Abraham out; Abraham did not seek God out. Two, Abraham actually lived before the existence of the Law; therefore, according to Jewish reasoning, he was unable to perform the obedience and good works required by the law to make him appear righteous before God.

Verse 3 *For what does the Scripture say? "And Abraham believed God, and it was reckoned to him as righteousness."*

Paul, speaking to Philemon of the debt of Onesimus, says, *"**charge that to my account**,"* (Philemon 1:18; i.e., "impute it to me"). The concept that Paul uses in Philemon is the same as that which occurs in Genesis 15:6: *"**God reckoned Abraham's faith for righteousness.**"* The meaning is that God accepted that Abraham believed God and was willing to act upon that belief allowed God to declare Abraham righteous before Him. We need to remember that Abraham's confidence in God's promises was in promises he never saw fulfilled.

Verse 4 *Now to the one who works, his wage is not reckoned as a favor, but as what is due.*

The significance of the use of the word "***one***" should not be ignored, as it clearly tells us that God is concerned with individuals, not as part of a greater group.

*"**Now to the one who works**,"* literally, "To him who does all that is required of him." *"…**his wage is not reckoned as a favor**,"* but rather, what was due them. Works yield wages that are treated as an obligation by an employer. Work necessarily incurs a debt from a person or group for whom the service is done.

Verse 5 *But to the one who does not work, but believes in Him who justifies the ungodly, his faith is reckoned as righteousness,*

At this point we need to understand justification. It is the act of being justified in one's actions thereby being acquitted of wrongdoing. For believers, it is an act whereby a just God is able to absolve us of our guilt and sins in His eyes, and to stand sinless before Him.

It is our faith in Christ and the recognition that He died for our sins that allows God to declare us righteous in his eyes. It is not the works of the law, but our belief in God's Son, Jesus, that allows us to appear righteousness before God. Our works provide the visible proof of the reality of the presence of Christ within us and come from the consequence of a changed life because of our desire to please a loving God.

Verse 6 just as David also speaks of the blessing upon the man to whom God reckons righteousness apart from works:

Forgiveness, granted and experienced by God, then, is not the result of human work, but of God's divine grace. David pleased God, and yet he could not boast of a just life before God. Abraham and David have something in common. Both were the recipients of God's, unearned forgiveness. Both received God's blessings because the believed God.

Verse 7 "Blessed are those whose lawless deeds have been forgiven, and whose sins have been covered."

Psalms 32:1: *"How blessed is he whose transgression is forgiven, Whose sin is covered!"* **"Blessed"** is the highest expression a Greek could use to express joy. In this verse, David, who was Israel's greatest king and was under the Law, could still sing of the forgiveness of his sins against the law. David had broken the law in his taking of Bathsheba. He even set his own penalty (2 Samuel 12:6: *"And he must make restitution for the lamb fourfold, because he did this thing and had no compassion."*). As a result, four of his sons died. He rejoiced knowing God forgave him. Sin in the life of a believer does not cancel God's forgiveness.

Verse 8 "Blessed is the man whose sin the Lord will not take into account."

Psalms 32:2; *"How blessed is the man to whom the Lord does not impute iniquity, And in whose spirit there is no deceit!"* This verse is in the future tense, meaning that at a future time, God will not reckon sin to the believer when he stands before the judgment seat of God. David's happiness came from one who understood he had sinned and yet, when he repented before God, he was confident his sins had been forgiven. David understood the concept of God's not taking our sins into account that allows us to appear righteous before Him.

Some Observations Regarding Verses 1 – 8

Man likes to feel that he can control his own destiny. Paul points out that it is God alone who controls our destiny. Paul uses two examples to illustrate this. First, he points out that Abraham was considered righteous in the eyes of God before the existence of the Law, which was the defining document of the "good" works in the Jews eyes. Second, David's life was not one of unbroken meritorious good works, yet David was able to express his confidence that God forgave him of his sins.

Our understanding of the principle Paul is trying to make here it is essential in having a right relationship with Jesus Christ. Their justification before God was initiated, not in response to something they did to earn it, but in the confident belief that God would do what He promised.

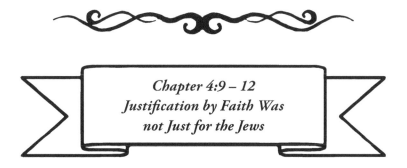

Chapter 4:9 – 12
Justification by Faith Was
not Just for the Jews

Verse 9 ***Is this blessing then upon the circumcised, or upon the uncircumcised also? For we say, "Faith was reckoned to Abraham as righteousness."***

The question Paul wanted the Jews to consider was if Abraham was circumcised or uncircumcised when God declared him righteous. Circumcision was of critical importance to many in the early Church, especially the Jewish believers. The Jews felt that only the circumcised could expect God's blessings. In the Jewish mind, circumcision was the first meritorious act of obedience to the law for an individual.

Nothing is more natural to man than the idea that righteousness is the result of meritorious action on their part. Many believers still consider circumcision, baptism, the Lord's Supper, prayer, and fasting as works making us worthy of righteousness. This stumbling block has caused many to fail to receive the blessings God had in store for them as they failed to totally understand that righteousness was a gift from God.

Verse 10 ***How then was it reckoned? While he was circumcised, or uncircumcised? Not while circumcised, but while uncircumcised;***

Consider the following chronology of events:

a. When God made his covenant with Abraham (see Gen. 15:18), and *"Abraham believed the Lord, and it was reckoned to him for righteousness"* (Gen. 15:6) Ishmael had not yet been conceived (see Gen. 15:2,3; 16:4)

b. Abraham was ninety-nine years of age when he was circumcised. On that same day, God told Abraham to circumcise Ishmael as well (see Gen. 17:24 - 25). Ishmael was then thirteen years of age.

Consider! Between the day when the blessings of Genesis 15:6 was pronounced upon Abraham and the day he was circumcised, there was an interval of at least fourteen years. Therefore, it was when Abraham was still uncircumcised that God pronounced the covenant promise and his blessings.

***Verse 11** and he received the sign of circumcision, a seal of the righteousness of the faith which he had while uncircumcised, that he might be the father of all who believe without being circumcised, that righteousness might be reckoned to them,*

A sign is a symbol of a reality that existed before the sign.

A stop sign is significant only when everyone who sees the sign knows that there is a law that says you must stop when you see the sign. Without the law, the sign is insignificant. So it is with circumcision. It was intended to be a symbol, recognized by all who saw, as evidence of God's promise to Abraham and his descendants. All the privileges and promises the Jew connect with circumcision were really due to the faith that Abraham exhibited while uncircumcised. A seal presupposes the pre-existence of the thing being sealed and does not add to that which is sealed. Abraham's seal of righteousness existed prior to his circumcision (while he was a Gentile).

Now Paul explains the significance of this symbol of circumcision given to Abraham by God: *"...that he might be the father of all who believe without being circumcised."* Are you paying attention? The key word here is **all** -- Jew or Gentile. The seal of circumcision was to identify Abraham as the predecessor of **all** who exhibited their faith in God, without necessarily being circumcised. Remember God's promise was that **all** nations would be blessed through him and his seed. Abraham's descendants were set apart as an example of a people God would bless when they lived in obedience to Him. It follows then that Abraham was chosen by God to be the representative father of both the circumcised and uncircumcised who exhibited faith in the promises of God.

***Verse 12** and the father of circumcision to those who not only are of the circumcision, but who also follow in the steps of the faith of our father Abraham which he had while uncircumcised.*

God delayed the circumcision of Abraham, in order to make it evident that faith leading to righteousness was independent of circumcision. The real descendants of Abraham are those who emulate and share his faith.

Note Galatians 3:29: *"And if you belong to Christ, then you are Abraham's offspring, heirs according to promise."*

Some Observations Regarding Verses 9 - 12

Since Abraham is the father of both the circumcised and the uncircumcised, then it follows that becoming righteous before God is open to everyone who exhibits the faith of Abraham.

Paul says it best in his letter to the Galatians' church. Galatians 3:24 – 29: *"Therefore The Law has become our tutor to lead us to Christ, so that we may be justified by faith. But now that faith has come, we are no longer under a tutor. For you are all sons of God through faith in Christ Jesus. For all of you who were baptized into Christ have clothed yourselves with Christ. There is neither Jew nor Greek, there is neither slave nor free man, there is neither male nor female; for you are all one in Christ Jesus. And if you belong to Christ, then you are Abraham's descendants, heirs according to promise."* To the Jew, God's righteousness was imputed as a result of ancestry. Paul wants us to understand it is a matter of personal faith.

Romans 4:13 – 25
Righteousness by Faith
Is For Everyone

Verse 13 For the promise to Abraham or to his descendants that he would be heir of the world was not through the Law, but through the righteousness of faith.

Finally we see Paul's admonition that covenant promise *"was not through the Law."* God's promise to Abraham contained the following items:

- title to the land of Canaan;
- the assurance that his seed would be without number;
- the guarantee that in Abraham's seed, all the people of the earth will be blessed.

The Jews had decided that the promises made to Abraham were realized through circumcision and obedience to the Mosaic Law. They glossed over the fact that it was an uncircumcised Abraham (as a Gentile) who received God's promise and the blessing, and failed to take into account that it was over 700 years later before the Mosaic Law was given to them. God's promise was clearly before the Mosaic Law and, therefore, not dependent on it.

Here is step one in the legal argument that righteousness is gained independent of the law. Abraham gained his righteousness before God before God's law was in existence.

Verse 14 For if those who are of the Law are heirs, faith is made void and the promise is nullified;

The Mosaic Law is not the source of gaining righteousness before God. If this were not true, then the faith exhibited by Abraham and God's promise to Abraham before the existence of the law was no longer valid.

To the Jews who considered themselves heirs of the Law, they were attempting to substitute their own will to gain the unconditional promises of God, when the reality was that God only required a simple declaration of confidence and faith in Him.

Here is step two in the legal argument that righteousness is gained independent of the law. If it was dependent on the law, then the promises God made to Abraham were of no value.

Verse 15 for the Law brings about wrath, but where there is no law, neither is there violation.

The Law expresses what may be done, or what may not be done. Since no man can completely keep the Law, it can only be a source for incurring God's wrath. *"Cursed is every one who continueth not in all things written in the book of law to do them,"* (Galatians 3:10).

Here is step three in the legal argument that righteousness is gained independent of the law. When there is no Law, there is no standard whereby God can judge man and visit His wrath upon unbelievers.

Verse 16   *For this reason it is by faith, that it might be in accordance with grace, in order that the promise may be certain to all the descendants, not only to those who are of the Law, but also to those who are of the faith of Abraham, who is the father of us all,*

If salvation were dependent on the merit or natural goodness of man, it would be utterly unattainable. No person could boast of obtaining an inheritance by complete obedience to the law since this is impossible.

Abraham was not born a Jew. He was born a Gentile, and by following God's directions was later called a Hebrew (literally an immigrant) by someone in whose land he was living.

Paul identifies two classes of people in this verse: first, those who base their salvation on absolute obedience to the Law; second, those who base their salvation on exhibiting the faith of Abraham.

Here is step four in the legal argument that righteousness is gained independent of the law. Abraham was the recipient of God's favor, not because of his sinless character but because of a loving God's divine grace.

Verse 17   *(as it is written, "A father of many nations have I made you") in the sight of Him whom he believed, even God, who gives life to the dead and calls into being that which does not exist.*

Genesis 17:5 says, *"No longer shall your name be called Abram, But your name shall be Abraham; For I will make you the father of a multitude of nations."* The fatherhood that God refers to is spiritual, as Abraham was the first to be called out by God and to exhibit the faith to believe God and accept His calling,

Here is step five in the legal argument that righteousness is gained independent of the law. If Abraham were to become "the father of many nations," it implies that these nations would have to include other than just Israelites.

Two essential attributes of GOD are: He gives life to the dead, and He calls into being that which did not previously exist. The first attribute gave authenticity to Jesus Christ as God's Son. John 5:21: *"For just as the Father raises the dead and gives them life, even so the Son also gives life to whom He wishes."* The second attribute refers to the work of creation.

Verse 18   In hope against hope he believed, in order that he might become a father of many nations, according to that which had been spoken, "So shall your descendants be."

It was not logical for Abraham to believe God, since he had experienced nothing of the promises God had made to him. In spite of all this, Abraham believed God's promises.

Verse 19   And without becoming weak in faith he contemplated his own body, now as good as dead since he was about a hundred years old, and the deadness of Sarah's womb;

Genesis 18:11: *"Now Abraham and Sarah were old, advanced in age; Sarah was past childbearing."* Up until now, Abraham and Sarah all natural hope for even one heir was seemingly gone.

Here is step six in the legal argument that righteousness is gained independent of the law. It is only when we accept that we cannot accomplish our righteousness on our own that God's grace can come into play, and we can appreciate what God can do for us.

Verse 20   yet, with respect to the promise of God, he did not waver in unbelief, but grew strong in faith, giving glory to God,

This does not imply that there was never any doubt in Abraham's mind. It only says that his faith triumphed because he accepted it was God who made the promise. The true way to have your faith strengthened is not to consider the difficulties of the thing promised, but rather to consider the character and resources of God. To give glory to God is to show by our conduct that we acknowledge that He will, and can, do what He says. Abraham's belief in God should become the standard for all believers.

Verse 21 *and being fully assured that what He had promised, He was able also to perform. and being fully assured that what He had promised,*

Genesis 18:14: *"Is anything too difficult for the Lord? At the appointed time I will return to you, at this time next year, and Sarah shall have a son."* God does not expect us to believe what is irrational, but He promises blessings granted by methods we cannot understand. Abraham was convinced God could deliver on His promises.

Here is the final step in the legal argument that righteousness is gained independent of the law: the need to accept by an unwavering faith that God will deliver on His promises.

Verse 22 *Therefore also it was reckoned to him as righteousness.*

Faith is the foundation of justification. Faith cannot make us righteous; only God makes us righteous. Because Abraham was confident that what God promised He could do, his faith resulted in his salvation.

Verse 23 *Now not for his sake only was it written, that it was reckoned to him,*

Abraham was a representative type. What was true of him can true of all others. If Abraham was justified by faith, we can all be justified by faith.

Verse 24 *but for our sake also, to whom it will be reckoned, as those who believe in Him who raised Jesus our Lord from the dead,*

The foundation of the Christian's faith is the same as the foundation of Abraham's, that is the confidence that God will deliver on His promises.

While Abraham looked forward to something God would do in the future, the Christian looks back to that which God has already done. The believer's faith should be *"as those who believe in Him who raised Jesus our Lord from the dead."* The provision for the believer's justification before God has never changed. 1 Peter 1:21: *"who through Him are believers in God, who raised Him from the dead and gave Him glory, so that your faith and hope are in God."*

Verse 25 *He who was delivered up because of our transgressions, and was raised because of our justification.*

These words stand out like a mountain peak in a valley of promises. This verse is a comprehensive statement of the gospel. Jesus' resurrection was necessary: first, as proof that His death had been accepted as the propitiation for our sins, and second, His resurrection was the assurance to believers of their justification and righteous appearance in the eyes of God.

As it was required under the law, that the high priest, not only slay the sacrifice at the altar but also carry its blood into the most holy place and sprinkle it upon the mercy seat. So it was necessary that our great High Priest, Jesus, should present his sacrifice before God that **we** might appear righteous before God. The resurrection is unique to Christianity. The resurrection of Christ proves the authenticity of the Christian message, and at the same time proves all other so-called religions false. Every other religion or religious movement has a dead founder.

As surely as Christ has risen, so surely shall believers be raised to an eternity with Him.

Final Thoughts on Chapter 4:

In this chapter, Paul was writing chiefly to the Jews. However, there is much in here that is meant to encourage all believers as well. The Jews based their privileged position with God on four items.

1. A covenant promise made to Abraham by God, that through him his descendants would be blessed and live in a land chosen by God.
2. That they were descendants of Abraham.
3. That Abraham was told by God that circumcision would be a sign that he and his descendants were children of the promise.
4. They were given the Mosaic Law by God and were told to obey it.

Paul explains that there was both a spiritual and a physical aspect of Abraham's fatherhood and God's covenant with him. The spiritual transcended the physical, and included the declaration of righteous before God to anyone who exhibited Abraham's faith in God. He does that by showing that God's reckoning righteousness to Abraham occurred before circumcision and before the giving of the Mosaic Law. Therefore, God's reckoning of righteousness was granted to both Jew and Gentile, who exhibited the confidence and faith of Abraham, a faith of unwavering confidence that God would fulfill His promises.

Chapter 5

The Benefits of Justification by Faith

Introduction:

In the previous chapter, Paul established that "justification by faith" was independent of heritage, the Law, circumcision, and works. The emphasis in this chapter is on what the blessings of justification by faith are for the believer in Christ. In the first verses of this chapter, Paul identifies some specific benefits.

- We have peace with God (an end of our search for peace)
- We have access to God
- We have the assurance of future glory
- Triumph over tribulation builds our faith and confidence in the love of God
- Knowing God gives us confidence in our salvation
- The Holy Spirit bears witness in us that we are the objects of the love of God
- We have the assurance of deliverance from God's wrath and judgment
- We have a joy only those who trust in God can appreciate

Note the transition from "faith" (see verses 1 and 2) to "hope" (see verses 3 through 5) to "love" (see verse 5). From the twelfth verse to the end of the chapter, Paul illustrates the logic of the imputation of righteousness through faith.

Chapter 5:1 – 11
*The Benefits of Justification
by Faith*

*Verse 1 Therefore having been justified by faith, we have peace with
God through our Lord Jesus Christ,*

The first blessing conveyed by justification by faith is "***peace with
God***." This peace comes to those who have trusted Christ as Savior and
know God no longer has any charge of sin against us and as a result, we
no longer fear the divine wrath of God. Our sins have been forgiven, the
justice of God satisfied, and His law honored and vindicated. God has
declared our righteousness before Him and now we live as part of God's
family. This peace results in the tranquility of mind that comes when our
search for God our for the meaning in life has ended.

*Verse 2 through whom also we have obtained our introduction by
faith into this grace in which we stand; and we exult in hope
of the glory of God.*

The second blessing is "access" to God. Ephesians 3:12; "*…in whom
we have boldness and confident access through faith in Him.*" This access is
gained because we now have an "introducer," God's Son, Jesus Christ. It
is important to recognize that this privilege is only for those who have
declared their faith in Him. The result is that we can stand before God,
knowing our sins have been forgiven.

The child of God has a future. You and I are living in a day when man
has all the comforts of life in an affluent society, but sees no future beyond
the present. However, as believers, we can glory in our future, knowing
that when God appears, we will join Him and share in His glory.

*Verse 3 And not only this, but we also exult in our tribulations,
knowing that tribulation brings about perseverance;*

Once our relationship to God has changed, our relationship to the things around us should also change. Tribulations that we used to think were an expression of God's displeasure or punishment now become opportunities to grow in our faith and confidence in Him.

Facing tribulations with God helps produce a Christian character built on a growing faith in Him. James 1:2 – 3: *"Consider it all joy, my brethren, when you encounter various trials...knowing that the testing of your faith produces endurance."* The endurance of trials provides Christians with visual, physical, and spiritual evidence of the depth of their relationship to God.

Verse 4 *and perseverance, proven character; and proven character, hope;*

One of the key ingredients for nearly any sort of success is perseverance, the ability to "keep on keeping on." Failure comes when we get impatient and take the problem back from God, thinking He isn't responding quickly enough.

The Greek word for "proven character," "*dokimē,*" denotes a person who has been found reliable, tested in battle, and found to be trustworthy, of proven value. James 1:12: *"Blessed is a man who perseveres under trial; for once he has been approved, he will receive the crown of life, which the Lord has promised to those who love Him."* Tribulations partnered with God will produce within us a process that builds our Christian character. This, then, is our hope, knowing that when we stand before God, having been faithful and persevering in our trials, we will share an eternal life with Him.

Verse 5 *and hope does not disappoint, because the love of God has been poured out within our hearts through the Holy Spirit who was given to us.*

Note the masterful transition from *faith* (verses 1 and 2) to *hope* (verses 2 and 4) to *love* (verse 5). "*Agapan*" is the Greek word used for love in this verse. It literally means unconditional love. God's unconditional love has been literally "poured out" within us.

Here Paul reminds us of the workings of the Holy Spirit is every believer. Titus 3:5,6: *"He saved us, not on the basis of deeds which we have done in righteousness, but according to His mercy, by the washing of regeneration and renewing by the Holy Spirit whom He poured out upon us richly through Jesus Christ our Savior."* Sinners may hear about the love of God and His Son hundreds of times, but until the Holy Spirit produces within them the awareness of God's love they are never affected by it. Here we see two of the ministries of the Holy Spirit; the imputation within us of the spirit of knowledge and an understanding of God.

Verse 6 For while we were still helpless, at the right time Christ died for the ungodly.

For while we were still helpless is intended to mean one who has no understanding of God. It is only when a sinner recognizes his need of God that he will discover God has already made a provision for his forgiveness. God demonstrated His unconditional love for you and me when He gave His Son to die for our benefit. Galatians 4:4: *"But when the fullness of the time came, God sent forth His Son, born of a woman, born under the Law."* As the love of a mother for her child, God's love is often strongest when its object is seemingly the least worthy. That God could love our unrighteous life would never enter into the heart and mind of natural man without the prompting of the Holy Spirit.

Verse 7 For one will hardly die for a righteous man; though perhaps for the good man someone would dare even to die.

A "good man" is a definition of the quality of a man according to man's set of values. It is a person who commands our admiration and affection because his actions are benevolent, kind, and reflect personal humility.

A righteous man is a definition of the quality of a man according to God's set of values. A righteous man's actions are guided by standards of justice, morality, and forgiveness toward others, as he lives a life pleasing and acceptable to God. It would be rare for a man to lay down his life for someone who is motivated to live a life pleasing to God, but maybe not so rare to lay down his life for a person who lives a life that is making a valuable contribution to the world. according to the world's and societies standards.

Verse 8 But God demonstrates His own love toward us, in that while we were yet sinners, Christ died for us.

The use of the present tense in the phrase "***while we were yet sinners***" is worth noting. We did not possess the capacity to love God when God chose to have His Son die for us. What renders God's love unique is that He sent his Son to die on the cross for those He knew to be without present merit.

John 3:16; *"For God so loved the world, that He gave His only begotten Son, that whoever believes in Him should not perish, but have eternal life."* Jesus did not die for us because we had demonstrated some worth to Him, but because of the anticipation of what our worth to Him could become.

Verse 9 Much more then, having now been justified by His blood, we shall be saved from the wrath of God through Him.

Christ's death puts sinners on a new footing before God. Christ's death on the cross for our sins and our acceptance of that sacrifice now allows believers to appear righteous before God, as God now sees believers through the sacrificial blood of His Son.

In addition, the believer now has the assurance of deliverance from the wrath of God. 1 Thessalonians 1:10: *"…and to wait for His Son from heaven, whom He raised from the dead, that is Jesus, who delivers us from the wrath to come."* Paul's *we* in this verse assumes that those addressed in this epistle have received and are enjoying the same provision of God that he is.

Verse 10 For if while we were enemies, we were reconciled to God through the death of His Son, much more, having been reconciled, we shall be saved by His life.

"***Enemies***" is a term Paul uses to refer to the fact that our actions as unbelievers have resulted in God's hostility and alienation from us. Reconciliation reflects a change in the attitude of parties previously at enmity, so that they are now at peace with one another. The removal of

God's alienation from us depends entirely upon God, the offended One, taking the initiative in restoring our relationship with Him.

The death of Christ does not remove the enmity of man towards God, but provides the means whereby man can secure the favor of God. The death of Christ was the sacrifice necessary to satisfy divine justice and the means of reconciliation with God. 2 Corinthians 5:18: *"Now all these things are from God, who reconciled us to Himself through Christ, and gave us the ministry of reconciliation."* Christ' death was man's propitiation to God.

Verse 11 And not only this, but we also exult in God through our Lord Jesus Christ, through whom we have now received the reconciliation.

God's Son's work on behalf of the believer has removed every trace of sin from the heart of the believer, and means that all believers can rejoice in God's goodness. God's offer of reconciliation is not a change in our position toward God, but a change in His attitude toward us.

2 Corinthians 5:18-20: *"Now all these things are from God, who reconciled us to Himself through Christ, and gave us the ministry of reconciliation, namely, that God was in Christ reconciling the world to Himself, not counting their trespasses against them, and He has committed to us the word of reconciliation. Therefore, we are ambassadors for Christ, as though God were entreating through us; we beg you on behalf of Christ, be reconciled to God."*

Some Observations Regarding Verses 1 – 11

In previous chapters, Paul has patiently explained that our righteous appearance before God is not a matter of our actions or heritage, but a matter of God's selection. Paul pointed out that Abraham's righteousness before God was obtained before the existence of the Law or circumcision. This was tough for the Jews to accept, so their natural question was that if this was true, then God's promise to Abraham of making him the father of a great nation was void. Paul answered that since God chose them to be the recipients of His law, they now knew what God expected of man. This was all well and good, but what they also needed to understand was the benefits of justification by faith, which they could not gain though simple obedience to the Law. Paul addresses that issue by noting that, in justification by faith:

1. They can now be at peace in their relationship with God, knowing He has permanently forgiven their sins, and they can now stand righteous before God.
2. They now have an eternal future with God.
3. Knowing that God has now forgiven them should give them the power to triumph over tribulation, which gives them confidence of their salvation.
4. They can now be confident of their deliverance from God's wrath and judgment.

Forgiveness and justification under the Law was temporary and unsatisfactory. Forgiveness and justification by faith is permanent. Christ's death and resurrection actually completed the law by making what the law hinted at become real and permanent.

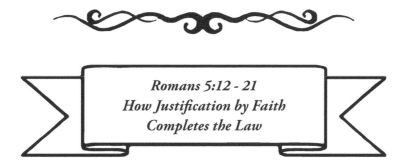

Romans 5:12 - 21
How Justification by Faith
Completes the Law

Verse 12 Therefore, just as through one man sin entered into the world, and death through sin, and so death spread to all men, because all sinned

Paul is developing the doctrine that death came to all men because of the sin of Adam, recognizing that Adam was the father of the human race; therefore, what he did, his descendants, who were still in him participated in as by proxy. The argument of Paul recognizes that Jesus was a historical person, just as Adam was a historical person.

Consider that Adam, unlike Eve, was not deceived (see 1 Timothy 2:14), but sinned deliberately, as God had expressly told Adam not to eat of the fruit of the tree of the knowledge of good and evil (see Genesis 2:16 - 17) before the existence of Eve. Therefore, all of Adam's descendants were introduced to sin by Adam's failure to obey God. The actions of those who went before us have a significant part in who we are now. Let me give a personal illustration. My great-grandfather lived in Sweden. In his day, he suffered religious persecution because he was a Baptist and so immigrated to the United States. When he left Sweden, in a sense I left also, as I was still within him. I really appreciate what my grandfather did for me. The reason I was born in America is because of what he did. In this same hereditary way, Adam's sin is imputed to us.

In today's society, we hear slums, poor housing, lack of education and recreation are the contributing factors in the immoralities of our society. There were no slums or delinquents, juvenile or adult, in the Garden. Yet in the midst of such a paradise, Adam and Eve yielded to the sin of disobedience. In Genesis 2:17, life was promised to Adam as the reward for obedience, and death was threatened as the punishment for disobedience. Adam disobeyed God, and death resulted. Recognize that God did not create man to die. He did not tell Adam to avoid eating of the tree of life.

We inherited from Adam a natural desire to sin and rebel against God. The question we must ask ourselves is, "Do we think we can better control our sinful nature, in a sinful environment, than Adam did, with a sinful nature in a perfect environment?"

Verse 13 *for until the Law sin was in the world; but sin is not imputed when there is no law.*

Paul now expands on the reasoning that death was passed on to all men, on account of one man.

Before the law, sin was not in the nature of actual disobedience to a command, except in the case of Adam. From Adam to Moses, sin was in the world as an unconscious act of rebellion against God, but it was not a transgression against God's commandments, because the Mosaic Law had not yet been given.

It is important that we understand the difference between disobedience and rebellion. Disobedience is the refusal to carry out a specific request given to us. Rebellion is actively defying the authority of someone who is over us. Adam's sin was an act of disobedience as he refused to accept a specific command given to him by God. However, our sins are usually an act of rebellion as our sins come from a refusal accept God's authority over us.

Verse 14 *Nevertheless death reigned from Adam until Moses, even over those who had not sinned in the likeness of the offense of Adam, who is a type of Him who was to come.*

Paul understood that God regards all men, from the first moment of their existence, as being out of fellowship with Him. Hosea 6:7: *"But like Adam they have transgressed the covenant; There they have dealt treacherously against Me."* As a result of Adam's sin subsequent generations are born in a state of spiritual separation from God and an unavoidable physical death. Even infants, who have not yet disobeyed or rebelled against God, have within them the natural desire to rebel against any authority.

Notice the expression in verse 14, *"a type of Him."* In the religious sense this term is intended to indicate an individual who represents someone who is to follow. Adam, as a human, was not a type of Christ; however, only one who had authority over sin could vanquish the results of Adam's sin. (1 Corinthians 15:22: *"For in Adam all die, so also in Christ all will be made alive."* And 1 Corinthians 15:45: *"So also it is written, 'The first man, Adam, became a living soul. The last Adam became a lifegiving spirit.'"*)

Verse 15 *But the free gift is not like the transgression. For if by the transgression of the one the many died, much more did the grace of God and the gift by the grace of the one Man, Jesus Christ, abound to the many.*

The parallel of Adam to Christ is mainly one of contrast. Adam's sin of disobedience brought death into the world to all mankind. Christ, with His one act of obedience to God (His death and subsequent resurrection), vanquished the effects of sin in the lives of all who were willing to accept His offer of grace. Adam's sin resulted in the birth of an involuntary sinful nature in subsequent generations, while God's provision for man's sin requires a voluntary action on the part of man.

God's grace is more abundant than the offense of Adam because we gain more through the actions of Christ than we lost through the actions of Adam. Ephesians 2:4-7: *"But God, being rich in mercy, because of His great love with which He loved us, even when we were dead in our transgressions, made us alive together with Christ (by grace you have been saved), and raised us up with Him, and seated us with Him in the heavenly places in Christ Jesus, so that in the ages to come He might show the surpassing riches of His grace in kindness toward us in Christ Jesus."*

Verse 16 **And the gift is not like that which came through the one who sinned; for on the one hand the judgment arose from one transgression resulting in condemnation, but on the other hand the free gift arose from many transgressions resulting in justification.**

In this verse, Paul contrasts between God's judgment of death because of Adam's sin and the free gift of God's grace, between condemnation and justification, and between the one and the many. The result of Adam's sin was death (i.e., the judgment). The result of the gift of God's grace is offer of eternal life (i.e., the free gift). It was through the actions of one, Adam, that all are subject to death; and it is through the actions of One, Christ, that eternal life became available to all.

The sentence of death, which was passed on to all men by Adam, was for one offense, whereas, we are justified by Christ before God in spite of our many offenses, through His one act of obedience. The resulting appearance of righteousness by God means He treats us as though we had not sinned, because of the righteousness of Christ. Depending on man's personal relationship with Jesus Christ he may appear righteous and unrighteous before God.

Verse 17 **For if by the transgression of the one, death reigned through the one, much more those who receive the abundance of grace and of the gift of righteousness will reign in life through the One, Jesus Christ.**

Christ's death on the cross dealt with the problem of mankind's sins, while Christ's subsequent resurrection dealt with God's stamp of approval of the judgment of forgiveness of man's sins. Jesus took upon Himself the responsibility of satisfying the sins of for all who accept God's offer of grace through the death of His son. God's grace gives the human race an opportunity to be delivered from the *guilt* of sins, not their *sinful nature*, and enables man to appear before God in a state of innocence in the eyes of a loving God.

Verse 18 So then as through one transgression there resulted condemnation to all men, even so through one act of righteousness there resulted justification of life to all men.

The one transgression of Adam caused the disruption of man's personal relationship with God. If, by the one act of Adam, all men were opened to sin, then it can be acknowledged that one act of perfect obedience (the voluntary death of Christ on the cross) can make it possible for all men to be saved. The "*all*" in this verse accents the universality of God's offer of grace.

Verse 19 For as through the one man's disobedience the many were made sinners, even so through the obedience of the One the many will be made righteous.

It is imperative that we, as Christians, view both Adam and Christ as actual historical people. The theory of evolution is designed to preclude the reason for the existence of God, thereby rendering the need for man's forgiveness by God, null and void.

Adam's direct disobedience to the revealed will of God, and Christ's perfect obedience to the revealed will of God must be understood for what they are. Adam's sin resulted in God's sentence of death, while Christ's obedience resulted in satisfying the demands of God regarding the forgiveness of sin. Those of the lineage of Adam are constituted sinners in a legal sense, as those who believe in Christ are now considered legally righteous in the eyes of God.

Verse 20 And the Law came in that the transgression might increase; but where sin increased, grace abounded all the more,

This verse and the verse that follows refer to the part that the Law plays in God's overall plan for mankind. The Law is the revelation of God's will for us and its purpose was to reveal our responsibilities toward God. Unfortunately, this increase in knowledge of what God desires of us invariably shows that we cannot completely obey the law in every aspect. It is by man's conscious awareness of that, that man realizes his need for one who can deliver him from the permanent consequences of his sin could only come from God.

Verse 21 that, as sin reigned in death, even so grace might reign through righteousness to eternal life through Jesus Christ our Lord.

For the believer, the reign of death is in the past tense. The design of God in permitting man to sin was to make it the occasion whereby he would recognize his need for God's grace in providing man with the opportunity to appear righteous before Him. Grace is the provision of a righteous God. 1 Timothy 1:14: *"and the grace of our Lord was more than abundant, with the faith and love which are found in Christ Jesus."*

— — — — — — — — — — — —

Final Thoughts on Chapter 5

Paul has two purposes in this chapter. In the first 11 verses, he wanted his Jewish readers to understand that the benefits of justification by faith were greater than the justification the Jews were able to obtain through a strict interpretation and obedience to the Mosaic Law. It had to be clear to them that strict complete obedience to the Law was impossible. The receipt of God's forgiveness of their sins was only as effective as their last sacrifices at the temple. Therefore there had to be something more, and that something could only come from God. Justification by faith provided the means whereby we can know that God has permanently forgiven us.

We can now stand righteous before Him, confident we will be delivered from His wrath and judgment, and we have an eternal future with Him.

In the remainder of the chapter, Paul wanted us to understand that it was the one act of the disobedience of Adam that condemned man, and it is therefore logical that it must be by one act of perfect obedience by Jesus Christ that man is justified.

The following chart is intended to show how Jesus' actions contrasted, yet superseded, the actions of Adam.

	ADAM	**JESUS**
Nature of action	Human	Divine
Relation to God	Created by God, yet seeks an equality with	Equal to God, yet humbled Himself before God
Response To God	Disobedient to	Obedient to
By One Act	Condemned man before God	Justified man before God
The Result	Subjected man to the judgment of God	Provided man with the grace of God
The Judgment	All men subject to death	All men subject to eternal life
In Conclusion	Man separated from God	Man brought into fellowship with God

Chapter 6

Understanding Sanctification

Introduction:

Up to this chapter, Paul has dealt with the need for salvation for sinners and their subsequent justification by faith. For many Jews, his emphasis on divine grace as the only source of salvation was something new. It seemed to them as if Paul was minimizing the value of works. This led some to reason, "If works mean so little, why perform them at all?" Paul is concerned that his readers understand how the righteousness that results from our justification by faith must be reflected in evidential changes in our lifestyle. In the next three chapters, Paul explains how a believer is to live a life of sanctification by faith. A life of sanctification is the visible reality that demonstrates that we are the children of God.

While they are both justification and sanctification may be at work in a believer, there are significant differences that we must understand. Paul tells us in Romans 1:16 -17: *"For I am not ashamed of the gospel, for it is the power of God for salvation to everyone who believes, to the Jew first and also to the Greek. For in it the righteousness of God is revealed from faith to faith; as it is written, 'But the righteous man shall live by faith.'"* Faith to faith; the first faith is clearly that which produces within us the power to believe in Jesus Christ (our justification). The second faith is the faith that empowers the believer to live a righteous life (our sanctification). The two actions together represent the evidences of a true born-again believer.

Justification by faith is a one-time act; sanctification by faith is a lifelong work in progress. The chart below illustrates the comparisons between "Justification by Faith" and "Sanctification by Faith."

The Important Question	Justification By Faith	Sanctification By Faith
How long does it take?	It takes place the moment you place your faith in Jesus Christ. (Luke 7:50)	It is a lifelong process of trying to be more like Jesus. (Habakkuk 2:4; Romans 1:17)
What does it cost?	It is God's gift to us. (Romans 3:24)	It is our gift to God. (2 Timothy 2:21)
How does it meet our needs?	It arises from a need in our heart to accept that there is a Creator. (Romans 1:20, 25)	It arises from a need to feel that we have a purpose in life. (1 Thessalonians 4:7)
What are its results in regard to sin?	It removes the guilt and penalty of sin from us. (Acts 26:18)	It removes the power of sin over us. (Romans 6:22)
How does it reflect in our appearance?	It declares us "righteous" in the eyes of God. (Romans 3:22)	It makes us appear "righteous" in the eyes of man. (John 13:35)
What does it mean to our salvation?	It is the source of our salvation. (Romans 1:16)	It is the goal of our salvation. (Hebrews 12:14; James 1:22)

To help us understand the significance of this, we need to review our understanding of what faith is and what faith is not. Faith is not a simple belief of certain dogmas and/or doctrines, nor is it demonstrated by the repetition of a creed or prayer. Faith is something we cannot experience by our physical senses. Hebrews 11:1 says, *"Now faith is the assurance of things hoped for, the conviction of things not seen."* To a Christian, the acceptance of Christ as our Savior by faith is only authenticated in a lifestyle that reflects obedience to and a desire to please Jesus Christ. James 1:22 says, *"But prove yourself doers of the word, and not merely hearers who delude themselves."* James 2:26 goes on to say, *"For just as the body without the spirit is dead, so also faith without works is dead."* Christianity does not minimize works; it just puts them where they belong (as evidence of a changed life).

Note that the verbs in the first few verses in this chapter are in the past tense, indicating something that God has already accomplished, not something God is doing now. Verses 1 -- 11 teach us that such in a relationship with Christ; his living in sin is not merely an inconsistency, but a contradiction, such as a live dead man, or a good bad man. In the final verses in this chapter, note some of the contrasts: formerly bondage > now freedom; formerly slaves of sin > now servants of God; formerly shame > now peace of mind; formerly wages > now free gift; formerly death > now life everlasting.

Finally, in this chapter and the two that follow, take note of the three deaths of the Christian believer: Chap. 6:11: dead to sin; Chap. 7:4: dead to the Law; Chap. 8:13: dead to the flesh. A study these chapters we will what these 'deaths' should mean to the believer.

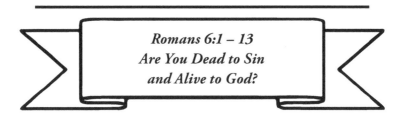

Romans 6:1 – 13
Are You Dead to Sin
and Alive to God?

Verse 1 What shall we say then? Are we to continue in sin that grace might increase?

In the preceding chapter Paul emphasized how God's grace was sufficient to forgive all our sins. The key word in this verse is "continue." Some reasoned that we are doing God a favor by sinning, rationalizing that the more God has to forgive; the more it emphasizes His forgiving nature. The Russian monk Rasputin, who was an influential favorite of Czar Nicholas II, espoused the doctrine, "The more a person sins, the more grace he will receive, so sin with enthusiasm." Clearly he espoused a doctrine of self-indulgence.

Verse 2 May it never be! How shall we who died to sin still live in it?

Here is Paul's answer to verse 1. To have *"died"* to something means we have eliminated its influence in our lives. The act, which should have initiated our dying to sin, was our accepting Christ as our Savior. It is separation from sin that constitutes the identity of a believer. Continuing in sin merely emphasizes the incongruity of claiming you are a Christian while living a life of self-indulgence and pleasure. A relationship with God requires us to eliminate those things from our lives that used to have power over us, and to refocus on those things that are pleasing to God.

Verse 3 Or do you not know that all of us who have been baptized into Christ Jesus have been baptized into His death?

The translators did not translate the Greek word *"baptizō"*; they just spelled the Greek word out in English because it had so many meanings. The first "baptism" in this verse means a personal identification with Christ (i.e., in the eyes of God). Baptism was a highly cherished sacrament of the early Church because of its implications of identification. Baptism was the approved method of professing a public faith in Christ and of declaring allegiance to Him.

"We are baptized unto his death" The second "baptism" in this verse has an interesting connotation. It means that we are identified with Christ's death to the world. The things of the world should no longer have any hold on us. Baptism is a voluntary act of identification with Christ. It declares that from now on, we are to live a changed life. As believers God sees us through Christ and the forgiveness that Christ purchased by His death on the cross. For Christians, baptism should identify a turning point in their lives that shows that we identify with Christ in a way that reflects how Christ changed our lives. Galatians 3:27: *"For all of you who were baptized into Christ have clothed yourselves with Christ."*

Verse 4 Therefore we have been buried with Him through baptism into death, in order that as Christ was raised from the dead through the glory of the Father, so we too might walk in newness of life.

Colossians 2:12: *"…having been buried with Him in baptism, in which you were also raised up with Him through faith in the working of God, who raised Him from the dead."* Acts 2:24: *"And God raised Him up again, putting an end to the agony of death, since it was impossible for Him to be held in its power."* It was the resurrection of Christ that authenticated who he was, the Son of God. So it is that by our resurrection to a new life that authenticates who we are, a child of God.

The phrase ***"in newness of life"*** indicates the quality of the lifestyle to be found in the life of the baptized believer. 2 Corinthians 5:17: *"Therefore if any man is in Christ, he is a new creature; the old things have passed away; behold, new things have come."* Ephesians 4:24: *"…and put on the new self, which in the likeness of God has been created in righteousness and holiness of the truth."* Beginning with the act of baptism, the world should see the process of "sanctification" (living a changed life) in our lives.

Verse 5   For if we have become united with Him in the likeness of His death, certainly we shall be also in the likeness of His resurrection,

Likeness is not identical to, but similar in appearance. Paul is not speaking of our physical death and resurrection; he is dealing with our death to the things of the world and our resurrection to new life.

The Greek word for "united" expresses a process by which a graft develops in a tree or a bush. The life or death of a tree necessitates the life or death of the branches and the graft. We actually share the life of Christ, much as a limb grafted into a tree shares the life of the tree. Philippians 3:10: *"that I may know Him, and the power of His resurrection and the fellowship of His sufferings, being conformed to His death;"*

Verse 6   knowing this, that our old self was crucified with Him, that our body of sin might be done away with, that we should no longer be slaves to sin;

The believer, though a new man, is not yet perfect; he is still capable of committing sin. It is the responsibility of the believer to live like the person God desires him to be.

The Greek word "*katargeo,*" here translated *"done away with,"* literally means, "to make of no effect." If we acknowledge Christ's forgiveness of our sins, we must also accept that now we are no longer slaves to sin. Galatians 2:20: *"I have been crucified with Christ; and it is no longer I who live, but Christ lives in me; and the life which I now live in the flesh I live by faith in the Son of God, who loved me, and delivered Himself up for me."*

Verse 7 *for he who has died is freed from sin.*

Here Paul again reminds us that with the death of Christ, our sins have now been forgiven, therefore freeing us from the burden of our sins. . 1 Peter 4:1: *"Therefore, since Christ has suffered in the flesh, arm yourselves also with the same purpose, because he who has suffered in the flesh has ceased from sin."* Freedom from sin is a matter of our choosing to live to please Christ.

Verse 8 *Now if we have died with Christ, we believe that we shall also live with Him,*

2 Timothy 2:11: *"It is a trustworthy statement: For if we died with Him, we shall also live with Him."* To live with Christ includes two ideas: association *with* Him, and identification *with* Him. Secure in the knowledge that Christ freed us of our sins we can be confident that we will spend eternity with Him.

Verse 9 *knowing that Christ, having been raised from the dead, is never to die again; death no longer is master over Him.*

"Death no longer is master over Him" implies that death did at one time have mastery over him. Why? Because by being in a human body in a sinful world, Jesus was Himself subject to the power of death caused by Adam's sin. However, Christ was not raised, like Lazarus, to a mere extension of a natural life, only to succumb once more to death. His resurrection was to an eternal life; that resurrection authenticated that He was God and demonstrated that He was no longer subject to the power of death. Acts 2:24: *"And God raised Him up again, putting an end to the agony of death, since it was impossible for Him to be held in its power."*

Verse 10 *For the death that He died, He died to sin, once for all; but the life that He lives, He lives to God.*

Christ did not sin, but He voluntarily accepted the responsibility for mankind's sin and, as a result, paid the penalty for sin (death). This act was Christ's "propitiation" to God. In other words, it was the gift that was able to satisfy God's demands. The work of the cross was the atonement for man's sin, but His resurrection was the elimination of the power of death over man. The significance of Christ's death and resurrection was so utterly decisive and final that there can be no question of the need of its being repeated. He now lives with God and his resurrection is His guarantee to every believer that they too can live for and with God.

Verse 11 *Even so consider yourselves to be dead to sin, but alive to God in Christ Jesus.*

We cannot be dead and living with respect to the same thing at the same time. Galatians 2:20: *"I have been crucified with Christ; and it is no longer I who live, but Christ lives in me; and the life which I now live in the flesh I live by faith in the Son of God, who loved me and gave Himself up for me."* Believers are to look upon themselves as being free from sin's penalty and dominion, and free to live to please God.

Verse 12 *Therefore do not let sin reign in your mortal body that you should obey its lusts,*

Sinners are servants of sin. If we are trying to live pleasing to God, we cannot allow our natural desire to sin to triumph over us. The slave who is set free is free must exercise the privileges and rights of his freedom to appreciate them. The Christian must realize that Christ has enabled him to resist the desires he once indulged in, but he must exercise his will to do so.

The Greek word for *"lust"* means earnest desire, irregular or violent desire. Lust is sensual in its every aspect. Paul does not teach that the body is the source of sin, but it is the source of its manifestation. In our society, criminals are quick to excuse their actions by saying they are victims of their environment. Unfortunately, many buy into that thinking, when the reality is that criminal are actually the victims of their own decisions.

Sanctification, the process of growing closer to Christ, does not determine our salvation, but it surely measures our relationship to God.

Verse 13 *and do not go on presenting the members of your body to sin as instruments of unrighteousness; but present yourselves to God as those alive from the dead, and your members as instruments of righteousness to God.*

Christianity is an unending offensive warfare against sin. In this warfare, we must recognize our innate desire to serve self. We will only discover freedom from sin as we voluntarily seek to serve God and others instead of ourselves.

Christianity has both a negative and a positive side. The first half of this verse is the negative side, what we must not do: *"neither present your members unto sin"*; the last half is the positive, what we must do: *"…but present yourselves unto God."* There is no room for neutrality.

Some Observations Regarding Verses 1 – 13

Two interesting questions that we must ask ourselves:

Question No. 1: Christ accepted the responsibility for our sins by dying on the cross. Have we acknowledged this, or are we still living in bondage to our sins?

Question No. 2: Christ died for our sins on the cross to appease God's demands regarding sin. Are we living your life to please God? Freedom from sin can only be realized when we change our focus away from pleasing our own desires.

The reason most of us get into trouble is because we stay too close to our old nature. A little girl fell out of bed one night and began to cry. Her mother rushed into her bedroom, picked her up, put her back in bed, and asked, "Honey, why did you fall out of bed?" And she said, "I think I stayed too close to the place where I got in." That is true of many Christians today.

Colossians 3:5: *"Therefore consider the members of your earthly body as dead to immorality, impurity, passion, evil desire, and greed, which amounts to idolatry."* True Christianity is the willingness to yield up our body, with all its inherent abilities, to God.

Romans 6:14 – 23
A Choice of Masters

Verse 14 For sin shall not be master over you, for you are not under law, but under grace.

The virtue of grace is that it can do what the Law cannot. The Law can only define our sins and condemn us. Grace allows for the forgiveness of our sins and provides the promise that they will be remembered no more. Hebrews 8:12: *"For I will be merciful to their iniquities, And I will remember their sins no more."* The life of the Christian is not meant to be one of constant conflict with sin, but rather one in which our victory over sin is certain. For the Christian, obedience to God is an expression of our thankfulness to God for His forgiveness of our sins.

Verse 15 What then? Shall we sin because we are not under law but under grace? May it never be!

The reality is that those who are under grace should evidence a manner of life superior to the standard of those who are under Law. The Law presents a standard of perfection as the expression of God's will for our lives, and not a means of salvation. Man cannot achieve that standard of perfection required by the Law. Their desire to show their appreciation of God's grace and love should necessarily be that of naturally avoiding any pretense of sin

***Verse 16** Do you not know that when you present yourselves to someone as slaves for obedience, you are slaves of the one whom you obey, either of sin resulting in death, or of obedience resulting in righteousness?*

Every person is a bondservant to someone or something. When a person voluntarily sold himself as a bond-slave during the time of Jesus, this action could never be nullified. The first time a person lies, he may feel remorse; the second time, some qualms of guilt; the third time, it all seems natural and easy. John 8:34: *"Jesus answered them, 'Truly, truly, I say to you, everyone who commits sin is the slave of sin.'"* Christians should view themselves as individuals who now allow God to be the master of their life rather then just seeking to please themselves. Living to please one's desires may seem normal, but leads to destruction; the desire to do someone else's will may seem abnormal, but in the end leads to a life of righteousness. The question implied in this verse is, "Who is the master of your life, self or God?"

***Verse 17** But thanks be to God that though you were slaves of sin, you became obedient from the heart to that form of teaching to which you were committed,*

It is one thing to receive a new nature, and quite another to learn how to walk in it. Christians should recognize that their deliverance from sin was through the grace of God and should therefore have a heart that is desirous of pleasing Christ.

***Verse 18** and having been freed from sin, you became slaves of righteousness.*

Notice that this is in the past tense. Faith in Christ does not make one free *to* sin, but free *from* sin. There is no place in the Christian experience where one is free to set his own standards and go his own way. Service to righteousness means reflecting positive lifestyle actions that add meaning to the ministry of Christ. Freedom from sin means we now have the opportunity to serve God and our fellow believers. In doing so we now become slaves of a life of righteousness.

Verse 19 I am speaking in human terms because of the weakness of your flesh. For just as you presented your members as slaves to impurity and to lawlessness, resulting in further lawlessness, so now present your members as slaves to righteousness, resulting in sanctification.

Paul does much of his teaching by showing contrasts. Where we were once willing to surrender ourselves become slaves of sin, so now we are to be willingly surrender ourselves to a life of righteousness. Obedience to something is the common to both sides of the contrast. That contrast appears in who the service is rendered to, self or God. When we commit sin, we are servants of that sin.

Paul is saying that we should become obedient servants to our new Master. To serve our new Master should be a joy and a privilege. John 8:32: *"…and you shall know the truth, and the truth shall make you free."* This service of righteousness is a continual process in the life of every believer leading to a life of sanctification.

Sanctification (noun): the process of making oneself more like God. Sanctification denotes a process. It reflects a purposeful lifestyle, evident in the life of the believer. It is a continual process in which believers strive to become more like Christ.

Verse 20 or when you were slaves of sin, you were free in regard to righteousness.

When a man is the slave of sin, he commonly thinks himself free and is proud of his condition. He thinks of himself as free from any restraints except his own.

Verse 21 Therefore what benefit were you then deriving from the things of which you are now ashamed? For the outcome of those things is death.

The pre-Christian lives of believers leave many with memories of a past life, in which they look back on with guilt and shame. To be ashamed of one's past is a vital element in the beginning of the process of sanctification. Ezekiel 16:63: *"'…in order that you may remember and be ashamed, and never open your mouth anymore because of your humiliation, when I have forgiven you for all that you have done,' the Lord God declares."* As believers, we can now be confident that God no longer remembers the things in our past.

Verse 22 *But now having been freed from sin and enslaved to God, you derive your benefit, resulting in sanctification, and the outcome, eternal life.*

Paul's conclusion is that living a life of sanctification results in the confidence of our spending an eternity with a loving God. Galatians 6:8: *"For the one who sows to his own flesh shall from the flesh reap corruption, but the one who sows to the Spirit shall from the Spirit reap eternal life."* Here is the greatest benefit of sanctification – an eternity spent with God.

Verse 23 *For the wages of sin is death, but the free gift of God is eternal life in Christ Jesus our Lord.*

Note again the contrasts: wages vs. free gift; death vs. life everlasting. The contrasts between the two are immeasurable. Receiving our just due is the principle by which we become heirs of death. Death is the result of God's justice: eternal life is the result of God's grace. The choice is ours – life or death.

Final Thoughts on Chapter 6

Who or what is master over our life. To the Jew it is living in strict obedience with the Law because they feared God. To the Christian it is living a life pleasing God as an expression of our thankfulness for His forgiveness of our. In the end, it is a question of what are the benefits of living under the Law versus living under grace.

Paul challenges us with the thought that we cannot claim a relationship with God and continue to live a sinful life. We are all servants to someone or something that requires our time and obedience. Life is a series of choices, and how we make them will determine whether we are living under the law and condemnation or under grace and sanctification. Our lives are contradictory when we say we are living under grace as Christians, yet we live a life that is inferior to those who are living under the law and those who are living by the standards of the world.

FOCUS	LAW (requires a commitment)	GRACE (requires a decision)
Its Objective	Defines sin	Defines God's nature
Its view of sin	Condemns sin	Forgives sin
Defines the power of sin	A life of bondage to sin (verses 16, 19)	Frees us from the power of sin (verses 17 -- 18)
How it defines our attitude toward our life.	Causes us to feel guilty of our sins (Verse 21)	Allows us a life of victory over sin (Verse 19)
The Final Outcome	condemnation and separation from God (verses 16, 21)	Eternal life spent with God (verses 16, 22 -- 23)

Chapter 7

Spiritual Freedom

Introduction:

Paul continues his explanation of the fruits of justification. He already considered peace (chapter 5) and holiness (chapter 6).

In this chapter, Paul considers the believer's freedom from bondage to the Law. The Law can only show us that it is impossible to live a sanctified life by our own efforts. Paul asserts that the inner sinful nature of man will never completely go away, and so they can never fulfill all the demands of the Law,, and will always remain imperfectly sanctified. The Law's power resides in its ability to convict one of sin, but at the same time is powerless to save the sinner (see 7:1-13) and impotent to remove the sin that remains in the life of the believer (see 7:14-25).

Most Christians are living in bondage to someone or something. It is for that very reason that they find it difficult to live a life of freedom. Paul wants believers to understand the source of their bondage. In this chapter, verses one through six explain how the believer receives his freedom, while verses seven through twenty-five show the believer how to live with the reality of that freedom. While justification sets us free, it is a life of sanctification that shows we are living in freedom.

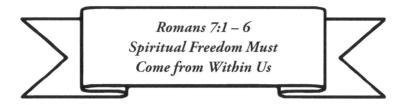

**Romans 7:1 – 6
Spiritual Freedom Must
Come from Within Us**

***Verse 1 Or do you not know, brethren for I am speaking to those who
know the law, that the law has jurisdiction over a person as
long as he lives?***

Paul is addressing the Jews. The knowledge of the law binds a man
to the law as long as he lives. It is only when he dies that man's required
obedience to the law is dissolved. In addition, Jewish religious leaders
burdened the Mosaic Law with oral traditions and regulations touching
just about every human activity and sphere of life. It had reached the point
that Jesus commented in Matthew 15:6, "*… And you invalidated the word
of God for the sake of your tradition.*" For the Jews, bondage to the Law is
required of them until the coming of their Messiah, and they believe the
Messiah has not yet arrived.

***Verse 2 For the married woman is bound by law to her husband while
he is living; but if her husband dies, she is released from the
law concerning the husband.***

Paul uses the illustration of a marriage to clarify the concept of bondage
to the Law. The idea is that when a woman enters the contract of marriage
under her own free will, she also accepted the obligation of bondage to her
husband, which accompanied this decision. In the eyes of God, only if the
husband dies is a married woman free to remarry. 1 Corinthians 7:39: "*A
wife is bound as long as her husband lives; but if her husband is dead, she is
free to be married to whom she wishes, only in the Lord.*"

***Verse 3 So then if, while her husband is living, she is joined to another
man, she shall be called an adulteress; but if her husband dies,
she is free from the law, so that she is not an adulteress, though
she is joined to another man.***

Verses two and three serve to illustrate the principle that the occurrence of a death affects a decisive change in respect to an individual's bondage to the law. In the illustration it is only the husband's death that ends the bondage relationship and legally opens the way for his wife to enter into another such relationship. The verse closes with the insinuation that in this illustration, a remarriage had already take place after the husband has died.

Paul wants his Jewish believers to understand who the characters in this marriage are: A. The wife - those who recognize their bondage relationship with the object of their choice; B. The first husband - the Mosaic Law; and C. The second husband – Jesus Christ. The idea is that when a Jew becomes a believer, he dies to his bondage to the Law and binds himself to another, i.e., Jesus Christ. Just as in a marriage contract, our choice of bondage is a matter of voluntary choice.

Verse 4 *Therefore, my brethren, you also were made to die to the Law through the body of Christ, that you might be joined to another, to Him who was raised from the dead, that we might bear fruit for God.*

Notice, we are made dead; we do not make ourselves dead. Galatians 2:19: *"For through the Law I died to the Law, that I might live to God."* In accepting the death and resurrection of Christ, we obtain our release from the Law and the permanent forgiveness of our sins. In doing this we acknowledge our bondage to Christ through our desire to please Him.

The purpose of marriage is to reproduce and bear fruit. Note the shift from the second person to the first: "so that *you* might belong to another -- in order **that *we* might bear fruit for God"** Jesus tells us in John 15:16, *"You did not choose Me, but I chose you, and appointed you, that you should go and bear fruit, and that your fruit should remain, that whatever you ask of the Father in My name, He may give to you."* The best evidence of our bondage to Christ is in bearing spiritual fruit acceptable to God.

Verse 5 *For while we were in the flesh, the sinful passions, which were aroused by the Law, were at work in the members of our body to bear fruit for death.*

When we begin life, we are under the control of our human nature. The prohibitions of the Law excite our human nature to rebel against the laws of God. When called into question, our nature seeks to self-righteously defend itself. As a result, spiritual fruitfulness was often impossible under the Law.

Verse 6 **But now we have been released from the Law, having died to that by which we were bound, so that we serve in newness of the Spirit and not in oldness of the letter.**

The argument goes along these lines: A. The Law imposes a lifetime obligation on its subjects; B. The Law has authority over a person as long as he remains in bondage to the Law; C. The believer is released from bondage to the Law through the death of Christ and His resurrection, which showed His power to break the bond of death, considered the outcome of disobedience to the law; D. Therefore the believer is no longer in bondage to the Law.

"…so that we serve in newness of the Spirit and not in oldness of the letter." "Newness of the Spirit" is the new nature that the Holy Spirit instills within us, the desire to return God's love by voluntarily seeking to please Him. The believer's new concern is to decide how they can now live to please their new Master, Christ, because of what He has done for them.

Some Observations Regarding Verses 1 – 6

Spiritual freedom is not freedom from responsibility, but a release from the bondage of living under the Law. This obedience was not voluntary, but was required by the Law. Any forgiveness of one's sins under the Law was only temporary. The death of Christ on the cross and His resurrection offered man another alternative. Christ's victory over death put an end to the inevitable result of following the Law, which was death. Now man could, by accepting the salvation Christ offered, rejoice in the knowledge that he would enjoy an eternity with Christ. Also, because of this gift of love by God, man could return this love by doing those things that would please his Savior. What Jesus is most pleased at is when we produce fruit in our lives. Galatians 5:22: *"But the fruit of the Spirit is love, joy, peace, patience, kindness, goodness, faithfulness, gentleness, self-control; against such things* there is *no law.* "Notice that these are all evidences of changes in our internal character and attitudes.

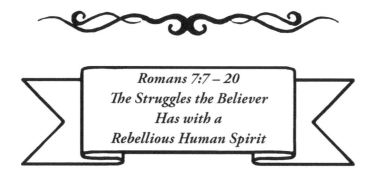

Romans 7:7 – 20
The Struggles the Believer
Has with a
Rebellious Human Spirit

Verse 7 *What shall we say then? Is the Law sin? May it never be! On the contrary, I would not have come to know sin except through the Law; for I would not have known about coveting if the Law had not said, "You shall not covet".*

Paul is giving his own religious experiences regarding the operation of the law, because he feels that his experience is common to all true Christians.

The Law cannot be identified with sin. However, the Law provides an awareness of sin. Can an x-ray machine be said to cause a disease because it reveals a diseased condition? Where there is no knowledge of the Law, there can be no consciousness of sin. It is only in the light of the commandments of the Law that we can recognize sin for what it is: an act of disobedience to God. Sin is not just an action taken, but may include action not taken when we know it should be taken. James 4:17 defines sin as *"When you know to do good and don't do it."*

The tenth commandment is used as an example because it directs attention to the inward root of man's outward actions. Exodus 20:7: *"You shall not covet your neighbor's house; you shall not covet your neighbor's wife or his male servant or his female servant or his ox or his donkey or anything that belongs to your neighbor."* The Law reveals our inborn desire to please ourselves rather than God. In doing so, it also reveals that the source of our guilt is within us.

Verse 8 *But sin, taking opportunity through the commandment, produced in me coveting of every kind; for apart from the Law sin is dead.*

An old writer confessed, "The permitted is unpleasing; the forbidden consumes us fiercely." In Genesis, Eve was faced with knowledge of a commandment from God. It was similar to our saying, "Don't do something" to a small child. When we lay down rules and regulations for our children, its intended purpose? is to protect our children from unnecessary harm, to help them grow strong, mature, and sense the importance of responsibility? And yet, their reaction is often feelings of rebellion, resentment, disobedience, and an attitude that says we don't understand their needs. Often they view this as a challenge to do something they may not even have contemplated before we forbade it.

It is not surprising that it was this tenth commandment that stopped Paul in his tracks. First in our nature comes a desire for something, and then comes the action taken to acquire it. The other commandments forbid transgressions that are, or seem to be, more or less external in character. But the tenth commandment strikes directly at the very root of sin, namely, man's own desires. The Law, then, by making us conscious of the existence and power of our sinful nature, acts just like the x-ray when it shows the existence of a previously undetected disease within our bodies.

Verse 9 *And I was once alive apart from the Law; but when the commandment came, sin became alive, and I died;*

The problem is we think freedom from the Law frees us from all restrictions. Paul's intimate knowledge of the Law gave him a feeling of self-righteousness, but when the Holy Spirit revealed the significance of the Law, he became aware of his inherent sinful nature. The result was that guilt and conviction came with the awareness that his sins could only result in death and separation from God comes from within us.

Verse 10 and this commandment, which was to result in life, proved to result in death for me;

The concept of strict obedience to the law was the priority in the life of a Pharisee like Paul. What consternation Paul must have faced when he realized his inability to totally obey the law and produced an awareness that within him that he lacked the ability to totally satisfy God.. The fault was not in the Law, but in the one who thought perfect obedience to the Law would bring life and power. In the final analysis, the law became the means of making the apostle Paul miserable and filled with the guilt of unforgiven sin.

Verse 11 for sin, taking opportunity through the commandment, deceived me, and through it killed me.

The Law completely failed to meet Paul's expectations by leading him to expect one thing, while it yielded the opposite. He expected life, and found death; he expected happiness, and found misery; he looked for holiness, and found feelings of guilt and the certainty of his inability to please God.

Verse 12 So then, the Law is holy, and the commandment is holy and righteous and good.

The conclusion is that the Law is not evil; the evil is the selfish nature of man, which is revealed by the Law. The Law is the still small voice of God, reminding humanity that their sinning will result in death. The ultimate achievement of the Law, then, is to make the sinner aware that he can only enter into a complete relationship with God by the acceptance of God's offer of grace for the forgiveness of sins past, present, and future through the death of His Son, Jesus, on the cross.

Verse 13 Therefore did that which is good become a cause of death for me? May it never be! Rather it was sin, in order that it might be shown to be sin by effecting my death through that which is good, that through the commandment sin might become utterly sinful.

Nothing so completely reveals our sin nature as the commandments of God. It is when we recognize that sin arises from a desire within us and not from the Law, that become open to take our first steps in receiving freedom from the Law.

Paul portrayed himself as one who, while his will desires that which is good, his sinful nature causes him to ignore that which he wills. There was a time when Paul was exclusively a sinner. Now, as he was dictating this letter, he is a sinner-saint, and this is the reason for his inner conflict. Paul understood that his carnal nature was still a part of his nature.

Verse 14 *For we know that the Law is spiritual; but I am of flesh, sold into bondage to sin.*

"The Law is spiritual" refers to its divine origin. The Law is a reflection of the character of God. As believers, we find that our human (fleshly) spirit instinctively rebels against God's Law. The apostle does not say, "I am *in* the flesh," but *"I am of flesh."* To be of the flesh means one's sinful nature is inherently present within us. The more one grows and strives to live in grace, the more sensitive and aware he becomes of his sinful nature. When Christians fail to accept that they still possess a sinful nature, they are deceiving themselves.

The positive declaration of this nature is due to the intensity of Paul's feeling against his partial bondage to the flesh. We are often subject to a power we cannot effectually resist, notwithstanding all our efforts. This is the kind of bondage of which Paul speaks in Galatians 4:3: *"So also we, while we were children, were held in bondage under the elemental things of the world."* Think again of how children instinctively rebel against actions they are told to avoid, or immediately desire that which they are denied.

Verse 15 *For that which I am doing, I do not understand; for I am not practicing what I would like to do, but I am doing the very thing I hate.*

Visualize the three distinct periods of Paul's life: First, as a Pharisee, he was confident that bringing the sacrifices to the temple and strict obedience to the Mosaic Law made him right with God. Second, he turned to Christ as his Savior and that living the Christian life was a matter of allowing the Spirit of God to live through him. Third, he found that he still struggled with a sinful nature that was ever present within him.

Galatians 5:17: *"For the flesh sets its desire against the Spirit, and the Spirit against the flesh; for these are in opposition to one another, so that you may not do the things that you please."* As Christians, we often do those things that, upon reflection, we realize we should not have done, but then try and excuse our actions by saying we didn't mean it. We often act before we think of the consequences of our actions. If we would take time to think first, we probably would avoid many embarrassing experiences.

As sincere believers, our ethical standard should be nothing short of moral-spiritual perfection. But when, at the close of the day, we review our actions, we are often discouraged by our shortcomings.

Verse 16 But if I do the very thing I do not wish to do, I agree with the Law, confessing that it is good.

Eventually, we discover that if we do what our conscience tells us to do, and not our will, we find that our actions are in accordance with the spirit of the Law. There is no conflict between the Law and the believer; the conflict is what the Law expects of us and what we actually do.

Verse 17 So now, no longer am I the one doing it, but sin which indwells me.

The apostle is saying that his new nature ("I") is not the one practicing sin, but his old sinful nature and human weakness. If sin still exerts its power over us, then it is clear that we must look for a solution inside ourselves. We cannot use the excuse, "It's not my fault, Lord!"

Verse 18 For I know that nothing good dwells in me, that is, in my flesh; for the wishing is present in me, but the doing of the good is not.

There is in this verse a truth that is often used by Christians: "It's not my fault; the devil made me do it!" Even though we are born again, we still have to fight the sin nature that abides in our flesh. Paul sees this as a battle between our desire to do good and our actual actions.

"*In my flesh*" means our natural human nature. Paul's care in distinguishing "*in me*" from "*in my flesh*" is significant. This is a confession that we have a natural desire to please God; yet at the same time possesses the desire to live to please ourselves. We must recognize that in ourselves we cannot win the battle over our flesh by ourselves but must look to Jesus Christ and to His strength. Our victory over sin comes as Christ gives us strength.

Verse 19 *For the good that I wish, I do not do; but I practice the very evil that I do not wish.*

Paul admits that he is not always act according to God's desires for him. As believers, we must often confess our inability to conform to God's commandments. We must accept that no amount of knowledge or self-will is sufficient to give victory over sin. We can only accept that the unsuccessful resistance of Satan's temptations and harassments serve to keep us humble.

Verse 20 *But if I am doing the very thing I do not wish, I am no longer the one doing it, but sin which dwells in me.*

The things that I do, when contrary to the desires and purposes of my heart, are the acts of a slave. There is a story told from the frontier days, and it goes something like this. A man asked a missionary to the Indians, what their religion was like that it allowed them to act the way they did. The missionary replied that he had asked an Indian medicine man that very same question. The medicine man replied that within every Indian there is a white dog, representing that which is good, and a black dog, representing that which is evil. The dogs are constantly fighting. The missionary asked him which dog usually won. The medicine man replied, "The one which is fed the most." Truly, each one of us has that same moral struggle within us. The question is, "Which one are we feeding the most?"

Some Observations Regarding Verses 7 – 20

These verses are a powerful testimony to the reality that our fleshly nature never leaves us. In these verses, Paul, a Jew of Jews, a Pharisee, and an example of an exemplary Christian, admits that he still struggles with his fleshly nature. Paul admits to the fragilities of being human. He still has feelings of guilt, as he sometimes does those things that he knows do not please God, even while he knows better. This should be a warning to all believers that we cannot become complacent in our desire to please God. Paul points out that the problem lies within each of us. The sins that lie within us are not the reason for our failures; rather, it is our lack of resistance to them and lack of focus on what should be our new nature. We need to be careful which dog we are feeding!

Romans 7:21 – 25
How to Live Free

Verse 21 I find then the principle that evil is present in me, the one who wishes to do good.

It is in the light of the Law that we recognize sin for what it is: disobedience of God's will. Every child of God, regardless of our seeming maturity, must be aware that the desire to do evil is always present within us. However, we cannot forget that within us also exists the Holy Spirit, who plants within us a desire to please God in gratitude for what His Son has done for us.

Verse 22 For I joyfully concur with the law of God in the inner man,

The "*inner man*" is the desire within us to please God, and is put there by the Holy Spirit. The apostle recognized that within the believer, there are two persons: the individual's fleshly desires, and the Holy Spirit. This conflict between the flesh and the Spirit continues in us as long as we live. 2 Corinthians 4:16: *"Therefore we do not lose heart, but though our outer man is decaying, yet our inner man is being renewed day by day."*

Children who love their parents find pleasure in showing their parents how much they love them through their acts of obedience and expressions of love. In this same manner, the believer find joy in acting in obedience to God as an expression of our love for Him.

Verse 23 *but I see a different law in the members of my body, waging war against the law of my mind, and making me a prisoner of the law of sin which is in my members.*

By the term the "*law of my mind*," Paul is referring to his born-again nature. Within him is still his fleshly nature which wars against his new nature. Galatians 5:17: *"For the flesh sets its desire against the Spirit, and the Spirit against the flesh; for these are in opposition to one another, so that you may not do the things that you please."* James 4:1: *"What is the source of quarrels and conflicts among you? Is not the source your pleasures that wage war in your members?"*

Verse 24 *Wretched man that I am! Who will set me free from the body of this death?*

It is not Paul's doctrine that the body is evil, or that it is the seat of sin. It is the human will within us that contaminate the body and places within us fleshly desires. The Greek word, (ταλαιπωροζ) translated "*wretched,*" is only used twice in the New Testament -- here and in Revelation 3:17. This is not the cry of an unsaved man: "*O wretched man that I am*"; this is a true believer calling for help. Paul could only groan under the pressure of indwelling sin, and yet possess a longing for deliverance by a power greater than his own. Paul genuinely deplores the fact that he is unable to serve God as completely and wholeheartedly as he desires. What he longs for is a redemptive power that will end the struggle that inhabits the physical body, in whose members the laws of sin are still operative.

Verse 25 *Thanks be to God through Jesus Christ our Lord! So then, on the one hand I myself with my mind am serving the law of God, but on the other, with my flesh the law of sin.*

The implication in this verse is that Paul is confidant that God can and will deliver him from the power of sin. It is a promise given by God Himself, through the sacrifice of His Son.

1 Corinthians 15:57: *"but thanks be to God, who gives us the victory through our Lord Jesus Christ."* This conclusion does not cloak the painful fact that the Christian, so long as he remains in this present life, still possesses a fleshly nature, but expresses the gratitude of a mature believer for Christ's strengthening.

Final Thoughts on Chapter 7

Paul begins by stating that the only escape we have from our bondage to the Law is death. The problem with the Law is that it only defines what we need to do to please God and shows us how we are not to live. Since we cannot perfectly meet its demands, the end result is death. The Law also cannot provide a way to receive permanent forgiveness of our sins. Paul reminds us that when we accept God's offer of grace through His Son Jesus Christ, we become dead to the law. God's grace also promises the permanent forgiveness of our sins, so we are now free from the guilt of realizing that we can never completely fulfill the demands of the law.

Paul than then tells us that in freeing ourselves from the law, we will still find within us a natural desire to do those things that please us, not God. However, in accepting God's grace, the Holy Spirit implants within ourselves a growing desire to please God because of what He has done for us. Unfortunately, this conflicts with an inner desire to please ourselves and often cause us to do things that conflict with our new nature. In his humility, Paul admits that he also suffers from this inner conflict. The believer must accept that this strange duality in our allegiance will continue until the day we stand in the presence of Jesus and receive our heavenly bodies. It is only then that our fleshly nature will totally be put to death.

Paul ends this chapter by telling us that this inner conflict while in this world will only be resolved when we ask God for help. The failure of many Christians today desiring to live a life pleasing to God, lies in their failure to turn to God for help. We must rid ourselves of the pride that lays within us and that says, "I can do it without help." Surely, if Paul can humbly admit that he had to have help from God, we can do no less.

Chapter 8

A Life of Victory

Introduction:

Paul's theme in this chapter is the security of the believer, not only from present condemnation but also from future judgment. Verses 1 -- 11 contain the development of the apostle's doctrine that those who are in Christ Jesus will never be condemned if they choose to walk the walk of righteousness under God's direction. Verses 12 – 30 acquaints us with four of God's promises to fill the life of the believer with the assurance of His presence and our salvation. Verses 31 – 34 assures believers that since Christ died for their sins, He now intercedes for them before God. Finally, verses 36 – 39 contain the assurance that nothing can ever separate the believer from the love of God.

A special reassurance is given to all believers in verses 36 – 37. It is the assurance that we are overwhelmingly conquerors.. *"But in all these things we overwhelmingly conqueror through him who loved us."*

It is worth noting that the Holy Spirit is mentioned in this chapter no less than nineteen times, whereas it was mentioned only once in the previous seven chapters.

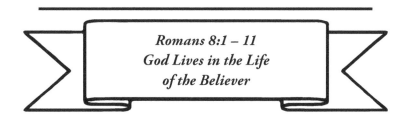

Romans 8:1 – 11
God Lives in the Life
of the Believer

Verse 1 *There is therefore now no condemnation for those who are in Christ Jesus.*

The word "*therefore*" indicates that what follows is a continuation of the previous chapter. That chapter made it clear that believers are now free from the guilt of sin and have been assured of a life of victory.

Previously, it was Satan who condemned us before God. In Revelation 12:7 – 11, we read that because of the shed blood of Christ on the cross, the angels in heaven were able to overpower Satan and throw him down to the earth so that he no longer had access to God and, therefore, no longer has the power to condemn us before God. The result is that when the believer now stands before God, he will do so free of the condemnation of past sins. And, of course, the term "***in Christ Jesus***" is a critical reminder that this assurance is only for those who have accepted Christ and are endeavoring to live a righteous life before God.

Verse 2 *For the law of the Spirit of life in Christ Jesus has set you free from the law of sin and of death.*

The Spirit of Christ in the life of the believer activates the "Spirit of life." Because the Spirit of Jesus Christ has set us free from the power of sin over us, and since the Spirit is under the direction of God, there is no one to condemn us before God.

"*The law of sin and death*" is the power that sin had over our old nature. Romans 7:6 says it best: "*But now we have been released from the Law, having died to that by which we were bound, so that we serve in newness of the Spirit and not in oldness of the letter.*" Keep in mind that it is not through our own strength, but by the power of the Spirit that lives within us that we are set free from the Law. It was Christ's power over death that set us free from the condemnation that the Law produces. John 8:36 says, "*If therefore the Son shall make you free, you shall be free indeed.*" And John 8:32 says, "*…and you shall know the truth, and the truth shall make you free.*" Believers are free from the guilt of the condemnation of sin and its penalty.

Verse 3 For what the Law could not do, weak as it was through the flesh, God did: sending His own Son in the likeness of sinful flesh and as an offering for sin, He condemned sin in the flesh,

The purpose of the Law was to reveal to man his inadequacy before a holy God. The Law is impotent against the sinful nature of man and has no provision for the eternal forgiveness of sins. Hebrews 10:1: *"For the Law, since it has only a shadow of the good things to come and not the very form of things, can never by the same sacrifices year by year, which they offer continually, make perfect those who draw near."*

When the Father sent the Son, it was for the purpose of providing man with the ability to obtain eternal forgiveness of sin. Christ was God's sacrifice so that the requirements of the law, which demanded a perfect sacrifice for the forgiveness of man's sin, would be fulfilled. Two things are implied concerning Christ's actions. First is the form under which He appeared in the world. (Christ took upon Himself our human nature, recognizing that the release of the guilt of man's sinful nature must be accomplished in the nature in which man had sinned.) Second is the object for which He was sent. (Christ acted as the propitiation gift that would appease God by bearing the curse of sin for all mankind.). Hebrews 4:15: *"For we do not have a high priest who cannot sympathize with our weaknesses, but One who has been tempted in all things as we are, yet without sin."*

It was only through Christ's voluntarily limiting His power to ours, and at the same time maintaining His obedience to the will of God to the point of death, that He was able to satisfy the requirements of the Law on our behalf.

Verse 4 in order that the requirement of the Law might be fulfilled in us, who do not walk according to the flesh, but according to the Spirit.

This statement refers to the work of the Holy Spirit within the believer. The Greek word translated "requirement" means justice, equity, so "the requirement of the law" is understood as meaning the justice (or righteousness) of the Law.

Two classes of people are identified: A. those who walk according to the flesh (our sinful nature); and B. those who walk according to the Spirit (our desire to please God). Galatians 5:16: *"But I say, walk by the Spirit, and you will not carry out the desire of the flesh.*

The Holy Spirit enables us to live a life pleasing to God, but the ultimate choice of how we live our life is ours: whether according to our natural desires or in righteousness before God.

Verse 5 For those who are according to the flesh set their minds on the things of the flesh, but those who are according to the Spirit, the things of the Spirit.

Paul tells us that when we choose our master, we also choose our nature and lifestyle. We either have our minds set upon the things of the flesh or fixed upon things of the spirit.

Here is presented the answer to the age-old question, "How can I know whether I am a Christian?" Galatians 5:19 – 21: *"Now the deeds of the flesh are evident, which are: immorality, impurity, sensuality, idolatry, sorcery, enmities, strife, jealousy, outbursts of anger, disputes, dissensions, factions, envying, drunkenness, carousing, and things like these, of which I forewarn you just as I have forewarned you that those who practice such things shall not inherit the kingdom of God."*

On the other hand, Galatians 5:22 -- 25 tells us, *"But the fruit of the Spirit is love, joy, peace, patience, kindness, goodness, faithfulness, gentleness, selfcontrol; against such things there is no law. Now those who belong to Christ Jesus have crucified the flesh with its passions and desires. If we live by the Spirit, let us also walk by the Spirit."*

Verse 6 For the mind set on the flesh is death, but the mind set on the Spirit is life and peace,

Here we find the results of our choice identified in verse 5. Our choice results in either death (eternal separation from God) or peace with God and eternal life. Galatians 6:8: *"For the one who sows to his own flesh shall from the flesh reap corruption, but the one who sows to the Spirit shall from the Spirit reap eternal life."* A *"mind set on the Spirit"* enjoys the peace that arises from the assurance that past sins are forgiven, and that nothing in the future can separate us from the love of God.

Verse 7 because the mind set on the flesh is hostile toward God; for it does not subject itself to the law of God, for it is not even able to do so;

In these next two verses, we see the results of a mind set on self. The first is that one rebels against God's commandments and is hostile towards God. James 4:4: *"You adulteresses, do you not know that friendship with the world is hostility toward God? Therefore whoever wishes to be a friend of the world makes himself an enemy of God."*

Verse 8 and those who are in the flesh cannot please God.

The second is man's aversion to God, which makes him unwilling to try and please God. The mind set on the self cannot subject itself to the will of God because it is dedicated to obedience to self-will, which can only result in willful insubordination to God's Law.

Verse 9 However, you are not in the flesh but in the Spirit, if indeed the Spirit of God dwells in you. But if anyone does not have the Spirit of Christ, he does not belong to Him.

Herein lies the great distinction of true believer; the one who allows God's Spirit to live within them allows the Holy Spirit to speak to them through their lives. 1 Corinthians 3:16: *"Do you not know that you are a temple of God, and that the Spirit of God dwells in you?"* If the Holy Spirit dwells in us, then we are naturally careful lest anything in our thoughts or feelings would be offensive to this divine Guest.

Quite the opposite is true of one who is living a life in the flesh his actions show he is not allowing the Spirit of God to speak to Him. The strength of the expression "*he does not belong to Him,*" leaves no room for doubt that God has rejected the person living in the flesh.

Verse 10 And if Christ is in you, though the body is dead because of sin, yet the spirit is alive because of righteousness.

The spirit, as it is used in this verse, is not to be understood as the Holy Spirit, but the human spirit. Paul is saying that if you have accepted Christ, your sinful nature still lives within you, and your natural body is still subject to death because of its sinful nature. However, where the Spirit of God dwells there is life.

Verse 11 But if the Spirit of Him who raised Jesus from the dead dwells in you, He who raised Christ Jesus from the dead will also give life to your mortal bodies through His Spirit who indwells you.

The resurrection of the believer is assured in this statement. Consider the following:

1. The Spirit of the Father raised up Christ from the dead.
2. The Holy Spirit is the Spirit of the Father.
3. This same Holy Spirit dwells in believers.
4. Therefore, this same Spirit who raised Jesus, guarantees the believer's resurrection from the dead.

Here we can see the unity existing between Father, Son, and Holy Spirit, a unity not only of essence but also of operation in the interest of our salvation. We are living in an age in which some evangelistic circles show a disproportionate focus on Jesus; others emphasize that all men are brothers, as the same God is the Father of them all; finally, a third party cannot stop talking about the Spirit. All of them are attempting to separate the Trinity of God, instead of recognizing that each is an expression of the same God, who is the sum of all three.

Some Observations Regarding Verses 1 – 11

Justification is a once-and-for-all action that God performs on believers when they acknowledge their faith in His Son. As believers, God no longer condemns us for our sins. They have been forgiven through the sacrifice of His Son, Jesus Christ. However, Paul reveals in these verses that the believer will always face a struggle as to whether he allows the Holy Spirit to control our life, or allow our sinful nature to "do it our way."

The following table will help you to see the
results of the decision that you make.

WALKING ACCORDING TO THE FLESH	THE CHOICE	WALKING ACCORDING TO THE HOLY SPIRIT
set their minds on things of the flesh (those things that please self)	**The evidence** (verse 5)	set their minds on things of the Spirit (those things that please God)
finds death	**The result** (verse 6)	finds life and peace
are hostile toward God	**Because they** (verses 7 - 9)	seek to please God
rejection by God	**God's Judgment**	appear righteous before God (Verses 9 - 10)

It's your choice!

Romans 8:12 – 17
God's First Promise to Those
Who Believe
(He has adopted us as His
children and heirs in His kingdom)

Verse 12 So then, brethren, we are under obligation, not to the flesh, to live according to the flesh

The apostle now challenges believers to accept the assurances that God gives them. We are debtors, not to the flesh but to the Spirit, which sets the believer free from the desires of the flesh. Colossians 3:5: *"Therefore consider the members of your earthly body as dead to immorality, impurity, passion, evil desire, and greed, which amounts to idolatry."*

Verse 13 for if you are living according to the flesh, you must die; but if by the Spirit you are putting to death the deeds of the body, you will live.

Remember, we are talking about professing believers here. If that person is still living according to his natural desires, he will surely die in his sins. However, if the professing believer rejects his natural desires and lives according to the desires of the Holy Spirit, then he will experience the promise of eternal life. The inclusion of *"by the Spirit"* emphasizes the principle that it is not by our own strength that we can live a life of self-righteousness. Our success in accepting the help of the Holy Spirit separates us from the consequences of sin in God's eyes. Here again we see the principle that it is not proclamation which identifies the believer, but production.

Verse 14 For all who are being led by the Spirit of God, these are sons of God.

John 1:12: *"But as many as received Him, to them He gave the right to become children of God, even to those who believe in His name."* Verses twelve through fourteen make our obligation to God clear: if we are to be the recipients of His promise to make us sons and heirs, we must permit our lives to be led by the Holy Spirit. God does not drive His sheep; He leads them. John 10:27: *"My sheep hear my voice and I know them and they follow me."* Believers will receive eternal life, not because they possess the Spirit of life, but because they are the sons of God. Sons are the objects of affection by their parents and share in the possessions of their parents. 2

Corinthians 6:18: *"And I will be a father to you, And you shall be sons and daughters to Me,' says the Lord Almighty."*

Verse 15 *For you have not received a spirit of slavery leading to fear again, but you have received a spirit of adoption as sons by which we cry out, "Abba! Father!"*

The Holy Spirit is called "the Spirit of adoption" because He creates in the children of God the spirit of joy and confidence in knowing they are God's children. The relation of God to us is the counterpart of ours to Him. If we feel He is our friend, then He reciprocates that feeling towards us. However, if we think of ourselves as a member of His family, He will feel toward us as a father. A spirit of fear, far from being evidence of piety, is evidence of a poor relationship with the Father. 2 Timothy 1:7: *"For God has not given us a spirit of timidity, but of power and love and discipline."*

"Abba! Father!" Abba is the Syrian and Chaldean form of the Hebrew word by which Jewish children address their earthly father. Expressions of tenderness are the last words children give up; in times of excitement they are sure to come back to them. The application of this intimate phrase by Jesus to God suggests an intimate Father-child. "Abba" is the Aramaic word Jesus used to address His Father in prayer in Mark 14:36: *"And He was saying, 'Abba! Father! All things are possible for Thee; remove this cup from Me; yet not what I will, but what Thou wilt.'"* Galatians 4:6: *"And because you are sons, God has sent forth the Spirit of His Son into our hearts, crying, 'Abba! Father!'"*

Verse 16 *The Spirit Himself bears witness with our spirit that we are children of God,*

According to Jewish Law, from the mouth of two or three witnesses a matter is to be considered established (see Deuteronomy 19:15). In the case presented here, these witnesses are inner in nature and not dependent on others. The Holy Spirit abides in every truly born-again believer, and never leaves. Acts 5:32: *"And we are witnesses of these things; and so is the Holy Spirit, whom God has given to those who obey Him."* Assurance of salvation has a two-fold foundation: the evidences of a changed life, and the witness of the Holy Spirit within us.

"Children of God" denotes a legal relationship, by nature, birth, and origin. John 1:12: *"But as many as received Him, to them He gave the right to become children of God, even to those who believe in His name."*

Verse 17 and if children, heirs also, heirs of God and fellow heirs with Christ, if indeed we suffer with Him in order that we may also be glorified with Him.

Christians are people who should have great expectations based upon their being sons of God. Under Jewish Law, as the Father's only begotten Son, Christ inherits all things. Since believers are in Christ, they are therefore co-heirs to His kingdom. Galatians 4:7: *"Therefore you are no longer a slave, but a son; and if a son, then an heir through God."*

Just as the cross preceded the crown, in the experience of Christ, so His people must first suffer with Him before they can be glorified with Him. It could even be implied that those who have never suffered for Christ have never openly identified themselves with Christ. 1 Peter 4:13: *"…but to the degree that you share the sufferings of Christ, keep on rejoicing; so that also at the revelation of His glory, you may rejoice with exultation."*

Some Observations Regarding Verses 12 - 17

These verses reflect God's first promise to those who would follow Him. If we choose to allow our lives to be guided by the Holy Spirit, He will adopt us as His children and co-heirs. If we do this, the Holy Spirit will fill us with the confidence and assurance of our adoption. Finally, as children of God, any persecution we receive as a result of our identity with Christ is insignificant in comparison to the eternal reward we will receive as children of God.

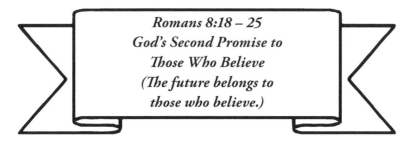

Romans 8:18 – 25
God's Second Promise to
Those Who Believe
(The future belongs to
those who believe.)

Verse 18 For I consider that the sufferings of this present time are not worthy to be compared with the glory that is to be revealed to us.

In this verse, we are told that the sufferings we can expect from the previous verse must be put in perspective. How can one fully appreciate a mountaintop experience unless one has previously experienced the valley? This is what the Apostle is saying when he makes the comparison between our suffering for Christ's sake and the glory that awaits us. 2 Corinthians 4;17: *"For momentary, light affliction is producing for us an eternal weight of glory far beyond all comparison."* 1 Peter 4:13: *"…but to the degree that you share the sufferings of Christ, keep on rejoicing; so that also at the revelation of His glory, you may rejoice with exultation."* While we wait to share in God's glory, we must also be willing to accept this world's sufferings.

Verse 19 For the anxious longing of the creation waits eagerly for the revealing of the sons of God.

The phrase "waits eagerly" literally means to watch with neck outstretched. All creation therefore waits and watches with outstretched neck, waiting in anticipation of restoration to an everlasting life in the future. When God created the earth and all life on the earth they were not created with a built in life expectancy. The believer's status as sons of God will be fully revealed to all creation at the rapture and will be a sign to all creation that an eternal life awaits them. Colossians 3:4: *"When Christ, who is our life, is revealed, then* **you** *also will be revealed with Him in glory"* *(emphasis added).*

Verse 20 For the creation was subjected to futility, not of its own will, but because of Him who subjected it, in hope

This verse is not meant to imply that *"creation"* possesses a will, but rather that its condemnation to death is not final. Creation was placed under the dominion of Adam. Genesis 1:28: *"God blessed them; and God said to them, 'Be fruitful and multiply, and fill the earth, and subdue it; and rule over the fish of the sea and over the birds of the sky and over every living thing that moves on the earth.'"* However, creation was subjected to the futility and frustration of death because of the sin of Adam. Genesis 3:17-19: *"Then to Adam He said, 'Because you have listened to the voice of your wife, and have eaten from the tree about which I commanded you, saying, "You shall not eat from it"; Cursed is the ground because of you; In toil you shall eat of it All the days of your life. Both thorns and thistles it shall grow for you; And you shall eat the plants of the field; By the sweat of your face You shall eat bread, Till you return to the ground, Because from it you were taken; For you are dust, And to dust you shall return.'"*

Verse 21 that the creation itself also will be set free from its slavery to corruption into the freedom of the glory of the children of God.

Bondage, which leads to corruption, must be taken in the sense of the decay and death apparent in all creation. Deliverance is certain, but it must wait for the appointed time. The disintegration of created nature yearns in anticipation of the birth throes of a better order of things. Its anticipated freedom, shared with the children of God, is the final freedom from death.

Verse 22 For we know that the whole creation groans and suffers the pains of childbirth together until now.

In this verse, we are introduced to the first of the three groanings: the groaning of creation. That it groans like a woman in travail shows that the groaning will inevitably result in new life. The groaning is neither final nor fatal. The word *"together"* has reference to all creation being united in its suffering.

Verse 23 And not only this, but also we ourselves, having the first fruits of the Spirit, even we ourselves groan within ourselves, waiting eagerly for our adoption as sons, the redemption of our body.

In this verse, we are introduced to the second of the three groanings: the groaning of God's children. 2 Corinthians 5:2, 4: *"For indeed in this house we groan, longing to be clothed with our dwelling from heaven; For indeed while we are in this tent, we groan, being burdened, because we do not want to be unclothed, but to be clothed, in order that what is mortal may be swallowed up by life."*

"Having the first fruits of the Spirit" is not something offered by man to God, but rather something given by God to man. For the Jews, the "first fruits" were the first production of the earth, which was offered to God. The Holy Spirit is the first fruits or promise of Christ's return for His believers. 2 Corinthians 1:22: *"…who also sealed us and gave us the Spirit in our hearts as a pledge."* The possession of the first fruits of the Spirit arouses within the Christian an awareness and anticipation of God's promise of deliverance of man from death.

Christians are like minor children who must patiently wait for their maturity to gain the inheritance they have been promised. We have been adopted, but our adoption has yet to be completed. The Greek word for redemption means to loosen or to unbind, to set free. The redemptive process we, as Christians, are waiting for is the transformation of our present body into the likeness of the body of Christ, and it is for that the sons of God eagerly wait for.

Verse 24 For in hope we have been saved, but hope that is seen is not hope; for why does one also hope for what he sees?

When we were saved, salvation came to us "with a promise of more to follow." Had the object we longed for already been realized, hope would not be necessary. Hebrews 11:1: *"Now faith is the assurance of things hoped for, the conviction of things not seen."* It is for the final fulfillment of the promise of the resurrection of the body unto eternal life that the Christian eagerly anticipates in hope. Titus 3:7: *"…that being justified by His grace we might be made heirs according to the hope of eternal life."*

Verse 25 But if we hope for what we do not see, with perseverance we wait eagerly for it.

The Christian life is characterized by a patient hope in that which has not yet been openly revealed. Only a Christian can look forward to the future without apprehension, fear, or doubt. 1 Thessalonians 1:3: *"…constantly bearing in mind your work of faith and labor of love and steadfastness of hope in our Lord Jesus Christ in the presence of our God and Father."* Faith is not only the ability to accept what we do not yet see, but also the ability to see what we do know as God sees them.

Some Observations Regarding Verses 18 – 25

We see in these verses God's second promise to the believer – a promise of a glorious future. However, as believers we must be willing to wait for this promised future, both eagerly and yet with patience. If we do so, God has said we will be revealed before all creation as His sons. We are also assured that all creation waits for this same moment, as it knows it will then be free from its present existence of corruption and death.

Romans 8:26 – 28
God's Third Promise
to Those Who Believe
(The Holy Spirit intercedes
for us before God.)

***Verse 26** And in the same way the Spirit also helps our weakness; for we do not know how to pray as we should, but the Spirit Himself intercedes for us with groanings too deep for words;*

In this verse, we are introduced to the third of the three groanings – the groanings of the Holy Spirit. Classical Greek gives a second meaning to the word translated as groaning; it is

"unutterable" or "cannot be uttered." Have you ever gone to God in prayer when you have been uncertain as to how to pray and what to pray for? We often do not pray as we should because we are uncertain of God's will.

"To intercede for" is to act the part of advocate in behalf of another. The Spirit does for us what an advocate does for his client (i.e., advise them of how they should present their cause). While we may not know how to plead our cause the Holy Spirit does. John 14:16: *"And I will ask the Father, and He will give you another Helper, that He may be with you forever;"*

The Spirit's groanings are not spoken, because they do not need to be, since God knows the Spirit's intentions on our behalf without them being expressed.

***Verse 27** and He who searches the hearts knows what the mind of the Spirit is, because He intercedes for the saints according to the will of God.*

God looks down deep into our hearts and sees our unexpressed desires breathed into our hearts by His Spirit, as prayers offered in accordance with His own will. When we allow our prayers to be prompted by the Holy Spirit, they will always be according to God's will. Psalm 139:1: *"O Lord, Thou hast searched me and known me."*

The Holy Spirit's intercession may be compared to a mother kneeling at the bedside of her ailing child and, in her prayers, presenting that child's needs to the heavenly Father.

***Verse 28** And we know that God causes all things to work together for good to those who love God, to those who are called according to His purpose.*

In some ways, this is a summary of the twenty-seven verses that precede it. Paul reassures us that those who love God and do God's work will experience all things working together for their good, according to God's divine purpose. Even the greatest afflictions may produce good according to God's will for us. *"For those who love God"* describes the fraternity of believers and it is only those who can claim this promise.

Some Observations Regarding Verses 26 – 28

These verses present God's third promise to the believer -- the promise that the Holy Spirit intercedes for us before God. To take advantage of this promise, we are under an obligation to pray. God's promise to us is that when we pray, the Holy Spirit will look into our hearts and translate our prayers and present them to God so they reflect our real needs and desires in a way that is according to God's will for us. He understands that often our prayers are not so much *"Your* will be done" as they are *"my* will be done." When the Holy Spirit intercedes for us, God assures us that everything that happens is intended for our good.

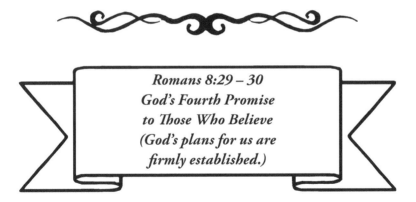

Romans 8:29 – 30
God's Fourth Promise
to Those Who Believe
(God's plans for us are
firmly established.)

Verse 29 For whom He foreknew, He also predestined to become conformed to the image of His Son, that He might be the firstborn among many brethren;

When the apostle says that God "foreknew" and also "predestined," he means God is acting according to His foreknowledge and choice. *"He predestined us to adoption as sons through Jesus Christ to Himself, according to the kind intention of His will,"* (Ephesians 1:5). In other words, before we were born, God in His infinite wisdom knew the intent of our hearts and whether or not we would believe in His message and accept it.

The evidence of the genuineness of our call is our perseverance in trying to be more like Christ. A life of sanctification can be thought of as a life of progressive conformity to be like Christ.

Verse 30 and whom He predestined, these He also called; and whom He called, these He also justified; and whom He justified, these He also glorified.

Paul's words indicate that before the world was created, God foresaw who would believe in Him and who would not. On the basis of that knowledge, salvation was predestined for those people God knew would accept his offer of salvation. Galatians 1:15: *"But when He who had set me apart, even from my mother's womb, and called me through His grace, was pleased."* This doctrine means that the Lord will be coming home with 100 sheep; none will be lost.

Those whom He called, He made sure received His message. The calling results in justification, which is the first step of obedience to God. Our justification makes us appear righteous in the sight of God. 1 Corinthians 6:11: *"And such were some of you; but you were washed, but you were sanctified, but you were justified in the name of the Lord Jesus Christ, and in the Spirit of our God."*

The past tense of "glorified" indicates the certainty that this is a future event that will take place. The future glory of believers is a present reality in the mind of God, though its completion will not happen until Christ's return. 2 Thessalonians 2:14: *"And it was for this He called you through our gospel, that you may gain the glory of our Lord Jesus Christ."*

Some Observations Regarding Verses 29 – 30

In these verses, we saw God's fourth promise to believers – His plans for us are already established. The foundation of God's plan was based on His knowing all those who would accept His offer of salvation before they were even conceived or born. Therefore, God placed within each believer the desire to become more like Him. The result was that the believer will ultimately be glorified (i.e., able to stand in the presence of God, knowing he has been made to appear righteous in the sight of God because of his acceptance of God's Son's offer of salvation through His death on the cross.

Romans 8:31 – 39
The Super Invincibility
of the Believer

Verse 31 What then shall we say to these things? If God is for us, who is against us?

If God is for us, then, in order to harm the believer, the enemy must be stronger than God, and that just isn't possible; therefore, no adversary has any power over us when God is for us. If God's love, displayed in the sacrifice of His Son on the cross, shows that He is concerned only in what is good for us, then what have we to fear from God for the future?

Verse 32 He who did not spare His own Son, but delivered Him up for us all, how will He not also with Him freely give us all things?

God did not spare His Son when He delivered Jesus up to die on the cross. He spared Abraham's son, but not His own. If the Father did not spare His own Son but delivered Him up to the agony of Calvary, how will He not fail to complete the purpose of the sacrifice: the forgiveness of our sins? If God did this, then surely He will not withhold anything from His chosen ones.

Verse 33 *Who will bring a charge against God's elect? God is the one who justifies;*

The elect are those God has chosen out of the world to be members of His family. All sin is committed against God; therefore, only God is in a position to bring charges against us. However, because we are God's elect, Jesus acts as our advocate before the Father. Since God now sees us through the sacrifice of His Son, all charges lose their validity. When God justifies someone, he need not be concerned if they are condemned by the world.

Verse 34 *who is the one who condemns? Christ Jesus is He who died, yes, rather who was raised, who is at the right hand of God, who also intercedes for us.*

Four things that Christ has done or is doing for us:

- He died for us: it was by His death, in atonement for our sins, that all grounds for our condemnation have been removed.
- He was raised from the dead for us: The resurrection of Christ is proof of the validity of His claim that He was God and has power over death. (Acts 2:24: *"And God raised Him up again, putting an end to the agony of death, since it was impossible for Him to be held in its power."*)
- He is at the right hand of God: He shares God's authority over creation. (Mark 16:19: *"So then, when the Lord Jesus had spoken to them, He was received up into heaven, and sat down at the right hand of God."*)
- He intercedes for us: He acts as our advocate and pleads our innocence before God. (Hebrews 7:25: *"Hence, also, He is able to save forever those who draw near to God through Him, since He always lives to make intercession for them."*)

Note the ascending order of theological importance: He died for us; He was raised from the dead for us; He sits at the right hand of God for us; He intercedes before God for us.

1 John 2:1: *"My little children, I am writing these things to you that you may not sin. And if anyone sins, we have an Advocate with the Father, Jesus Christ the righteous;"*

These statements provide the final evidence in support of verse one in this chapter: *"**There is therefore now no condemnation for those who are in Christ Jesus**".*

Verse 35 *Who shall separate us from the love of Christ? Shall tribulation, or distress, or persecution, or famine, or nakedness, or peril, or sword?*

Paul reminds us that the tribulations Christians face cannot separate us from Christ's love. No one can accuse us, no one can condemn us, and no one can separate us from the love of Christ.

Notice "who can separate us from the love of God" progresses in difficulty to our likelihood to weaken in the face of these experiences:

- Tribulation – physical trials
- Distress – mental and emotional trials
- Persecution – physical abuse caused by others
- Famine -- hunger
- Nakedness – exposure to the elements without protection
- Peril – danger, threat of death
- Sword -- death

The world sees these afflictions as proof that Christ has removed His favor from us. Paul saw these same afflictions as opportunities to bring us into closer fellowship with God. (Philippians 3:10: *"…that I may know Him and the power of His resurrection and the fellowship of His sufferings, being conformed to His death."*)

Whatever we may be called upon to suffer in this life, nothing can deprive us of the love of Him who died for us, and who now lives to plead our cause in heaven.

Verse 36 Just as it is written, "For Thy sake we are being put to death
all day long; We were considered as sheep to be slaughtered."

There is nothing strange or unexpected about our present-day suffering for the Lord's sake. To suffer for Christ's sake is the very situation in which we discover that the love of Christ is most real and His presence most felt. For most of the Old Testament times, death was thought of as the final separating destiny of man. Psalm 44:22: *"But for Thy sake we are killed all day long; We are considered as sheep to be slaughtered."* Paul is saying that any suffering because of our belief in Christ is to be considered expected of the world.

Verse 37 But in all these things we overwhelmingly conquer through
Him who loved us.

However, Paul continues, assuring us that whatever comes our way; we can conquer it through the strength of God who loves us. What does it mean to overwhelmingly conquer? It means that we not only achieve victory over trials, but those trials are deprived of their power to do us harm. It is important to note that it is not by our strength that we are able to conquer.

Verse 38 For I am convinced that neither death, nor life, nor angels,
nor principalities, nor things present, nor things to come,
nor powers,

The Greek that is translated "***I am convinced***" is in the perfect indicative passive tense, so the apostle is actually saying, "I have been convinced." His confidence is founded on the fact that we was confronted with these same experiences he came away from them feeling God's hand of love on him strengthening him. Notice how he groups the items together:

1. Death and Life = The state of our physical existence Christ has vanquished death and robbed it of its sting (1 Corinthians 15:54 – 55: " *But when this perishable will have put on the imperishable, and this mortal will have put on immortality, then will come about the*

saying that is written, "DEATH IS SWALLOWED UP in victory. "O

DEATH, WHERE IS YOUR VICTORY? O DEATH, WHERE IS YOUR STING?") Remember, as believers, physical death results in our being in the presence of God.

2. Angels and Principalities = The interference from other God-created beings Even angels, however mighty, whether good or bad, or any superhuman power, will ever be able to separate us from the love of God. (Ephesians 6:12: *"For our struggle is not against flesh and blood, but against the rulers, against the powers, against the world forces of this darkness, against the spiritual forces of wickedness in the heavenly places."*)
3. Present and Future = time and history
4. Powers = mighty works or miracles

***Verse 39** nor height, nor depth, nor any other created thing, shall be able to separate us from the love of God, which is in Christ Jesus our Lord.*

Paul concludes by adding "nor height no depth," which were technical terms in astrology. The reference here would be to the movements of the planets, which were thought to control the destiniy of mortals. Paul concludes by declaring that nothing in God's creation will be able to separate us from the love of God as expressed by His Son, Jesus Christ.

Final Thoughts on Chapter 8

This chapter began with the statement that there is no condemnation of those who believe in Jesus Christ (verse 1). Paul than goes on to share the promises God has made for those who believe in Him and in His Son. First, God has adopted us as His children and heirs. Second, God promises that we have a great future before us. Third, God promises that the presence of the Holy Spirit within us will intercede in our prayers to God. Fourth, God promises that His plans are certain as shown by His the provision of Christ for the forgiveness of our sins..

Paul next assures believers that the provision of God's Son, Jesus Christ, now means His Son now intercedes for us before God. Therefore, there is no longer anyone who can condemn believers before God. Paul ends the chapter by showing us that since God so loved us, there is nothing that exists that can separate us from the love of God.

This chapter is the high-water mark in Romans, as it points to the results of the believer's justification by faith. We begin this chapter with no condemnation; we close with no separation from God; in between, we read that all things work together for good to those who love God. How could it be any better than that for the believer?

Chapter 9

Understanding God's Sovereignty

Introduction:

There is a clear change of theme between chapters 8 and 9. Chapter 8 closes on a note of triumph at the promise that nothing can separate us from the love of God. In contrast, Chapter 9 opens with a description of sorrow and despair.

Chapters 9 through 11 represent a "trilogy" that taken as a whole and is intended to clarify the position of the Jews and their relationship with the gospel Paul preaches. In Chapter 9, Paul wants us to understand God's sovereignty. In Chapter 10, he wants the Jews to understand the meaning of God's apparent rejection of them. In Chapter 11, he wants the Jews to understand that God always keeps His promises. In these chapters Paul will show that Jesus' divinely offer of salvation to all men has a historic and Biblical foundation. He will show how the disobedience of the Jews opened the door of salvation to the Gentiles, and how that should cause the Jews to be filled with a jealousy that should result in their own salvation.

The promises of God were never intended solely for those who were Israelites by birth, but for all who displayed Abraham's faith (i.e., those willing to believe God's promises). Paul makes a distinction between "Israel" and those "who are of Israel," and between Abraham's "children" and Abraham's "seed." The distinguishing between these groups is a feature of biblical history.

Paul shows the gospel does not annul God's special covenants with Israel. if God's will would have been thwarted by the Jews' rejection of

Jesus, then what confidence could the Christians have that His will could not be thwarted again?

Paul will show that while God may give the appearance of rejecting the Jews and extending His blessings to all men (verses 1 - 24), His actions were distinctly predicted in the Old Testament (verses 25 - 29). The conclusion of his reasoning is in verses 30 - 33. If the descendants from Abraham are unable to secure God's favor through their heritage and works, how foolish are those individuals who rely on outward ordinances and church relations or membership as the grounds of their acceptance by God. Finally, in this chapter Paul reassures his Jewish brethren of his love for them and respect for their national identity.

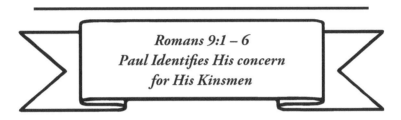

Romans 9:1 – 6
Paul Identifies His concern
for His Kinsmen

Verse 1 I am telling the truth in Christ, I am not lying, my conscience bearing me witness in the Holy Spirit,

In Acts 23:12, Paul shared that many Jews thought of him as an enemy of his people. As a result, Paul begins by expressing his concern for his people in Jewish legalistic terms by identifying two witnesses as to the truth of his feelings; "my conscience" and "the Holy Spirit."

Verse 2 that I have great sorrow and unceasing grief in my heart.

Next, Paul expresses his concern for his people in emotional terms. Paul's sorrow reflects the gravity in which he viewed Israel's unbelief. With all the advantages the Jews enjoyed, they had rejected the Messiah and were therefore left without hope, either for this world or the next. For him, his grief was in response to the Jews' continuing rejection of Christ.

Verse 3 For I could wish that I myself were accursed, separated from Christ for the sake of my brethren, my kinsmen according to the flesh,

Finally, Paul expresses his concern in terms of self-sacrifice in his willingness to forfeit his personal salvation if would save his people. Paul qualifies his statement by noting that the brethren relationship is one of ancestry. Paul knows t he could never actually be separated from Christ; therefore, he says *"I could wish,"* if such a self-sacrifice would be in accord with God's will and plan. In this, he echoes the thoughts of Moses in Exodus 32:32: *"But now, if Thou wilt, forgive their sin and if not, please blot me out from Thy book which Thou hast written!"* Here are individuals concerned for those who are perishing without God.

Verse 4 who are Israelites, to whom belongs the adoption as sons and the glory and the covenants and the giving of the Law and the temple service and the promises,

Israel is a nation whose true destiny lies in the future fulfilling of God's purposes. Paul proceeds to identify the unique privileges of the Jewish people in God's eyes.

- To whom belong **the adoption as sons**. (Israel is the only nation God called as His son. Exodus 4:22: *"Then you shall say to Pharaoh, 'Thus says the Lord, Israel is My son, My firstborn.'"* And Deuteronomy 7:6: *"For you are a holy people to the Lord your God; the Lord your God has chosen you to be a people for His own possession out of all the peoples who are on the face of the earth."*)
- To whom belonged **the glory**, *a* visible manifestation of God. (Israel is the only nation to experience the visible presence of God. Exodus 13:21: *"The LORD was going before them in a pillar of cloud by day to lead them on the way, and in a pillar of fire by night to give them light, that they might travel by day and by night."* And 1 Kings 8:11: *"…so that the priests could not stand to minister because of the cloud, for the glory of the Lord filled the house of the Lord."*)

- To whom belonged *the **covenants***. (Israel is the only nation God specifically promised to make a great nation. Genesis 17:2: *"And I will establish My covenant between Me and you, And I will multiply you exceedingly."* Deuteronomy 29:12 – 15: *"… that you may enter into the covenant with the Lord your God, and into His oath which the Lord your God is making with you today, in order that He may establish you today as His people and that He may be your God, just as He spoke to you and as He swore to your fathers, to Abraham, Isaac, and Jacob. Now not with you alone am I making this covenant and this oath, but both with those who stand here with us today in the presence of the Lord our God and with those who are with us here today."* Acts 3:25: *"It is you who are the sons of the prophets, and of the covenant which God made with your fathers, saying to Abraham, 'And in your seed all the families of the earth shall be blessed.'"*)

- To whom belonged **the giving of the Law**. (Israel is the only nation to whom God directly gave a set of laws in order to govern their existence. Deuteronomy 4:13,14: *"So He declared to you His covenant which He commanded you to perform, {that is,} the Ten Commandments; and He wrote them on two tablets of stone. And the Lord commanded me at that time to teach you statutes and judgments, that you might perform them in the land where you are going over to possess it."*)

- To whom belonged **the temple service**. (Israel is the only nation God established as a nation of priests. Deuteronomy 7:6: *"For you are a holy people to the Lord your God; the Lord your God has chosen you to be a people for His own possession out of all the peoples who are on the face of the earth."*)

- To whom belonged **the promises**. (God promised Israel her own land; He promised to protect her; He promised her a kingdom with Jerusalem as its capital; He promised that from her would come the Messiah. *(Acts 13:32,33: "And we preach to you the good news of the promise made to the fathers, that God has fulfilled this promise to our children in that He raised up Jesus, as it is also written in the second Psalm, 'Thou art My Son; today I have begotten Thee.'"*)

Verse 5 *whose are the fathers, and from whom is the Christ according to the flesh, who is over all, God blessed forever. Amen.*

Finally, the last two advantages are listed in this verse.

- Whose are **the fathers**. It has been said, "If one wishes to be successful, he should choose his ancestors!" Paul was probably thinking of all the devout ancestors who played an important role in the history of redemption. *(The ancestors of the Israelite nation were men and women specifically called out by God.)*
- And **from them, as far as his human nature is concerned, is Christ**. When Paul reaches the climax, he does not say that Christ belonged to them but that Christ came from Jewish stock and, therefore, derived his human nature from the Israelites. Israel's greatest glory consists in Christ's consenting to be their kinsman "*as concerning the flesh.*"

When Paul says, "**Christ, who is over all God blest forever**," he confesses Christ's deity. Colossians 1:16-17: *"For by Him all things were created, both in the heavens and on earth, visible and invisible, whether thrones or dominions or rulers or authorities   all things have been created by Him and for Him. And He is before all things, and in Him all things hold together."* Paul has traced the salient points in Israel's history, and climaxes it by proving that the Messiah, according to His human nature, is Jewish, but at the same time is deity. Colossians 2:9: *"For in Him all the fullness of Deity dwells in bodily form."*

He ends this section with an "Amen," signifying with this Hebrew word that all he has said is "true."

Verse 6 *But it is not as though the word of God has failed. For they are not all Israel who are descended from Israel;*

Numbers 23:19: *"God is not a man, that He should lie, Nor a son of man, that He should repent; Has He said, and will He not do it? Or has He spoken, and will He not make it good?"* Paul warns his Jewish readers that simply because of their birth relationship to Abraham and outward obedience to Jewish law, they could not claim God's promises as exclusively theirs. The promises were addressed to those who shared their descent with Abraham by sharing his declaration of faith in God.

Some Observations Regarding Verses 1 – 6

Paul began this section by declaring his genuine concern for his fellow Jews. First, he expresses it with a vow, calling on his conscience and the Holy Spirit as his witnesses. Second, he expresses his personal sorrow over their existing situation. Finally, he expresses his grief by saying he would give up his own personal salvation (if that were possible) if it would ensure the salvation of his kinsmen. He then goes on to identify those gifts that God has given to His people. However, the Jews, as they considered that since God set them apart as a nation, this meant they were automatically God's chosen and did not bear a personal responsibility for their selection. Their calling as a nation was meant to insure their survival as a separate body of people; it was not intended to reflect the personal salvation of individual Jews. That could only by obtained through an individual's declaration of faith in God and a desire to live to please God.

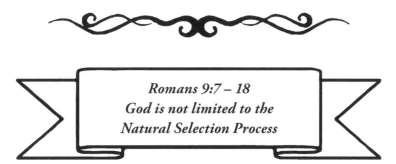

Romans 9:7 – 18
God is not limited to the
Natural Selection Process

Verse 7 neither are they all children because they are Abraham's descendants, but: "through Isaac your descendants will be named."

Natural descent from Abraham did not automatically secure a portion in the promised inheritance. Within the Jews there had been the distinguishing and separating of chosen individuals by God Himself. God rejected Ishmael, notwithstanding his natural choice as the firstborn of Abraham, but chose Isaac instead. Isaac was the child promised by God, and it was God, not man, who set the time of his birth. Apart from God's divine enablement of the parents, Isaac would never have been born. Isaac was God's choice, not Abraham's. Galatians 4:23: *"But the son by the bondwoman was born according to the flesh, and the son by the free woman through the promise."*

Verse 8 ***That is, it is not the children of the flesh who are children of God, but the children of the promise are regarded as descendants.***

The *"children of the flesh"* (i.e., Ishmael) represented Abraham's plan; *"the children of the promise"* (i.e., Isaac) represented God's plan. The birth of Ishmael was the result of Sarah's becoming impatient with God's timetable and taking matters into her own hands. God's judgment grieved Abraham's heart, as he loved his firstborn son. On the other hand, Ishmael was not ignored by God but was chosen to be the father of many of the Arab nations.

Natural descent from Abraham was no guarantee of a spiritual kinship with Abraham. God's choice is the important matter, not mere physical birth. Galatians 3:29: *"And if you belong to Christ, then you are Abraham's offspring, heirs according to promise."*

Verse 9 ***For this is a word of promise: "At this time I will come, and Sarah shall have a son."***

Genesis 18:10: *"And he said, 'I will surely return to you at this time next year; and behold, Sarah your wife shall have a son.' And Sarah was listening at the tent door, which was behind him."* Why is God so specific about the time and the season and the seed? It was because God wanted Sarah and Abraham to know that their son's birth would be according to God's plan and promise and human merit had nothing to do with it. Isaac's birth was meant to demonstrate the manifestation of God's power.

Verse 10 ***And not only this, but there was Rebekah also, when she had conceived twins by one man, our father Isaac;***

Not only does the case of Isaac and Ishmael prove that God's choice does not depend on natural descent, but the case of Esau and Jacob demonstrates this more clearly. With Abraham's two sons, there was one father and two mothers. In the case of Jacob and Esau, they were both children of the same mother, the same father, and the same conception. It was God's elective choice that decreed that Jacob, the younger, was to be served by Esau, the older.

Verse 11 *for though the twins were not yet born, and had not done anything good or bad, in order that God's purpose according to His choice might stand, not because of works, but because of Him who calls,*

God made His choice before there was any evidence of their character or achievements, but rather that God's electing purpose might reflect His independence of human merit.

Paul is quietly trying to show his readers that the choice of those who were to enter God's kingdom was according to the discretion and will of God.

Verse 12 *it was said to her, "The older will serve the younger."*

God rejected the line of primogeniture -- that is, the priority of the firstborn over those born later. Genesis 25:23: *"And the Lord said to her, 'Two nations are in your womb; And two peoples shall be separated from your body; And one people shall be stronger than the other; And the older shall serve the younger.'"* This declaration was contrary to Jewish custom, and the wisdom of God's choice was later reflected the subsequent actions of Jacob and Esau. An example was when Esau considered a bowl of stew more important that his birthright. Consider also the deception of Isaac when Jacob, with the help of his mother, obtained the firstborn's blessing from Isaac. It is well to remember here also God did not forget Esau, as he became the father of Edom.

Verse 13 *Just as it is written, "Jacob I loved, but Esau I hated*

This quotation comes from Malachi 1:2, 3: *"'I have loved you,' says the Lord. But you say, 'How hast Thou loved us?' 'Was not Esau Jacob's brother?' declares the Lord. 'Yet I have loved Jacob; but I have hated Esau, and I have made his mountains a desolation, and appointed his inheritance for the jackals of the wilderness.'"* Paul is quoting these verses about fifteen hundred years after God's original declaration. His purpose was to warn Israelites against presuming that simply because they were descended from Abraham, they could claim a share in the promises made to Jacob from God.

The use of the word "*hated*" was simply a way of saying that Esau was not the object of God's electing purpose; the same can be said of every man who perishes apart from God's favor. In this case, the word undoubtedly means to "love less." Thus, in Genesis 29:33, Leah says she was hated by her husband; while in the preceding verse, the same idea is expressed by saying, "*Jacob loved Rachel more than Leah.*" Yet in no way did Jacob let this distinction affect his responsibility to Leah as his wife, just as God bestowed many blessings on Esau and his descendants. God's preferential love of Jacob was shown, as it was through him that the nation of Israel was founded. The promises made to Jacob (i.e., Israel) were never intended for all who were descended from Jacob, any more than the promise made to Abraham was intended for all of his descendants. No one should assume that birth or blood relationships assure them of the privileges of a child of God. Ephesians 1:11: "*…also we have obtained an inheritance, having been predestined according to His purpose who works all things after the counsel of His will,*"

Verse 14 *What shall we say then? There is no injustice with God, is there? May it never be!*

The apostle, according to his usual manner, proposes an objection to his doctrine of God's election in the form of a question that denies its validity and then immediately gives his answer.

When God makes His choices independent of man's input, man immediately concludes that this is an injustice. Is a man unjust in choosing a a friend, a co-worker, a mate, in preference to another? Does God not have the same right as man? God acts in mercy and grace and love, and He does not make mistakes in His choices. It is remarkable how often we do not question the judgments of men, but do question the judgments of God.

Verse 15   For He says to Moses, "I will have mercy on whom I have mercy, and I will have compassion on whom I have compassion."

Paul now looks back at an event in the history of Israel, where if God had acted in justice without mercy, He would have completely blotted out His people. Exodus 33:19: *"And He said, 'I Myself will make all My goodness pass before you, and will proclaim the name of the Lord before you; and I will be gracious to whom I will be gracious, and will show compassion on whom I will show compassion and I will have mercy on whom I will have mercy.'"* These words from the Old Testament come from the time when the Jews erected a golden calf at Mount Sinai and began to worship it. God wanted to, could have, and maybe should have, destroyed them for their blatant act of rebellion against Him, but he didn't. Instead, He spared His people, recalled Moses to the mount, and for a second time, gave him the tablets of commandments.

Verse 16   So then it does not depend on the man who wills or the man who runs, but on God who has mercy.

Clearly God's mercy is something that man neither earns nor controls. God's mercy is not a reward for human righteous actions, but is intended to show mankind that they need be humble when they are the beneficiaries of God's mercy. Ephesians 2:8: *"For by grace you have been saved through faith; and that not of yourselves, it is the gift of God;"* There is no doubt that Paul was fully conscious of the fact that **his** welfare for time and eternity was subject to God's good pleasure.

Verse 17   For the Scripture says to Pharaoh, "For this very purpose I raised you up, to demonstrate My power in you, and that My name might be proclaimed throughout the whole earth."

Paul's second illustration of God's sovereignty was regarding Egypt's pharaoh of the exodus. Exodus 9:16: *"For this purpose have I raised thee up, and placed thee where thou art; and instead of cutting thee off at once, have so long endured the obstinacy and wickedness."* When God spared Pharaoh himself from the plagues, it was because of His choice.

"That My name might be proclaimed throughout the whole earth." Here is the reason God spared Pharaoh: it was so Pharaoh would be a personal witness -- albeit an unwilling, unbelieving, and ungrateful one -- to the authority and power of the true God and His evidential mercy over his chosen people. It is interesting to note that the reason this pharaoh is remembered throughout history was because he was the pharaoh of the Exodus.

Verse 18 So then He has mercy on whom He desires, and He hardens whom He desires.

Since no one knows who has been chosen to accept the message, it is imperative that it be proclaimed to all classes of people, everywhere, whenever possible and should be our greatest incentive for preaching the gospel.

When God hardened the Pharaoh's heart, it means that God allowed Pharaoh to make decisions based on his natural human nature. Exodus 4:21: *"And the Lord said to Moses, 'When you go back to Egypt see that you perform before Pharaoh all the wonders which I have put in your power; but I will harden his heart so that he will not let the people go.'"*

Some Observations Regarding Verses 7 – 18

The children of the promise, then, are those who, as a result of their lives of obedience to God, become co-heirs with Him in heaven. These are the true children of Abraham's faith. The main problem the Jews faced was that they didn't fully understand that they were special only because they were the first ones who received God's promise of blessing in response to their obedience. They failed to understand that God could chose whomever He wanted to bless.

God's choices are made to insure that His ultimate plan for mankind will succeed. His choices are not made on the basis of works, but of mercy. When God chooses us, He realizes that we are literally works in progress, living lives of sanctification. God's choices are made on the basis of what He knows we will accomplish in His plan when we become His followers.

Romans 9:19 – 33
We Must Understand the
Wisdom of the
Sovereignty of God

Verse 19 You will say to me then, "Why does He still find fault? For who resists His will?"

Here is the dichotomy the Jews felt they faced. If God alone decides what is best for us, how can we be held responsible for our actions? This is man's natural response when he considers the sovereignty of God. If one man believes and is saved, and another remains impenitent and is lost, and this is according to the will of God, how can God find fault in us?

Verse 20 On the contrary, who are you, O man, who answers back to God? The thing molded will not say to the molder, "Why did you make me like this," will it?

In Paul's response, we have both a reproof and an answer. The reproof to verse 19 is founded on ignorance of the true relation between God as the Creator and man as His created being. As the sovereign Creator, God has the Creator's right to do what He will with what He has Himself created.

For example only a foolish son would say to his father, "Why did you bring me into the world?" Or ask his mother, "Why did you give birth to me?" To further illustrate this, Paul uses the example of the potter. The potter makes his clay from the materials at hand, but God made both the potter and the clay. Isaiah 29:16: *"You turn things around! Shall the potter be considered as equal with the clay, That what is made should say to its maker, 'He did not make me'; Or what is formed say to him who formed it, 'He has no understanding'?"* Isaiah 64:8: *"But now, O Lord, Thou art our Father, We are the clay, and Thou our potter; And all of us are the work of Thy hand."*

Verse 21 **Or does not the potter have a right over the clay, to make from the same lump one vessel for honorable use, and another for common use?**

If a potter has the right to make one vessel for special use and another for common use out of the same lump of clay, then certainly God, as the Creator, has the right, out of the same mass of humanity, to elect some to everlasting life and to allow others to remain in rebellion against Him.

The potter's freedom of choice is not capricious. The potter must, as a condition of his craft, make this decision before he starts out. He does so by considering the material he has to work with. Can the clay, supposing it were endowed with intelligence, question the form it eventually becomes under the hand of the potter? And so it is with God; it is His right to shape individuals according to His will, some into honor and some into dishonor.

Verse 22 **What if God, although willing to demonstrate His wrath and to make His power known, endured with much patience vessels of wrath prepared for destruction?**

In this and the following verse, Paul shows that in the exercise of God's sovereignty, there is nothing unreasonable or unjust. Even in choosing of those scheduled for destruction, God deals with them with longsuffering and tenderness.

God did not create mankind in order to destroy them. Their resultant judgment of destruction is the result of choosing to defy God, in spite of their knowledge and conscience of Him. In Job 38, God asks Job where he was when He created the universe. In Matthew 15, Jesus talks of pruning the vine, not just for destruction of that which was pruned, but to improve the opportunity for the growth of the rest of the branches.

Paul warns his unbelieving kinsmen that God's patience is not an indication of His favor, but rather He is delaying the judgment until every opportunity has been given for repentance. If God bears with great patience those He knows will never be saved, should not we have patience with the unbeliever who may still, by God's grace, experience an eventual genuine conversion?

Verse 23 *And He did so in order that He might make known the riches of His glory upon vessels of mercy, which He prepared beforehand for glory,*

If the pharaoh of the exodus had been immediately destroyed, who in the history of the world would have been witness of God's mercy toward Israel? As the ten plagues followed each other, one by one, that mercy became increasingly evident. God plans and acts so that all creation is aware of His forgiving mercy and grace, which He freely offers.

Verse 24 *even us, whom He also called, not from among Jews only, but also from among Gentiles.*

"*Whom He also called*" is another manner of saying, "*whom He has elected.*" The call is where God convicts the minds and hearts of the sinners so that they are aware of their guilt and understand their need of Christ. Paul finds in the call of the Jews and Gentiles an illustration of God's grace. Israel was chosen by the sovereign will of God, not because of their merit. Therefore, no one should consider God as unjust if He rejects unbelieving Israelites and accepts Gentiles who turn to Him in faith. The New Testament Church was comprised of individual Jews and Gentiles, whom God had called unto salvation to make up one body.

Verse 25 *As He says also in Hosea, "I will call those who were not My people, 'My people,' And her who was not beloved, 'beloved.'"*

. Paul uses this Old Testament verse, Hosea 2:23, to apply to the Gentiles who have accepted Christ as Savior. Also as in 1 Peter 2:10: "*… for you once were not a people, but now you are the people of God; you had not received mercy, but now you have received mercy.*"

Verse 26 *"And it shall be that in the place where it was said to them, 'you are not My people,' There they shall be called sons of the living God."*

Hosea 1:10: *"…and it will come about that, in the place where it is said to them, You are not My people, it will be said to them, You are the sons of the living God."* As it was for the Jews, so it is to be for the Gentiles. Whether the restoration of the Israelites or the conversion of the Gentiles, the source of their restoration or conversion is the grace and mercy of God.

Verse 27 And Isaiah cries out concerning Israel, "Though the number of the sons of Israel be as the sand of the sea, it is the remnant that will be saved;"

Paul now proceeds to show that rejection of God by a great majority of the Jews was foretold in Scripture. Isaiah 10:22: *"For though your people, O Israel, may be like the sand of the sea, Only a remnant within them will return; A destruction is determined, overflowing with righteousness."* In the meantime, God watches over this remnant and preserves those within that remnant. This was meant as a reminder, to show that God never considered merely being a descendant of Abraham was sufficient to guarantee eternal redemption.

Verse 28 for the Lord will execute His word upon the earth, thoroughly and quickly."

If only a remnant of God's chosen people are to be saved, than how careful should we, as professors of Christianity, be of our salvation?

Verse 29 And just as Isaiah foretold, "Except the Lord of Sabbath had left to us a posterity, We would have become as Sodom, and would have resembled Gomorrah."

Isaiah 1:9: "Unless the Lord of hosts had left us a few survivors, We would be like Sodom, We would be like Gomorrah." The purpose of the quotation of this verse is to show that being an Israelite by birth was not enough to secure exemption from God's judgments or the receipt of God's favor. God guides the course of history so that, even though Israel would be severely punished, there would always be a faithful remnant left, thus fulfilling God's promises to the Jewish patriarchs. For us today it is becoming evident that unless God shortens man's days upon the earth it will become as Sodom and Gomorrah.

Verse 30 *What shall we say then? That Gentiles, who did not pursue righteousness, attained righteousness, even the righteousness which is by faith;*

It is a remarkable fact of religious history that mankind has often eagerly sought to win the favor of God by fasts, sacrifices and obedience to the Law and yet failed to secure peace with God. Others, seemingly indifferent to the various forms of religion, have by an act of simple faith have seemingly obtained peace. The Gentiles, through their declarations of faith in Christ, obtained that which satisfied the demands of the Law, and were therefore made acceptable in the sight of God. Galatians 2:16: "*…nevertheless knowing that a man is not justified by the works of the Law but through faith in Christ Jesus, even we have believed in Christ Jesus, that we may be justified by faith in Christ, and not by the works of the Law; since by the works of the Law shall no flesh be justified.*"

Verse 31 but Israel, pursuing a law of righteousness, did not arrive at that law.

The Gentiles, through their declarations of faith, attained the favor of God, while the Jews failed because they sought righteousness through living a formal observance of the law. However, since perfect obedience to the Mosaic Law was impossible, they failed to obtain the righteousness before God that they sought. It was not the function of the law to justify sinners, but to bring sinners under the conviction of their failure to reach its demand of perfection.

Verse 32 *Why? Because they did not pursue it by faith, but as though it were by works. They stumbled over the stumbling stone,*

No error is more destructive to humanity than the one that leads them to rely on their own power or merit to find favor with God. The tragedy of Israel was that, by fulfilling the demands of the Law, they thought they were putting God under obligation to accept their righteousness.

It was not the object of their pursuit that was wrong, but rather the way they pursued it. They were pursuing the Law, not the intent of the Law. Israel took it for granted that man would be able, by his own power and resources, to fulfill the Law's demands. To a Jew, so long as he felt he was morally upright before the law, he considered himself righteous before God.

The whole spirit, opinions, and expectations of the Jews were adverse to the person, character, and doctrines of the Messiah as a Redeemer. The Jews expected the Messiah; however, they expected Him as a conqueror on a throne, not a cross. Jesus was, therefore, a stumbling block, as He did not meet their presuppositions as to how the Messiah would appear to them. Isaiah 8:14: *"Then He shall become a sanctuary; But to both the houses of Israel, a stone to strike and a rock to stumble over, And a snare and a trap for the inhabitants of Jerusalem."*

Verse 33 just as it is written, "Behold, I lay in Zion a stone of stumbling and a rock of offense, And he who believes in Him will not be disappointed."

Jesus Christ was the stumbling stone for the Jews, as the cross offended them, because it was shocking and disgraceful. The message it conveyed was one of an infinite debt to Him, which no "works" could ever repay. There unbelief resulted in Israel's rejection of Jesus Christ as the Messiah. 1 Peter 2:6, 8: *"For this is contained in Scripture: 'Behold I lay in Zion a choice stone, a precious corner stone, And he who believes in Him shall not be disappointed; And a stone of stumbling and a rock of offense; for they stumble because they are disobedient to the word, and to this doom they were also appointed."* The individual accepting Christ today may face ridicule in the world, but his accepting of Christ's saving faith will be honored in the presence of God.

Final Thoughts on Chapter 9

The chapter begins by making it clear that God is not limited in His choices by the natural ancestry of man. It is important we understand this principle when we consider the promises that God made to man. Whether or not we are the chosen of God is determined by how we respond to His calling to us when we hear the gospel message. It is our acceptance or rejection of Christ, through faith, that will determine our final relationship before God.

Paul uses the example of the potter to illustrate that God, as the Creator of man, also has the same freedom in how He chooses to make men according to His purposes and will.

The Potter	God
makes the clay	makes both the potter and the clay
decides what to make with the clay	decides what to make of the potter
makes both great and common vessels from the same clay	makes both great and common potters

God alone knows of our acceptance of His calling, since He alone knows what our response will be. He alone knows the beginning from the end in our lives; therefore, He alone is qualified to make the right choices. The Scriptures assert that God punishes man because of his natural tendency to sin, and He punishes them in proportion to their sins.

Finally, Paul points out that while the Jews tried to obtain their righteousness before God by their works in obedience to the Mosaic Law, they failed, while the Gentiles obtained their righteousness before God in a simple act of faith.

Our growth and development as believers is in our response to the challenges that Christ places before us. First, we are to have the faith to believe in the message of Christ. Then that belief must be accompanied by a change in our lifestyle in conformance with that belief. Instead of living a life whose purpose is to please ourselves, we are to lead a life where we are concerned about pleasing God. True maturity shows itself in our service to God.

Chapter 10

Understanding God's Rejection of Israel

Introduction:

Paul now turns from the sovereignty of God to the responsibility of man regarding God's promises. The rejection of Israel as a nation was due entirely to the fault of the people themselves. In a sense, Israel felt that they were the masters of their own destiny. As a result, they lost their personal relationship with God, rejected Jesus as God's Son, and lost their favored position with God.

In this chapter Paul will show that the rejection of the ancient chosen people of God was in accordance with the predictions of the prophets of old. However, he will point out that their rejection was not complete, and that the way to salvation is still open to them. At the same time, Paul will point out that God's extending salvation to the Gentiles was intended motivate the Jews to renew their proper relationship with Him.

Paul wants the Jews to realize that the gospel message to the Gentiles was in accordance with God's promise to their ancestors.

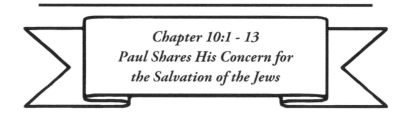

Chapter 10:1 - 13
Paul Shares His Concern for
the Salvation of the Jews

Verse 1 Brethren, my heart's desire and my prayer to God for them is for their salvation.

Paul begins by assuring his fellow Jews that regarding his feelings towards them, he earnestly desires their salvation. The word rendered "desire" is more properly translated "good-pleasure." By stating his "good-pleasure" to pray for them, he is implying his love for them. Although Paul was the "apostle of the Gentiles," he never lost a concern for his own people.

There are two interesting implications in this verse:

- The Jews, with all their religious knowledge, still needed a personal relationship with God.
- A personal relationship with God was available to those who accepted the gospel message of Jesus Christ, which Paul preached.

Verse 2 For I bear them witness that they have a zeal for God, but not in accordance with knowledge.

Paul endeavors to emphasize the things that are commendable about the Jews, and at the same time, diplomatically point out their weaknesses. For example, zeal to be acceptable to God or useful to men must be directed toward the right objective. Paul acknowledges that his kinsmen's zeal had the right object: zeal for God. The problem was that it was based on inadequate knowledge. Acts 21:20: *"And when they heard it they began glorifying God; and they said to him, 'You see, brother, how many thousands there are among the Jews of those who have believed, and they are all zealous for the Law;'"*

Before Paul's conversion, he was a perfect example of the perverse zeal for God that was destroying Israel. Misdirected zeal is the failure of many modern-day Christians and churches. Having a ministry that appeals to the world is not a substitute for a ministry that emphasizes a personal relationship with God. The quest for knowledge, apart from Christ and His Word, is evidence of a misdirected zeal.

Verse 3 For not knowing about God's righteousness, and seeking to establish their own, they did not subject themselves to the righteousness of God.

The major mistake of the Jews was not understanding justification. It is also the weakness of natural man, who seeks to justify himself before others; while remaining a stranger to God's offer of justification.

The Jews felt they would appear righteous before God by strict obedience to the Law. However, the sacrificial system under the Law only provided a temporary forgiveness of sins. In their misunderstanding of God's purpose in establishing the Law; they lost sight of their need for a permanent provision for the forgiveness of their sins by God. This led to their failure to comprehend and acknowledge God's offer of righteousness through His son, Jesus Christ. Note, that this is contrary to the thinking that ignorance is an excuse, and good intentions are all that is necessary to obtain righteousness before God.

Verse 4 For Christ is the end of the law for righteousness to everyone who believes.

This is the gospel message of the Bible. Christ fulfilled the requirements of the law so that everyone who believes in Him would receive permanent forgiveness of their sins, and so appear righteous before God. The accomplishments of the cross "tore the veil in the Temple," the veil representing the barrier separating God and man; this cleared the way for man to have a direct relationship with God.

The Mosaic Law was given to lead men to acknowledge their need for Christ; it wasn't intended to provide for man's eternal salvation. The Jews' rejection of Jesus Christ as the Messiah meant they remained shackled to a temporary righteousness under the Law. The Jews' acceptance of Christ as the Messiah would have resulted in their obtaining eternal righteousness in the eyes of God.

Verse 5 For Moses writes that the man who practices the righteousness which is based on law shall live by that righteousness.

Eternal righteousness worked out by man is impossible. To secure justification before the Law requires permanent and perfect obedience to the law. Nehemiah 9:29: *"… Yet they acted arrogantly and did not listen to Thy commandments but sinned against Thine ordinances, By which if a man observes them he shall live. And they turned a stubborn shoulder and stiffened their neck, and would not listen."*

Paul will now contrast justification by works of the Law, and justification by faith. He will show the former is impossible, while the other is freely available to all men, Jew and Gentile.

Verse 6 But the righteousness based on faith speaks thus, "Do not say in your heart, 'Who will ascend into heaven?' that is, to bring Christ down,"

The righteousness based on faith in Christ does not demand that man try and bring God down to their level of understanding. *"Who will ascend into heaven?"* Clearly this is a rhetorical question as it presents an absurdity of someone going to heaven and bringing Christ back to earth with them. Moses says it this way in Deuteronomy 30:11 – 12, *"For this commandment which I command you today is not too difficult for you, nor is it out of reach. It is not in heaven, that you should say, 'Who will go up to heaven for us to get it for us, and make us hear it, that we may observe it?'"* Christ's offer of salvation was done on man's level on the cross and in His resurrection.

Verse 7 "… or ' Who will descend into the abyss?' that is, to bring Christ up from the dead"

The expression used by the ancient lawgiver (Moses) was a familiar way of saying that a thing could not be done. We cannot go down to the abyss to find Christ any more than we can ascend to heaven for the same purpose. Paul is again trying to show the absurdity of trying to bring Christ down to man's level.

Verse 8 But what does it say? "The word is near you, in your mouth and in your heart"-- that is, the word of faith which we are preaching,

153

The gospel tells us that the thing required for our salvation is simple and easy. Deuteronomy 30:14: *"But the word is very near you, in your mouth and in your heart, that you may observe it."* The provision of righteousness offered by God is right there for the taking.

Verse 9 **that if you confess with your mouth Jesus as Lord, and believe in your heart that God raised Him from the dead, you shall be saved;**

Here is all that is necessary to find Christ. The two requisites for salvation is confession and faith. Confession is the necessary external evidence of the intent of your heart. Open confession of the acknowledgment of Christ's death and resurrection before men is an indispensable condition of authentic discipleship. Matthew 10:32: *"Everyone therefore who shall confess Me before men, I will also confess him before My Father who is in heaven."*

Saving faith is not the product of a mere intellectual assent as to who the person of Christ is. It is imperative to *"believe in your heart that God raised Him from the dead."* If you confess Christ and believe in Him in your heart, your life will show it. Profession without production is an empty vessel.

Verse 10 **for with the heart man believes, resulting in righteousness, and with the mouth he confesses, resulting in salvation.**

Paul wants us to understand that belief must precede confession in the true order of salvation. The heart and the mouth reveal what a person really accepts and believes. If there is faith in the heart, confession with the lips is a natural consequence of that faith. A silent Christian is an individual lacking in true faith. Confession without faith would be spurious, just as faith without confession would be an admission of a dead faith.

Verse 11 **For the Scripture says, "Whoever believes in Him will not be disappointed."**

This free translation of Isaiah 28:16 is intended to say as Isaiah says, that those who believe in the cornerstone, Jesus Christ, sent by God, will find themselves at peace with God.

Verse 12 For there is no distinction between Jew and Greek; for the same Lord is Lord of all, abounding in riches for all who call upon Him;

Belief in Him is the condition of acceptance and it doesn't matter who the individual is.

- **"For there is no distinction between Jew and Greek."** The Jews believed otherwise and maintained that a Gentile must become a converted Jew before he could be saved.
- **"For the same Lord is Lord of all."** God is the same for everyone.
- **"For all who call upon Him."** All that is necessary is for a person to "call" upon His name.

It was very difficult for Jews to accept this as they wrestled with whether Paul really meant to say that they, the highly privileged descendants of Abraham, were in God's eyes no better than the Greeks or Gentiles. Acts 10:36: *"The word which He sent to the sons of Israel, preaching peace through Jesus Christ (He is Lord of all)… abounding in riches for all who call upon Him."*

Verse 13 for "Whoever will call upon the name of the Lord will be saved."

The prophet Joel, after predicting the dreadful calamities that were about to come upon the people, prophesized that subsequent to those judgments would come a time of great blessings. This period would be characterized as one where God's divine truth and love would no longer be confined to the Jewish people, but would overflow to all nations. Thus Joel says in 2:28 and 32, *"It shall come to pass afterward, that I will pour out my spirit upon all flesh … and whosoever shall call upon the name of the Lord shall be delivered."*

Some Observations Regarding Verses 1 – 13

The average church today may be filled with self-righteous zeal and be busy performing self-righteous actions to demonstrate heir zeal to the world. However, it is possible to possess a zeal that does not include the message of Jesus Christ. The Jews had been experts at this. They performed all kinds of sacrifices, practiced devout religious ceremonies and special festivals required by the Law, but in the process had lost sight of who God was and His purpose in creating the Law. In the above verses, Paul attempted to reassure His readers that salvation was still available to them if they would but reconsider their relationship with God and the person of Jesus Christ. To do this they needed to stop trying to bring God down to their level. Then if they were willing to confess that Jesus was now their Messiah they would be saved. Finally, they needed to understand that God's offer of salvation through His Son was available to everyone.

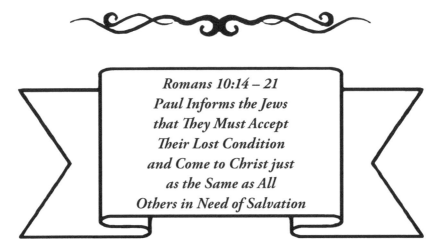

Romans 10:14 – 21
Paul Informs the Jews
that They Must Accept
Their Lost Condition
and Come to Christ just
as the Same as All
Others in Need of Salvation

Verse 14 How then shall they call upon Him in whom they have not believed? And how shall they believe in Him whom they have not heard? And how shall they hear without a preacher?

Paul identifies the steps necessary to discover one's need for salvation. The previous verses ended with our need to confess our sins before God and man. If God was open to all men to call upon Him, He must necessarily make His message available for man to understand their need of God and would also provide the necessary messengers carrying this message.

"And how shall they hear without a preacher?" Acts 8:30, 31: *"And when Philip had run up, he heard him reading Isaiah the prophet, and said, 'Do you understand what you are reading?' And he said, 'Well, how could I, unless someone guides me?' And he invited Philip to come up and sit with him."*

Verse 15 And how shall they preach unless they are sent? Just as it is written, "How beautiful are the feet of those who bring glad tidings of good things!"

To be **"sent"** suggests at least two things: first, that the one sent is submissive to a higher authority; and second, that his message was given him by the sending authority

What follows is from Isaiah 52:7: *"How lovely on the mountains Are the feet of him who brings good news, Who announces peace And brings good news of happiness, Who announces salvation, And says to Zion, 'Your God reigns!'"* This passage describes the joy with which the Israelite exiles welcomed the news of their imminent release from captivity. Paul thought of the "gospel" he preached as "good news" (i.e., **"glad tidings"**).

Verse 16 - However, they did not all heed the glad tidings; for Isaiah says, "Lord, who has believed our report?"

Paul noted that the rejection of the messenger by some was foreseen and predicted in Isaiah 53:1: *"Who has believed our message? And to whom has the arm of the Lord been revealed?"* Isaiah was referring to the rejection of the prophecies regarding his message of disaster coming upon the Jews because of their rejection of God. There is also an n inference here that implies that the person rejecting the message is also rejecting the messenger. Luke 10:16: *"The one who listens to you listens to Me, and the one who rejects Me; and he who rejects Me, rejects the One who sent Me."*

Verse 17 So faith comes from hearing, and hearing by the word of Christ.

Faith in Christ presupposes having heard the words that Christ proclaimed on earth. Giving the Jews (and some Gentiles) the chance to hear the gospel was the purpose of Jesus' ministry on earth. Faith does not come by preaching human values (philosophy, psychology, politics, etc.). Faith comes by preaching the Word of God through His messengers. The gospel is not a matter of intuition, imagination, conjecture, but of revelation.

Verse 18 But I say, surely they have never heard, have they? Indeed they have; "Their voice has gone out into all the earth, And their words to the ends of the world."

Paul asserts that the message was proclaimed to and heard by the Jews and there was no excuse for their unbelief. That the gospel was proclaimed to all nations was evident in that by the close of the Apostolic Period, the total number of Christians was estimated at over half a million.

Verse 19 But I say, surely Israel did not know, did they? At the first Moses says, "I will make you jealous by that which is not a nation, By a nation without understanding will I anger you."

Israel's rejection of God's provision of Christ's offer of salvation opened the way for the preaching of the gospel to the Gentiles. Israel as a nation was so insensible of God's mercies that they provoked Him to anger by their idolatry; therefore, they should not have been surprised when He chose to bless another people with his offer of salvation. Deuteronomy 32:21: *"They have made Me jealous with what is not God; They have provoked Me to anger with their idols. So I will make them jealous with those who are not a people; I will provoke them to anger with a foolish nation,"*

Verse 20 And Isaiah is very bold and says, "I was found by those who sought Me not, I became manifest to those who did not ask for Me."

This quotation confirms two great doctrines taught in this chapter:

- The Jews were no longer the exclusive beneficiaries of God's blessings,
- The blessings of God's kingdom were available to all mankind.

While God remains undiscovered by those who think he has already chosen them, those who may not seem to be looking for Him often discover God. Isaiah 65:1: *"I permitted Myself to be sought by those who did not ask for Me; I permitted Myself to be found by those who did not seek Me. I said, 'Here am I, here am I,' To a nation which did not call on My name."* Multitudes of people familiar with the gospel are indifferent to its message, while others who hear it for the first time eagerly accept the salvation it offers in the name of Christ.

Verse 21 But as for Israel He says, "All the day long I have stretched out My hands to a disobedient and obstinate people."

"The stretching forth the hands" is the gesture of invitation and supplication. Notice it is God who is trying to reach out to His people. The spiritual condition of Israel does not come from their lack of opportunity to hear the gospel, but from the same stubborn and rebellious spirit seen in the days of Moses and the prophets. Isaiah 65:2, indicates that God considers Israel fully responsible for the divine judgment pronounced upon it: *"I have spread out My hands all day long to a rebellious people, Who walk in the way which is not good, following their own thoughts."* It is not for want of knowledge, nor intelligence, but a willful and stubborn disobedience that excludes many from the Kingdom of Christ and all its blessings.

Final Thoughts on Chapter 10

The problem was that the Israelites (think a nation of Jews) wanted to feel that they were the masters of their own destiny. All they had to do was diligently follow the Mosaic Law. They practiced all kinds of religious forms and special festivals, but in the process lost sight of the lawgiver. When Jesus appeared on the scene, they rejected His offer of salvation to any who would accept Him as the Son of God. Paul wanted the Jews to realize that when they, as a nation, rejected Jesus' offer of salvation, God had no choice but to extend that offer to everyone, both Jews and Greek (pagans). All that was necessary for those who accepted His offer was to be willing to confess their sins before God and ask Him for the salvation provided through His Son, Jesus Christ.

Paul reminds the Jews that God had sent them many messengers in their prophets, warning of the consequences of their rejection of Him. He points out that Jesus was also a Messenger sent from God with His offer of salvation. All that was required was that they be willing to hear the message, accept His authenticity, and confess their belief in Him as God's Son. It was their corporate denial as a nation that denied them many of the blessings God had intended for them.

Finally, Paul wanted them to understand that it was up to them individually, to accept or reject Jesus as God's Son and the promised Messiah. Paul reminded them that many others had heard the message and repented, and had now received the promise of the permanent forgiveness of their sins and the promise of an eternal life spent with God. Now God was waiting patiently for His chosen people to determine their ultimate fate.

Chapter 11

God has not Forgotten His Chosen People

Introduction:

Within God's Church, the distinctions between Jew and Gentile do not exist. The only distinction that is important is the one between believers and unbelievers. Paul emphasizes the importance of the following doctrines as they apply to both the Jews and the Gentiles

- God has an unalterable plan for Israel
- The doctrine of election still applies to the Jews
- The sovereignty of God is absolute
- There is a plan for both the Gentiles and Jews in this dispensation or age
- All who reject God and His offer of salvation will face God's retribution

"God has not cast off His people whom He foreknew" could be the theme of this chapter. As the rejection of the Jews was not total, neither was it final. The gospel allows for individual Jews to be saved. Israel, as a nation, may be excluded from an automatic entrance to the Kingdom of Christ, but individual Jews who choose to believe in Jesus Christ will be admitted to His kingdom.

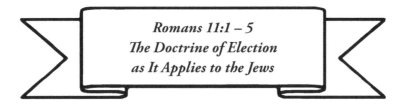

Romans 11:1 – 5
The Doctrine of Election
as It Applies to the Jews

Verse 1 I say then, God has not rejected His people, has He? May it never be! For I too am an Israelite, a descendant of Abraham, of the tribe of Benjamin.

"God has not rejected His people, has He?" Paul wants the Jews to understand the significance of this question. To the Jewish people, the rejection of Israel as a nation was inconsistent with the Word of God. For them, they applied the words of Samuel 12:22 to the nation of Israel: *"For the Lord will not abandon His people on account of His great name, because the Lord has been pleased to make you a people for Himself."*

Paul now goes on to clarify this apparent conflict by showing that the promises by God had reference, not to the Jewish nation, but to individual elect Jews.

"May it never be!" In Hebrew this is one word, and means "profane" or "profanity." Paul is saying it is profane to think that it would be possible for God to totally reject the Jews.

In support of this, Paul emphasizes his own Jewish ancestry, and being of the tribe of Benjamin was of particular importance. First, Benjamin was the only son of Jacob born in the land of promise; second, the tribe of Benjamin was one of the (Judah being the other) tribes that never seceded from the nation. After the exile of these two tribes to Babylon, it was their descendants that returned to the Promised Land and populated the theocratic nation of Israel that existed at the time of Christ. Paul was, therefore, considered himself "a Hebrew of Hebrews."

Paul began Romans by proclaiming his own acceptance of Christ, and his confidence in his acceptance by God. This reference to his own salvation was especially relevant to the Jews, as many remembered his previous opposition to the gospel. To Paul, therefore, his acceptance by God was proof that God had not abandoned all the Israelites.

***Verse 2** God has not rejected His people whom He foreknew. "Or do you not know what the Scripture says in the passage about Elijah, how he pleads with God against Israel?"*

Elijah, thinking he stood alone against the prophets of Baal, complained to God that too much was being expected of him. *(1 Kings 19:10: "And he said, 'I have been very zealous for the Lord, the God of hosts; for the sons of Israel have forsaken Thy covenant, torn down Thine altars and killed Thy prophets with the sword. And I alone am left; and they seek my life, to take it away.'"* Fear often drives people to wrong conclusions, and Elijah was no exception.

***Verse 3** - "Lord, they have killed Thy prophets, they have torn down Thine altars, and I alone am left, and they are seeking my life."*

The time referred to here was the great defection by the northern nation of Israel, under the reign of Ahab, in turning to worship the idol Baal and the murder of the prophets of God.

During the time of Paul it was much the same as God's chosen people had abandoned Him in favor of a religion that authorized the killing and persecuting of those who were preaching the words of God as spoken by Jesus Christ.

***Verse 4** - But what is the divine response to him? "I have kept for Myself seven thousand men who have not bowed the knee to Baal."*

Here is God's reply to Elijah's lament in 1 Kings 19:18: *"Yet I will leave 7,000 in Israel, all the knees that have not bowed to Baal and every mouth that has not kissed him."*) Note the "***I have kept for myself,***" Actually, Elijah should have known better because in the previous chapter of 1 Kings, he was told by Obadiah, one of the king's servants, that he was personally caring for over 100 prophets of God hidden in caves. How could Elijah think that he "alone" was left?

Verse 5 In the same way then, there has also come to be at the present time a remnant according to God's gracious choice.

That God would reject them all His people is incompatible with His electing love. As in the days of Elijah, the number of those who had not bowed the knee to Baal was far greater than the prophet believed it to be, so the number of those who had acknowledged Christ as the Messiah, in the time of Paul, was undoubtedly larger than he was aware of.

The last few words of this verse, ***according to God's gracious choice,*** explain it all. The preservation of the remnant has its origin in the saving action of God. That remnant then and now is composed of those individual Jews chosen for salvation according to God's election and grace, who have come to accept Christ as their Messiah.

Some Observations Regarding Verses 1 – 5

Paul wanted his readers to notice the distinction God made between Israel and His chosen people in Israel. Knowing that Israel, as a nation, would fail in her faithfulness to Him, God's plan of salvation made a provision for individual Jews to accept His offer. Psalms 94:14: *"For the Lord will not abandon His people, Nor will He forsake His inheritance."* The fact that God foreknew there would be some individuals who accepted Him excludes the idea of His rejecting them all. The phrase "His people" must not be limited to Israel, or the descendants of Abraham, as only those identified as God's chosen people.

The doctrine of election means that God alone chooses those He knows will be faithful to Him; it is not for us to know who they are. God has an invisible Church (individuals confident of their relationship with Christ) within the visible church.

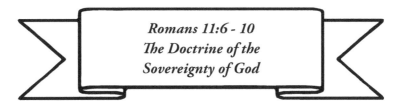

Romans 11:6 - 10
The Doctrine of the
Sovereignty of God

Verse 6 - But if it is by grace, it is no longer on the basis of works, otherwise grace is no longer grace.

There are only two possible sources of salvation: men's works or God's grace; these represent two mutually exclusive systems. Salvation by works was the very cornerstone of Judaism. As a result, the Jews could not comprehend the idea of grace (i.e., God's undeserved favor).

What they didn't understand was that for grace to be God's grace, no human could boast of God's offer of salvation through any merit or righteousness of his own, *"otherwise grace is no longer grace."* Salvation was not intended as a reward, but as a gift given according to the sovereignty of God.

Verse 7 What then? That which Israel is seeking for, it has not obtained, but those who were chosen obtained it, and the rest were hardened;

The Israelites zealously sought after righteousness, but failed to achieve it because they sought it by works. That Israel has not attained that righteousness is evident in that she remains scattered among the nations. At the same time, there are individual Jews, chosen by God, who have obtained it by faith.

The "hardening" refers to moral and religious insensitivity. Israel was hardened because they failed; they did not fail because they were hardened. They were blinded because they would not accept the light God gave them. 2 Corinthians 3:14: *"But their minds were hardened; for until this very day at the reading of the old covenant the same veil remains unlifted, because it is removed in Christ."*

Verse 8 just as it is written, "God gave them a spirit of stupor, Eyes to see not and ears to hear not, Down to this very day."

A stupor resembles a deep sleep in which a person is insensitive to impressions that come from outside. The average Jew is indifferent to the gospel and feels that it does not apply to him. They are insensitive to the reality of God's Word. Isaiah 29:10: *"For the Lord has poured over you a spirit of deep sleep, He has shut your eyes, the prophets; And He has covered your heads, the seers."* Many Jews even today refuse to accept what they hear and read from God's Word.

Paul quotes an Old Testament passage to support this hardening as an act of God. In this verse, Moses speaks to the hardening of the Israelites in Deuteronomy 29:4: *"Yet to this day the Lord has not given you a heart to know, nor eyes to see, nor ears to hear."*

Verse 9 And David says, "Let their table become a snare and a trap, And a stumbling block and a retribution to them."

The table in this verse represents the source of God's blessings and provision. The idea is that their perceived blessings from God became a curse because of their reliance on them as theirs by right. To the Jews, the Law represented their religious security. This would prove to be a stumbling block. Their fixation on obedience to the Law meant that they lost sight of the true source of God's blessing and His right to give or withhold those blessings according to His will. The result was a hardness of heart and in a people who have lost their way.

In the end, they discovered that what they had expected would be their salvation, instead led them away from the true source of salvation, namely a personal relationship with Christ. So it is in our day, where many take refuge in being a part of some ecclesiastical organization instead of a personal relationship with Christ.

Verse 10 "Let their eyes be darkened to see not, And bend their backs forever."

Psalms 69:23: *"May their eyes grow dim so that they cannot see, And make their loins shake continually."* Such is the pathetic picture of many today.

They seek to live righteous lives by trusting in their own strength, but soon discover they are forever burdened by their inadequacies.

Some Observations Regarding Verses 5 - 10:

In the example of the Jews, their slavish obedience to the Law meant that they lost sight of the Lawgiver and His purpose in giving the law. As a result, they were unable to accept the idea that their real salvation was a product of God's grace and not their own works. Therefore, they were unable to accept that Jesus Christ was the Son of God and were, unable to accept His offer of salvation. When we fail to accept the sovereignty of God and His provision for our salvation, then instead of finding freedom in Christ we find ourselves enslaved to a lifetime of unnecessary rules and regulations.

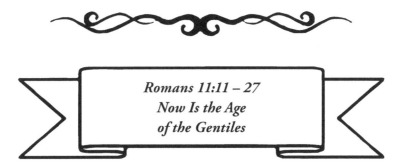

Romans 11:11 – 27
Now Is the Age
of the Gentiles

Verse 11 I say then, they did not stumble so as to fall, did they? May it never be! But by their transgression salvation has come to the Gentiles, to make them jealous.

The unbelief of Israel had a twofold purpose in God's plan. First, the rejection of the gospel by the Jews resulted in the preaching of the gospel to the Gentiles. Second, in offering His spiritual blessings to the Gentiles He hoped their jealousy would stir the Jews to seek repentance and accept the gospel message. This was God's way of giving the Jews a second chance.

This brings up an interesting thought. What would have happened if the Jewish nation had embraced Christ and Christianity? Good? Bad?

The Jews, who became Christians, tried to burden the gospel with the ceremonial observances of the law. If these had become a requirement of Christianity, it could have had disastrous consequences, as few Gentiles would have been willing to accept these added requirements. In reality, their inability to make Jewish ceremonial observances a requirement of Christianity (thank James, the brother of Jesus for this) was responsible for the rapid acceptance of the gospel among the Gentiles.

Verse 12 *Now if their transgression be riches for the world and their failure be riches for the Gentiles, how much more will their fulfillment be!*

Prior to the establishment of the Christian Church, the greatest revival took place when a man by the name of Jonah preached the message of repentance to the city of Nineveh and saw the entire city turn to God. Consider, if the rejection of the Jews of the gospel has been an occasion of the offering of God's grace to the world, how much more will God's grace abound in a world where the finally Jews accept the gospel? The greatest revival in the world will take place after the Church is raptured and God's Jews are left to evangelize those who remain.

Verse 13 *But I am speaking to you who are Gentiles. Inasmuch then as I am an apostle of Gentiles, I magnify my ministry,*

Paul's position as the Apostle of the Gentiles was unique, for he ministered as a Jew, a Christian, and an apostle. Acts 9:15: *"But the Lord said to him, 'Go, for he is a chosen instrument of Mine, to bear My name before the Gentiles and kings and the sons of Israel.'"*
Paul felt he was magnifying his ministry in just doing what Christ had ordered him to do in ministering to the Gentiles and his success was also assisting in the salvation of the Jews.

Verse 14 *if somehow I might move to jealousy my fellow countrymen and save some of them.*

Paul is operated under the principle that the more faithfully he discharged his mission to the Gentiles, the greater would be the certainty that some Jews will be stirred to jealousy, resulting in their salvation. 1 Timothy 2:3, 4: *"This is good and acceptable in the sight of God our Savior, who desires all men to be saved and to come to the knowledge of the truth."*

Verse 15 For if their rejection be the reconciliation of the world, what will their acceptance be but life from the dead?

"The reconciliation of the world" implies the conversion of multitudes of Gentiles who declare their faith in Christ. Imagine if the Jews were to experience *"life from the dead"* (i.e., a life-changing experience). This will happen when the Jews accept Jesus Christ as the promised Messiah. Luke 15:24: *"… for this son of mine was dead, and has come to life again; he was lost, and has been found.' And they began to be merry."* Jesus said this when describing a son who had left the family to go out on his own only to return when he realized the peace found in the sanctuary provided by the family. Imagine the impact it will have for the whole world if the Jews returned to the sanctuary of the family that included God and His son Jesus Christ!

Verse 16 And if the first piece of dough be holy, the lump is also; and if the root be holy, the branches are too.

Paul now uses a couple of common illustrations from everyday life to make his point. First, we need to understand that the first piece of dough and the cultivated olive tree represent the covenant promises God made to the forefathers of the Jews.

The word *"holy,"* means set apart for God. Paul is reassuring the Jews that the covenant promises are still considered "holy" by God. The lump and the branches, then, are understood as those who result from the covenant promises.

Verse 17 But if some of the branches were broken off, and you, being a wild olive, were grafted in among them and became partaker with them of the rich root of the olive tree,

For Paul, the cultivated olive tree represented Israel (God's chosen people), and the wild olive tree represented the Gentiles. Paul uses the illustration of a gardener taking some branches off the wild olive tree (the

Gentiles) and grafting them onto the cultivated tree (Israel). Notice that the branches of the wild olive tree were grafted onto the cultivated tree among the branches already on the cultivated tree.

The idea is simply this: The branch of one tree is engrafted onto another tree, and it has no independent life of its own but rather, derives its life from the life of the tree it is grafted into. In Paul's illustration, the Gentiles chosen to be grafted into God's covenant promises derive their life from the same covenant promises as the Jews do.

Don't overlook the word *"some"* in this verse. Not all the branches were broken off the cultivated tree, only those who had rejected the life-giving source of the Covenant promises. John 15:2: *"Every branch in Me that does not bear fruit, He takes away; and every branch that bears fruit, He prunes it, that it may bear more fruit."* Remember, branches are intended to produce fruit.

Verse 18   do not be arrogant toward the branches; but if you are arrogant, remember that it is not you who supports the root, but the root supports you.

There was a tendency for the Gentiles who had received salvation to look down upon the Jews who had rejected this same salvation offer. Paul reminds them that Gentile-Christian boasting cannot alter the fact that it was from their incorporation into the same covenant promises available to the Jews that the Gentiles derived their spiritual blessings. John 4:22: *"You worship that which you do not know; we worship that which we know, for salvation is from the Jews."* The Gentiles had no knowledge of this source of life until they were grafted into the cultivated olive tree and its life-giving source.

Verse 19   You will say then, "Branches were broken off so that I might be grafted in."

The Apostle also reminds the Gentile Christians that another had formerly occupied the place they now occupied on the cultivated olive tree. The Gentiles, therefore, are not to look with disdain upon the branch that had been broken off, as their position on the tree only came about through the death of another branch and it was by the grace of God that allowed them to be grafted in.

Verse 20 *Quite right, they were broken off for their unbelief, but you stand by your faith. Do not be conceited, but fear;*

God caused some of the Jews to be "***broken off***" because of their rejection of the true source of their life, Jesus Christ. The Gentiles are being warned not to become conceited, but to be aware that the same fate could await them if they reject Christ.

Verse 21 *for if God did not spare the natural branches, neither will He spare you.*

Here is a warning to Gentile Christians who may be repeating the same sin as the Jews, boasting of their privileged position. The dealing of God with his chosen people s teaches us that instead of being proud and self-confident, we are to be humble and thankful. God did not spare the nation of Israel when they rejected Christ, He will not spare a Gentile rejecting Christ.

Verse 22 *Behold then the kindness and severity of God; to those who fell, severity, but to you, God's kindness, if you continue in His kindness; otherwise you also will be cut off.*

Gentile Christians are reminded that any blessings they have received are due wholly to the grace of God and not to any merit of their own. Our security and blessings depend on the "continuing divine favor" of God; oor, we too may be cut off.

The Greek word for "severity" means to "cut off" or fall from a height, as falling off a cliff. Here we are reminded of God's nature: His kindness towards those who don't deserve it, and His severity towards those who do deserve it. The idea of a judging God is distasteful to many because it is a denial of man's independence and an assertion of God's sovereignty.

Verse 23 *And they also, if they do not continue in their unbelief, will be grafted in; for God is able to graft them in again.*

The principle the apostle just stated as applicable to the Gentiles is applicable to the Jews as well. Salvation is conditional in that its reception requires an expression of faith in the God who revealed Himself in His Son, Jesus Christ. Just as certainly as God broke off the unbelieving branches, God can and will graft them in again if they do not continue in their unbelief. Nothing but unbelief prevents the Jews from being brought back to the source of life.

Verse 24 *For if you were cut off from what is by nature a wild olive tree, and were grafted contrary to nature into a cultivated olive tree, how much more shall these who are the natural branches be grafted into their own olive tree?*

Paul recognizes only ONE (cultivated) olive tree. In Paul's illustration, the wild olive tree branch was grafted on to the cultivated tree because it was bearing fruit. The simple meaning of this verse is that the future restoration of the Jews is an easier event than the grafting in of the Gentiles into the cultivated olive tree.

If God made room for Gentile believers, by cutting off branches of the natural olive tree, has how much easier will it be for Him to restore the natural branches to their place in the cultivated olive tree? It is more natural for the Jews to be grafted back into the same olive tree from which they were originally taken than it is for Gentiles, taken from a wild olive tree, to be grafted into the cultivated olive tree.

Verse 25 *For I do not want you, brethren, to be uninformed of this mystery, lest you be wise in your own estimation, that a partial hardening has happened to Israel until the fullness of the Gentiles has come in;*

There is interdependence between the salvation of the Gentiles and that of Israel. Paul wants the Gentile Christians in Rome to know this because then they will be less likely to succumb to temptation and be conceited about their superior wisdom to that of the Jews.

Ephesians 3:3-6: "*… that by revelation there was made known to me the mystery, as I wrote before in brief. And by referring to this, when you*

*read you can understand my insight into the mystery of Christ, which in
other generations was not made known to the sons of men, as it has now been
revealed to His holy apostles and prophets in the Spirit; to be specific, that the
Gentiles are fellow heirs and fellow members of the body, and fellow partakers
of the promise in Christ Jesus through the gospel."*

By "fullness" the apostle means "full number." The grafting of the
Gentiles began with the calling out of the Church. John 10:16: *"And I have
other sheep, which are not of this fold; I must bring them also, and they shall
hear My voice; and they shall become one flock with one shepherd."* With the
gathering into the kingdom of the elect Gentiles (i.e., the Rapture of the
Church), the fullness of the Gentiles will be completed. After that event,
the responsibility for world evangelism will once again fall on the Jews,
until those prophecies that speak of the salvation of Israel are finally and
fully accomplished. Here, we see the fulfillment of Daniel's seventieth
week of prophesy.

Verse 26 *and thus all Israel will be saved; just as it is written, "The Deliverer will come from Zion, He will remove ungodliness from Jacob."*

"All Israel will be saved" refers to the turning of Israel to faith in Christ
and repentance and their restoration of God's favor and blessing. As their
rejection did not include every individual, so their restoration will not
include the salvation of every individual Jew. The term *"all Israel"* means
the total number of elect Jews, those chosen by God for salvation, just as
the fullness of the Gentiles was represented only by those chosen by God
for salvation.

Verse 27 *"And this is My covenant with them, When I take away their sins."*

The promise of their deliverance from ungodliness will begin
"whenever," in the life of individual Israelites, their sin is removed by their
acceptance of Jesus Christ as their Messiah. Jeremiah 50:20: *"In those days
and at that time,' declares the Lord, 'search will be made for the iniquity of
Israel, but there will be none; and for the sins of Judah, but they will not be*

found; for I shall pardon those whom I leave as a remnant.'" Hebrews 8:10, 12: *"For this is the covenant that I will make with the house of Israel. After those days, says the Lord: I will put My laws into their minds, And I will write them upon their hearts. And I will be their God, And they shall be My people. For I will be merciful to their iniquities, And I will remember their sins no more."*

Some Observations Regarding Verses 11 - 27:

The purpose of these verses was to explain to the Jews that the gospel message being communicated to the Gentiles was part of God's master plan for mankind.

There are three successive stages in God's divine master plan of salvation for mankind:

- The Jews rejection of Jesus resulted in the unbelief of the greater part of Israel being rejected by God. (This involved a divine hardening of the hearts of the Jews by God.)
- The communication of the gospel of Jesus Christ to the Gentiles would continue until all those Gentiles chosen by Christ have declared their faith in Him.
- After this time, God will then again work through His chosen people, the Jews, to evangelize the world. This will take place during Daniel's prophesized seventieth week. (Read Daniel 9:24 - 27.)

Romans 11:28 – 36
The Jews Will Be
Restored to God's Favor

Verse 28 From the standpoint of the gospel they are enemies for your sake, but from the standpoint of God's choice they are beloved for the sake of the fathers;

When Paul says that Israel is as an enemy of the gospel He is referring to their present state of alienation from God's favor and blessings. While God foresaw and predicted their present rejection of His Kingdom, He never contemplated their permanent exclusion from His love for them. God's attitude of the nation of Israel must be viewed in the light of the promises God made to their patriarchs. Deuteronomy 7:8: *"… but because the Lord loved you and kept the oath which He swore to your forefathers, the Lord brought you out by a mighty hand, and redeemed you from the house of slavery, from the hand of Pharaoh king of Egypt."* Deuteronomy 10:15: *"Yet on your fathers did the Lord set His affection to love them, and He chose their descendants after them, even you above all peoples, as it is this day."*

Verse 29 for the gifts and the calling of God are irrevocable.

The special gifts of God, His election, justification, adoption, and effectual calling, are irrevocable. These "gifts" were bestowed of the Jewish people as a result of God's "calling" of them to be His chosen people.

The Greek word translated "irrevocable" means "without change of mind." The purposes of God are unchangeable; consequently, those God has chosen for special blessing will not fail to receive it. 2 Timothy 1:9: *"… who has saved us, and called us with a holy calling, not according to our works, but according to His own purpose and grace which was granted us in Christ Jesus from all eternity,"*

Verse 30 For just as you once were disobedient to God, but now have been shown mercy because of their disobedience,

Prior to their conversion, the Gentiles were unaware of God's grace, yet the unbelief of the Jews provided them the opportunity to hear of God's mercy.

Verse 31 so these also now have been disobedient, in order that because of the mercy shown to you they also may now be shown mercy.

Because of the Jews unbelief God's mercy has been temporarily withheld from them, as a corporate body, that God's mercy might be shared with the Gentiles. We must understand that only "some of the branches from the cultured tree were broken off (Ref. verse 17). However, we must recognize that those branches that have been broken off from the cultured tree still have the opportunity to be grafted back on the tree, through God's mercy in the provision of His son Jesus Christ, and His offer of eternal forgiveness to all that would believe in Him.

Verse 32 For God has shut up all in disobedience that He might show mercy to all.

The first part of this verse is a statement of fact; the latter is a statement of purpose. It is only in the context of disobedience that mercy has relevance and meaning. There can be no exercise of mercy where there is no disobedience. God used both Jews and Gentiles disobedience to make evident His mercy to both. He allows their sinfulness to be revealed to them thereby setting the stage for both to comprehend their need for God's mercy and forgiveness thus resulting in their salvation. Galatians 3:22: *"But the Scripture has shut up all men under sin, that the promise by faith in Jesus Christ might be given to those who believe."*

Verse 33 Oh, the depth of the riches both of the wisdom and knowledge of God! How unsearchable are His judgments and unfathomable His ways!

The "riches" here refer to man's awareness of God's grace and mercy. This statement was prompted by Paul's awareness of man's inability to fully comprehend what God has revealed. Our salvation is not based on knowledge alone of God's provision of a His risen and coming Son, but must include actions based on the truth of that knowledge.

To appreciate what Paul is saying, we must understand the difference between wisdom and knowledge. Knowledge is the sum of the information that we have learned about a given subject. Wisdom is the ability to apply that knowledge in a useful and correct manner. Many people have an abundance of knowledge but are unable to use it in a practical way. My father used to say that wisdom was evident when we used our "common sense." God's wisdom is evident in His act of providing man with the means for the realization of their salvation.

We may not understand the things that happen to us, but we must believe that it is for our good, that God allows them. God' "judgments" may seem unfathomable to us. Job 5:9: *"… Who does great and unsearchable things, Wonders without number."* Job 11:7: *"Can you discover the depths of God? Can you discover the limits of the Almighty?"* We have no vantage point from which we can view God's judgments and ways (i.e., we cannot see the future). This limitation of the human intellect is the reason for many disagreements among Christians when they attempt to express their understanding of God.

Verse 34 *For who has known the mind of the Lord, or who became His counselor?*

This rhetorical question that Paul asks probably arose because some of the leaders of the local churches were acting in a manner that understood all that there was to know about God. Even today, we see some leaders in churches, because of their perceived importance, act as if God would be lost without them. They act as though they are waiting for a vacancy in the Trinity.

Have you noticed that Jesus Christ never asked for advice from men while He was here on earth? Isaiah 40:13, 14: *"Who has directed the Spirit of the Lord, Or as His counselor has informed Him? With whom did He consult and who gave Him understanding? And who taught Him in the path of justice and taught Him knowledge, And informed Him of the way of understanding?"*

Verse 35 *Or who has first given to Him that it might be paid back to him again?*

What do you have that God hasn't given you? Who can truthfully say that God owed them the things that they possess? Job 35:7: *"If you are righteous, what do you give to Him? Or what does He receive from your hand?"* Job 41:11: *"Who has given to Me that I should repay him? Whatever is under the whole heaven is Mine."*

There are some who believe that if they act in self-prescribed way that God owes them His blessings. The Jews, in their rigid obedience to the Law, felt that this alone was sufficient to assure them of God's blessings.

Verse 36 *For from Him and through Him and to Him are all things. To Him be the glory forever. Amen.*

God is the source of our salvation; through Him, our salvation becomes a reality, and to Him all glory is due. This is Paul at worship!

From Him -- Through Him -- To Him! The individual who trusts what he cannot understand, who loves when it cannot be explained, who reasons that nothing but good can ultimately come from God, is a person to whom God has revealed the gift of His Son.

Human knowledge, power, and virtue are reflections of God's divine power and glory. Colossians 1:16: *"For by Him all things were created, both in the heavens and on earth, visible and invisible, whether thrones or dominions or rulers or authorities all things have been created by Him and for Him."* Revelation 5:13: *"And every created thing which is in heaven and on the earth and under the earth and on the sea, and all things in them, I heard saying, 'To Him who sits on the throne, and to the Lamb, be blessing and honor and glory and dominion forever and ever.'"*

Final Thoughts on Chapter 11:

This chapter begins with a reminder to the Jews that it is God alone who chooses those He knows will be faithful to Him. In God's doctrine of election, it is not for us to know or question whom God chooses. This is an exercise of the sovereignty of God.

Paul goes on to remind his readers that it is in this sovereignty of God that we discover that salvation is the result of His grace, not our efforts. Paul points out that the Jews, in their slavish obedience to the Law, lost sight of the Lawgiver and His purpose in giving the law. As a result, they were blinded to the significance of Jesus Christ, refusing to accept him as God's Son.

Paul next reminds his Jewish readers that their rejection of Jesus Christ was, in fact, part of God's plan. He identifies three successive stages of God's divine plan of salvation:

- The Jews' rejection of Jesus resulted in the unbelief of the greater part of Israel. (A divine hardening of the hearts of the Jews by God is involved.)
- The communication of the gospel of Jesus Christ to the Gentiles, until such time as all who have been elected by Christ have declared their faith in Him.
- After this, God will again work through His chosen people, the Jews, to evangelize the world. This will take place during Daniel's prophesized seventieth week.

Paul closes this chapter by reassuring the Jews that God will again restore them to their favored position. They are reminded that their disobedience and separation from God was necessary to cause them to recognize their need for, and eventual acceptance of, the provision of God's mercy through His Son, Jesus Christ.

Chapter 12

A Transformed Life

Introduction:

The Apostle presented the major doctrines of the Christian faith as he understood them in the preceding chapters and now addresses himself to their effect on the conduct of the individual believer. The first eleven chapters made it clear that the life of a man who is righteous must be a life of evidential obedience to God. The life of a righteous man is complicated by the fact that they live in a world of unbelievers. Therefore the conduct of the Christian must be evident by his relationship to those with whom he comes in contact with in this world. In this chapter Paul wants us to see that this relationship must have guidelines. The non-Christian is not concerned about the doctrine you hold, but rather what your life says about you. In the next three and a half chapters, Paul gives us a series of practical exhortations intended to show us how Christian believers ought to live in the world.

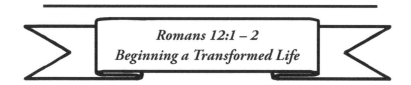

Romans 12:1 – 2
Beginning a Transformed Life

Verse 1 I urge you therefore, brethren, by the mercies of God, to present your bodies a living and holy sacrifice, acceptable to God, which is your spiritual service of worship.

In Greek philosophy, the ethical ideal was to be free from the body and its degrading influences. This is also true of most Eastern religions. For the Christian our body is the instrument through which we express ourselves to the world. We are to use our physical bodies and our lives to serve God in gratitude and love for what He has done for us. We do not serve God to win His favor; we serve God because we have already received His favor. This, then, is the first step in the Christian's transformation – the presenting of our body as a sacrifice of service to God.

"I urge you therefore…," "I urge you" is the language of grace, not Law, and emphasizes the voluntary nature of our subsequent response. *"To present your bodies a living and holy sacrifice."* The body is not evil in itself; if it were, God would not ask that it be offered to Him. This "living" sacrifice is in contrast with the ancient practice of sacrifices requiring that the life be taken before the offering was placed upon the altar.

"Acceptable to God…," For the body to be an acceptable sacrifice to God it must be "living and holy," i.e., separated unto and consecrated to God. When we accept God's offer of salvation through His Son we can now present our bodies as a "holy" sacrifice free from those defects that would cause an offering to be rejected by God. 1 Corinthians 6:20: *"For you have been bought with a price: therefore glorify God in your body."*

"Which is your spiritual service of worship." Service is the proper sequel to worship. A more literal rendering of *"spiritual"* would be "reasonable" or "rational." The believer is to exhibit a lifestyle in the world that reflects what God has done and is doing through him. This consecration to God, which Paul says is required, is a "reasonable service." This voluntary response to God is our first step in our transformation into a new creature.

Verse 2 *And do not be conformed to this world, but be transformed by the renewing of your mind, that you may prove what the will of God is, that which is good and acceptable and perfect.*

A transformation demands evidence of a change. It is a wonderful experience to have a baby in a home, but what a heartache it is for the parents when the infant does not mature! Think about God's heartache when His children remain spiritual infants and do not grow and mature and become transformed.

"And do not be conformed to this world…" The word "conform" is a word that we hear on every level of society. The world requires its citizens to conform to be acceptable. Paul urges believers not to fashion their lives and conduct by those around them. The phrase ***"this world"*** identifies a world from which God is excluded. Unfortunately, many spiritual leaders in this world today are more concerned about being conformed with the world than they are with living a life of evident transformation.

"But be transformed by the renewing of your mind…" The Greek word translated as "transformed" is "*metamorphoo,*" the word from which the English word "metamorphosis" is derived. Consider the definition of metamorphosis: a change in the form or nature of a thing or person into a completely different form or nature. It is the same word used to describe the transfiguration of Christ in Matthew 17:2 and Mark 9:2.

For the believer transformation requires a progressive life of sanctification. Sanctification is a process of constantly renewing the mind until it is transformed to be more like Christ. We are to be constantly renewing the source of our thoughts and understanding. The mind needs to be renewed to prevent the illusion that our natural conscience is a reliable guide to proper moral conduct.

"***To prove,***" in this instance, means to discover by experience what the will of God is and to learn that obedience to His will is good for us. ***"… that which is good and acceptable and perfect."*** The classical Greek word for "perfect" means to be finished, wanting nothing for completeness.

So Paul has placed before us the second step in our transformation: the renewing of our minds. The purpose of this transformation is that we might be made acceptable and perfect to God.

We need to be reminded that by doing nothing, God's will for our life cannot be discovered. God prefers to direct a body in the process of transformation.

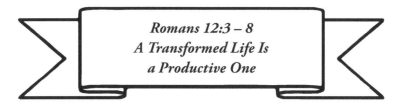

Romans 12:3 – 8
A Transformed Life Is
a Productive One

Verse 3 For through the grace given to me I say to every man among you not to think more highly of himself than he ought to think; but to think so as to have sound judgment, as God has allotted to each a measure of faith.

Paul begins by acknowledging that the office of apostle was bestowed on him through God's undeserved favor and not something he earned because of his righteous life. Paul was especially aware of this as he had been actively persecuting believers when Christ reached down with His offer of grace. Therefore we are not to think of ourselves as more important than another because God has chosen us for salvation because we exhibited a measure of God given faith. This realization should result in our using sound judgment when considering our actions.

Verse 4 For just as we have many members in one body and all the members do not have the same function,

In this verse and in the next one, three truths are identified: A. the unity of the body; B. the diverse functions of its members; and C. the interdependence of each member of the body.

Although the body has many members, the function and evidential production of individual members may seem to indicate that some are more important in the sustaining of life in the body than others. However, for the complete and proper functioning of the body all are equally necessary and interdependent. Ephesians 4:16: *"… from whom the whole body, being fitted and held together by that which every joint supplies, according to the proper working of each individual part, causes the growth of the body for the building up of itself in love."*

Verse 5 so we, who are many, are one body in Christ, and individually members one of another.

Paul now compares the interdependence of the members of our physical body to Christ's Body (the Church). As individual believers, while we differ from one another, we all are part of the same Body, the Church. The production of individual members in the Body must be for the benefit of the whole Body if the Church is to be successful. The relation of believers to each other is analogous to the mutual relation of the members of the same physical body, represented by one soul. 1 Corinthians 12:27: *"Now you are Christ's body, and individually members of it."*

Verse 6 And since we have gifts that differ according to the grace given to us, let each exercise them accordingly: if prophecy, according to the proportion of his faith;

Now Paul is getting to the substance of what a productive Christian does in the Body. "Gifts" is the Greek word "charismata," which comes from the same stem as the word for grace. Our gifts are given ***"according to the grace given to us."*** These gifts then, can be translated as the gifts which the Spirit of God through His grace endows in each of us. Every believer has one or more of these gifts that are to be used for the growth of the Body.

Finally, Paul introduces us to the first of seven spiritual gifts he wants to emphasize. ***"… if prophecy, according to the proportion of his faith;"*** The original meaning of the Hebrew word rendered *"prophet"* in the Old Testament is *"interpreter,"* or 'one who explains or delivers the will of another.' A prophet's authority was recognized not from their predicting of the future, but from interpreting and delivering messages from God. Their pronouncements were accepted according *"to the proportion of their faith"* as evidenced by these individuals.

The prophets of the Old Testament could best be viewed as the conscience of the people. Most of their pronouncements were a warning to the people or authorities that, if they continued in their present course of action, God would punish them. For this reason, the prophets were usually feared, despised, and sometimes killed or imprisoned. Also, keep in mind that the test of a prophet was this: 'if what they prophesized happened, they were true prophets; if not, they were to be killed.' Some of the prophets chosen by God were reluctant to deliver God's message because they were aware of what would happen to them personally.

Those who were considered prophets in the New Testament Christian Church were men who, while under the influence of the Holy Spirit, delivered divine communications relating to doctrinal truths, warned the people about their activities that were displeasing to God and the results thereof, and only rarely foretold future events. The message of the true prophet was the product, not of his own intuition or even of his own study and research, but of special revelation by the Holy Spirit. The prophet's message was intended by God to both convict and edify the Body and its members.

Verse 7 - *if service, in his serving; or he who teaches, in his teaching;*

"*…if service, in his serving…*" The apostle uses the word *diakonia* for one who is called to serve. What is intended here is service involved in meeting the needs of others in a practical way.

When people have this gift, they find themselves seeking ways to help others, and are sought out by others for their help. This is one of those gifts often exercised behind the scenes.

"*…or he who teaches, in his teaching…*" Teaching is the successful communication of knowledge. People with this gift are eager to share their knowledge with others, and are successful in communicating it. In Paul's day, the teacher mainly derived his knowledge from the study of the Old Testament and from studying the teachings of Jesus, in whatever form they were available to him. Teachers are not a source of new revelation, but a source of spiritual knowledge regarding God's Word within the church body. The important thing to look for in one who has this gift is their success at communicating their knowledge, and if others seek them out for edification regarding God's Word.

Verse 8 *or he who exhorts, in his exhortation; he who gives, with liberality; he who leads, with diligence; he who shows mercy, with cheerfulness.*

The final four gifts that Paul wants to emphasize are identified here. Note, the final three gifts identify the spirit and manner in which they are to be exercised.

"...he who exhorts, in his exhortation..." "Exhortation" is the Greek word *"paraklésis,"* literally, "a calling near." "Exhortation" refers to the ability to inspire others to a course of action. While teaching is addressed to the communication of knowledge, exhortation is addressed to the awakening of one's conscience and emotions. The successful gift of exhortation will results in the motivation of its hearers into a course of action. People with this gift are able to encourage and challenge others to apply their message, good or bad, to their lives. In today's world, they are known as motivational speakers. Within the body of the Church, the purpose of the gift of exhortation is to motivate Christians to actively live in obedience to God's Word. Acts 13:15: *"And after the reading of the Law and the Prophets the synagogue officials sent to them, saying, 'Brethren, if you have any word of exhortation for the people, say it.'"*

"...he who gives, with liberality..." Since giving is the sharing of one's personal possessions, the inclusion of motive and purpose is appropriate. Those with the gift of giving understand that all they have came from God. For them, their giving is not necessarily in proportion with the availability of excess possessions, but is as God moves their hearts (spontaneous benevolence). Those with this gift do so without the ulterior motive of acquiring influence or winning public approval. Here's a reminder of what our attitude should be in our giving. 2 Corinthians 9:7: *"Let each one do just as he has purposed in his heart; not grudgingly or under compulsion; for God loves a cheerful giver."*

"...he who leads, with diligence..." "Leadership" is the translation of a word that means, "to stand before others." When we have this gift, others seek us out for to exercise authority over them. Too many proclaim themselves leaders without the approval of those they have chosen to lead. In the church, some people are tempted to desire an office of authority for reasons other than as an avenue for service. *"...with diligence..."* literally means faithfully, without shirking their responsibilities because of "other" priorities. One of the problems we encountered as missionaries in another country was to make those chosen for leadership to understand that they were to make themselves available, whether it was "convenient" or not. 1

Timothy 5:17: *"Let the elders who rule well be considered worthy of double honor, especially those who work hard at preaching and teaching."*

"...he who shows mercy, with cheerfulness..." Showing mercy is not done out of a sense of duty, but out of a heart of compassion, with love and cheerfulness. Those with this gift have the ability to make those undergoing trials feel adequate. A particularly cheerful and agreeable disposition may well be evidence of the presence of this special gift (mercy) and marks a person out as having this gift. Mercy does not view the circumstances, but focuses on the building up of those who feel they have failed. These individuals understand that justice must be accompanied by understanding and compassion. One who has this gift is able to show concern for others, independent of their circumstances, and is able to encourage them in love.

Some Observations Regarding Verses 3 -- 8:

Spiritual gifts are one of the most misunderstood subjects in the Church. The first thing we must be understood is that everywhere they are mentioned in the Scriptures, they are identified as gifts. This means that one is not able to exercise these gifts on demand, but only when and as God gives them. Individuals have told me that I have the gift of teaching. Every time I speak, I make sure I have many hours of preparation behind what I will say. However, sometimes, when I am teaching, I feel that I am talking to the four walls, while other times I feel the presence of God and know the members of my audience are of one heart and mind, receiving what God has given me to pass on to them. The difference is that this is God's way of keeping me aware that people are moved only as He works in their hearts. The evidence of a spiritual gift by an individual does not set him apart as blessed by God, but as one God has chosen to work through.

The gifts are for the edification of the Body (i.e., the Church). If the exercise of a spiritual gift does not edify the Body, it is not legitimate. The exercise of a spiritual gift is intended to result in a transformed mind, productive for God.

In the above verses, seven specific spiritual gifts are identified. The description following the mention of each specific gift is self-explanatory. The one gift that many people are sometimes confused about is exhortation. It is not the same as the gifts of evangelism, preaching, teaching, or encouragement. It is the ability to motivate people to a positive response, to a call for action. We might call such an individual a "motivational" speaker.

It is evident from 1 Corinthians, chapters 12 and 14, that some gifts were coveted and exercised by many of the early Christians for the purpose of self-exaltation and self- gratification. Christians are neither to over-value, nor to under-value their gifts, but must assess them for their contribution to the function of the Body. Ephesians 4:7: *"But to each one of us grace was given according to the measure of Christ's gift."*

Many people ask how they can identify their spiritual gift. Some indicate that they have been much in prayer about it, and have asked for a sign from God so they will know what to do. These well-meaning people need to understand that the way for them to discover their gift is by actively doing something for the Lord; in the doing, they will find those endeavors that others will appreciate. Remember John 15:16: *"You did not choose Me, but I chose you, that you should go and bear fruit…"* When you are using your gift from God in the Body and seeing positive responses, you will experience the real joy of serving Him. As I see it, God doesn't call qualified individuals; God qualifies the individuals He calls.

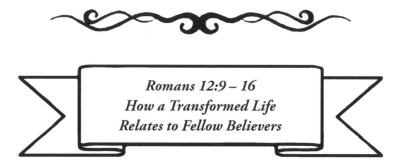

Romans 12:9 – 16
How a Transformed Life
Relates to Fellow Believers

The following series of verses are intended to provide the Christian with some fundamental practical principles that should dominate their Christians lives. First, Paul establishes a principle, and then he identifies the personal attitude that should accompany the exhibition of that principle in our life.

Verse 9 Let love be without hypocrisy. Abhor what is evil; cling to what is good.

In this verse, the apostle addresses the way the Christian life should be lived in the midst of a sinful world.

"Let love be without hypocrisy." Agape love is unconditional love. A love that is not evidential is not true love. True love is a decision made without conditions, and is not an emotional impulse, nor does it evidence itself only upon those who express a mutual love in return. 1 Timothy 1:5: *"But the goal of our instruction is love from a pure heart and a good conscience and a sincere faith."* Hypocrisy is a behavior or attitude that reflects a contradiction of what is true. God is able to differentiate between a true and hypocritical profession of love.

"Abhor what is evil..." To abhor something, expresses the highest degree of disgust or hatred toward something. The abhorrence of evil, then, must be expressed and evidential. The child of God cannot flirt with sin and serve God at the same time. Any evil, perceived practice or tolerance of evil completely negates one's Christian testimony.

"...cling to what is good..." The word *"cling"* in the active form means "to glue" or "to attach one's self to any person or thing." The same Greek word, here translated as "cling," is used to signify the permanence of the marriage relationship. 1 Thessalonians 5:21: *"But examine everything carefully; hold fast to that which is good."* Believers have an obligation to practice that which God recognizes as good.

Verse 10 Be devoted to one another in brotherly love; give preference to one another in honor;

"Be devoted to one another..." As Christians, we are to make it a priority to show concern for our fellow Christians. We are to do so *"in brotherly love."* The Greek word for love here is "phileo," meaning a love that we would express as if we were members of the same family. John 13:34,35: *"A new commandment I give to you, that you love one another, even*

as I have loved you, that you also love one another. By this all men will know that you are My disciples, if you have love for one another."

"...give preference to one another..." We should act toward our fellow Christians as if they are a priority in our life, and do so in a manner that shows that they are important to us. This is to be done "***in honor,***" meaning we should be done with a attitude of respect and appreciation of them and what they mean to us. Philippians 2:3: *"Do nothing from selfishness or empty conceit, but with humility of mind let each of you regard one another as more important than himself;"*

Verse 11 *not lagging behind in diligence, fervent in spirit, serving the Lord;*

Religion without enthusiasm is dead. These expressions are intended to remind us that our religious service is to be done in an enthusiastic spirit.

"...not lagging behind in diligence..." Paul states this principle in the negative; it would be better stated as "be diligent." Paul wants us to be faithful. A Christian may burn out, but he must never rust out. Total commitment to faithful service leaves neither the time nor the inclination to discover an alternate love.

"*fervent in spirit,*" The Greek word (*Teo*) from which "fervent" translated means to be "hot, zealous, ardent, burning." It also suggests that our zeal and enthusiasm should be under the control of the Holy Spirit. Acts 18:25: *"This man had been instructed in the way of the Lord; and being fervent in spirit, he was speaking and teaching accurately the things concerning Jesus, being acquainted only with the baptism of John;"* I am reminded of the words God spoke, regarding the church in Ephesus, in Revelation 3; the Ephesian church had lost its first love. Many new Christians lose the fervent spirit; in so doing, "lose their first love."

Finally, Paul tells us that our commitment to faithfulness with an enthusiastic spirit is to be directed at **"*serving the Lord.*"** The real proof of zeal is not in a demonstration of religious excitement, but in a demonstration of faithful service of the Lord Jesus. Acts 20:19: *"... serving the Lord with all humility and with tears and with trials which came upon me through the plots of the Jews;"*

Verse 12 rejoicing in hope, persevering in tribulation, devoted to prayer,

"rejoicing in hope," Circumstances may not seem to warrant rejoicing, but we Christians are urged to live with the certain knowledge that God has better things ahead for us. The believer's feet may be on the ground, but his eye is to be fixed on heaven in expectancy of the Lord's return.

"...persevering in tribulation..." Endurance and perseverance are the virtues one learns in the challenge of life's experiences. Hebrews 10:36: *"For you have need of endurance, so that when you have done the will of God, you may receive what was promised."* Our ability to persevere in the face of trials is often a measure of the closeness of our personal relationship with God. The believer never appreciates mountain-peak blessings until he has experienced the valleys of defeat.

"...devoted to prayer..." Intercourse with God is necessary to the growth of a personal relationship with Him. Therefore, the apostle emphasizes the necessity of prayer as a requirement for Christian living. One does not need to stop working or to cease whatever he is doing to pray. Acts 1:14: *"These all with one mind were continually devoting themselves to prayer, along with the women, and Mary the mother of Jesus, and with His brothers."* In the end, Paul is saying don't forget to pray.

Verse 13 contributing to the needs of the saints, practicing hospitality.

"...contributing to the needs of the saints..." Christianity is a faith evidenced by an open hand, an open heart, and an open door. We are to be open to identifying the needs of the saints, and be willing to make their needs our own. Hebrews 6:10 says, *"For God is not unjust so as to forget your work and the love which you have shown toward His name, in having ministered and in still ministering to the saints."*

"...practicing hospitality..." The Greek word *philoxenos,* translated "hospitality," literally means, "love for strangers." ." Without hospitality, the spread of the gospel during the early days of the Church would have been greatly impeded. The value that the early Christians placed upon the virtue of hospitality is plain, from Paul's enumerating it among the requisite qualifications of a bishop in Titus 1:8. Jesus expressed it as follows

in Matthew 25:35 *"I was a stranger, and you welcomed me."* When this sharing takes place under one's own roof, it is labeled hospitality. Hebrews 13:2 says: *"Do not neglect to show hospitality to strangers, for by this some have entertained angels without knowing it."* Do others feel welcome in your home, or do you project an attitude of just tolerating their presence?

Verse 14 Bless those who persecute you; bless and curse not.

This admonition can be a tough one for many of us. When others seem to be targeting us for persecution, it often provokes feelings of resentment, even in the minds of believers. ***"Bless,"*** in classical Greek, means to "speak well of someone." As Christians, Christ reminds us that persecution at the hands of the world is inevitable and is evidence that we are following in His footsteps. Instead of wishing or praying that our persecutors and enemies feel the wrath of God, we should pray for their good. Matthew 5:44: *"But I say to you, love your enemies, and pray for those who persecute you."* Luke 6:28: *"… bless those who curse you, pray for those who mistreat you."* Leave vengeance to God, as He is a wiser and better judge than we are. Frankly, the vengeance of God is far worse than anything we could perceive.

Verse 15 Rejoice with those who rejoice, and weep with those who weep.

Generally speaking, it is easier to weep with those who weep than to rejoice with those who rejoice, because human nature prompts the former, but envy may stand in the way of rejoicing at another's achievements or good fortune. The world's motto is "Laugh and the world laughs with you; weep and you weep alone." This should not be said about Christians. Instead, we are to feel the sorrows and joys of others as though they were our own; shared joy is doubled, so shared sorrow is halved.

Verse 16 Be of the same mind toward one another; do not be haughty in mind, but associate with the lowly. Do not be wise in your own estimation.

"Be of the same mind toward one another…" As Christians, we should acknowledge that we all share the common command of sharing God's Word and a common hope for an eternal future with Christ. Philippians 2:2: *"… make my joy complete by being of the same mind, maintaining the same love, united in spirit, intent on one purpose."* We are to be of one mind with our fellow believers in Christ.

"…do not be haughty in mind…" Feelings of superiority are an attitude or state of mind that has no place in the life of a true Christian. In God's eyes, we are all equal. 1 Peter 3:8: *"To sum up, let all be harmonious, sympathetic, brotherly, kindhearted, and humble in spirit…"* ***"but associate with the lowly."*** There is no aristocracy in the Church. A sign of worldliness in the Church is evident when its leaders no longer associate as readily with those considered of lesser importance, but rather seek out those they feel their social equal or of greater importance in the church.

"Do not be wise in your own estimation." The opinionated person is intractable and impervious to any advice but his own. Some believers may think of themselves as spiritual giants, but in the eyes of others, they are not. Just as there is to be no social aristocracy in the Church, so there is to be no spiritual aristocracy. Proverbs 3:7: *"Do not be wise in your own eyes; Fear the Lord and turn away from evil."*

Some Observations Regarding Verses 9 – 16:

The above verses are intended to give us some fundamental values to guide us in our actions and attitudes toward others. Too often, Christians act as if they are in some sort of exclusive club. We like to surround ourselves with those we feel our social, economic, and cultural equals. In doing so, we overlook the example of how Christ conducted His life while here on earth in His confrontations with others. He was not only willing to associate with others outside His circle of followers, but He went out of His way to meet and share with them. Christianity is not intended to be exclusive in nature, but inclusive. The question we must ask ourselves is, "Do others feel comfortable and welcome in our presence?" A positive answer to this question will only happen if others sense from us that our love and concern for them is genuine.

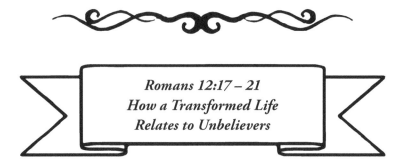

Romans 12:17 – 21
How a Transformed Life
Relates to Unbelievers

Verse 17 Never pay back evil for evil to anyone. Respect what is right in the sight of all men.

John Calvin, one of the major founders of the Christian theological reformation movement, summarized the meaning of this verse as follows: "What is meant is that we ought diligently labor, in order that all may be edified by our honest dealings -- that they may, in a word, perceive the good and the sweet odor of life, by which they may be allured to the love of God."

"Never pay back evil for evil to anyone." We must act in such a way as to commend ourselves to the consciences of all men. The nature in each one of us is to want revenge and recompense for every wrong done to us. Proverbs 20:22: *"Do not say, 'I will repay evil'; Wait for the Lord, and He will save you."* Remember as Christians you can expect to be persecuted by the world.

"Respect what is right in the sight of all men." You and I live in a world of unbelievers who are not concerned about the doctrine we hold. What they are concerned about is: Are we truthful or not? Will we pay our honest debts? Are we dependable? The norms of behavior governing Christian conduct must be norms that even unbelievers recognize as worthy of approval. God wants us to conduct our affairs in a manner that the public conscience will find acceptable. 2 Corinthians 8:21: *"… for we have regard for what is honorable, not only in the sight of the Lord, but also in the sight of men."* We are to live as if we are living in front of Jesus.

Verse 18 If possible, so far as it depends on you, be at peace with all men.

The admonition to live at peace with everyone has two qualifying statements: A. If it be possible; and B. So far as it depends on you.

"If possible…" The impossibility can come from two different sources. The first is when others flatly refuse to accept your offer of peace. The second comes when you discover that their price for peace comes with too high a price. For the Christian, too high a price is when the demand for peace (not offending another) requires compromising God's Word. ***"… so far as it depends on you…"*** We are not to let the source of discord be traceable to a failure on our part when it is compatible with God's commands for us in His Word. ***"… be at peace with all men."*** Those who are ambassadors of God's peace must necessarily be peaceably disposed toward all men. If the maintenance of peace means the sacrifice of God's truth and/or honor, then the price of peace is bought at too dear a cost. (Refer to Matthew 10:34-36 and Luke 12:51-53.)

Verse 19 Never take your own revenge, beloved, but leave room for the wrath of God, for it is written, "Vengeance is Mine, I will repay," says the Lord.

We must not forget what God did for us while we were His "enemies" (Romans 5:10: *For if while we were enemies we were reconciled to God through the death of His Son, much more, having been reconciled, we shall be saved by His life.)* We cannot ignore the possibility that His mercy may eventually embrace those we consider our "enemies."

Paul does not imply that divine vengeance will, of a certainty, overtake our enemies in our lifetime, but simply that we should not usurp the prerogative of God. The desire for vengeance in a Christian destroys an important Christian distinctiveness, which is the ability to win people for Christ

"… but leave room for the wrath of God…" Deuteronomy 32:35: *"Vengeance is Mine, and retribution, In due time their foot will slip; For the day of their calamity is near, And the impending things are hastening upon*

them." When we take revenge out of the hands of God, we are, in a sense, saying that God is either unwilling or unable to handle it Himself.

Verse 20 *"But if your enemy is hungry, feed him, and if he is thirsty, give him a drink; for in so doing you will heap burning coals upon his head."*

To fail to do good to our enemies when they are in need of it and when it is in our power to do so is a kind of indirect retaliation. Proverbs 25:21: *"… if your enemy is hungry, give him food to eat; And if he is thirsty, give him water to drink;"* Matthew 5:44: *"But I say to you, love your enemies, and pray for those who persecute you."* Remember, God may have them reserved for a day when He knows they will change their lives and ask Him into their hearts.

"… for in so doing you will heap burning coals upon his head." To "heap burning coals (of fire) upon his head" is a way saying that the results of acting well toward our enemies may make them feel a sense of shame and guilt (see 1 Peter 2:15). This does not mean that it will bring God's judgment upon them, but it could help bring about their repentance and salvation. Finally, recognize that when our enemies stand before God on their judgment day, we do not want them to be able to use our actions toward them as an excuse for their actions.

Verse 21 *Do not be overcome by evil, but overcome evil with good.*

The world's philosophy leads men to expect retaliation when they have wronged another. To receive kindness and love when retaliation is expected can sometimes melt the hardest heart.

The Christian's victory over evil consists in his refusal to become a party to the promotion of evil by returning evil for evil. By doing this he will lend authenticity to God's love to the world. Though he may not succeed in making the enemy cease to be an enemy, he can refuse to allow him to be *his* enemy.

"To overcome evil by good" means to live a life where true victory lies in refusing to let the evil that surrounds us transform the good that Christ wills us to do. The Christian should consider the presence of evil as

an opportunity, whereby Christ's love may be authenticated by our actions. Evil is not vanquished by retaliation, but it may be conquered by kindness.

Final Thoughts on Chapter 12

In this chapter, we discover that living a transformed life means living a life in conformance to God's desire for us. There are individuals who claim to be followers of Christ, yet they cannot point to a transformed life. Some say that they cannot specify a time when they accepted Christ, but they feel they are living a Christian lifestyle. Paul says that cannot be. In reality these are like those in Matthew 7:22 who, when confronting Jesus on judgment day, say to Him, "… *Lord, Lord, did we not prophesy in your name, and in Your name cast out demons, and in Your name perform many miracles?"* Jesus will answer them and say, "*I never knew you.*" It is one thing to proclaim the name of Christ, and quite another to be obedient and live a transformed life.

A person with a transformed life will exhibit those values and gifts that Christ deems important. A transformed life will result in God's blessing us with those spiritual gifts that will help others to grow in their belief. It is our life that is our greatest testimony of what and who God is to us. Among fellow believers, we are to be a source of encouragement and to exhibit love and compassion. Among unbelievers, our lives should be such that unbelievers will respect us. We are not to flaunt our relationship with God in such a way that we look down on our enemies as people who deserve God's vengeance. We are to leave their fate to God, and instead pray that they may see God's light through us.

We are told we must be transformed, unified, productive, and a positive example to those around us.

Chapter 13

Christians Living in the World

Introduction:

In the preceding chapter, we were told that Christians must be transformed, unified, productive, and an example to those around them. In this chapter, we will discover how the Christian life is to be lived in an unbelieving world. Paul is interested in the presentation of a positive example of Christianity to the world. It is only as the world sees Christianity in a positive light that the proclamation of the gospel will be successful. Reinforcing this idea, Paul reminds us that God ordained civil government and believers have a responsibility to that government. Remember that the authorities in Paul's day were known for their persecution of Christians and for having immoral personal lifestyles.

Christianity, when it enters any community, should not immediately assail their form of government, even if there is something in their institutions of authority inconsistent with Christ's spirit of righteousness. It is important we understand that it can only be changed through the changing of the hearts and conscience of the authorities. Direct denunciation will only be viewed as rebellion. Christians must live differently from those around them, and yet at the same time not appear rebellious against society. As Christians, we have special problems balancing our responsibilities to both God and human government, which can leave us feeling helpless. In the time that I am living, my country has deliberately turned away from God. Both the government and schools have decreed that there is no place in them for God. As a result, violence and rebellion are the norm, and the desires of a civilized society are completely ignored, while individual rights are declared supreme.

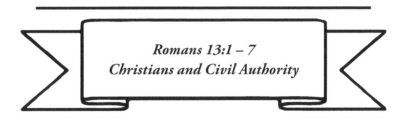

Romans 13:1 – 7
Christians and Civil Authority

Verse 1 Let every person be in subjection to the governing authorities. For there is no authority except from God, and those which exist are established by God.

To the Jews, religion and government were interrelated into a theocracy. At the same time, it was considered contrary to the teaching of the Torah to have a Gentile rule over the Jews. As a result, the Jews were continually in rebellion against Gentile rule, which eventually led to their expulsion from Rome and, finally, to the destruction of Jerusalem.

"Let every person be in subjection to the governing authorities." In God's master plan, civil authority was appointed over individuals with a specific role to fulfill. Obedience was not enjoined on the grounds of the personal merit of those in authority, but on the grounds of their official position. A circumstance may arise in which followers of God must choose between obeying God and obeying man (see Acts 5:29), but even then, they must understand that if their Christian convictions do not permit their compliance, they must be willing to accept the consequences of their refusal. While government is of God, the form is of men. Titus 3:1: *"Remind them to be subject to rulers, to authorities, to be obedient, to be ready for every good deed,"*

"For there is no authority except from God." In Paul's time, pagan as the Roman imperial government was, even Jesus acknowledged it as a divinely appointed authority. John 19:11: *"Jesus answered, 'You would have no authority over Me, unless it had been given you from above; for this reason he who delivered Me up to you has the greater sin.'"* Paul makes it clear that God recognized civil government as necessary to the existence of society.

"... and those which exist are established by God." We are to obey magistrates because they derive their authority from God. Not only is human government a divine institution, but the form in which that government exists and the persons by whom its functions are exercised are determined by His providence. The Church and civil government occupy different spheres, yet both are divinely established institutions.

Verse 2 ***Therefore he who resists authority has opposed the ordinance of God; and they who have opposed will receive condemnation upon themselves.***

In the eyes of God, civil authority is required to establish the rules of society so that all may live in harmony. Paul views ruling authorities as performing their duty of preserving order, approving good behavior, and punishing evil; therefore, Paul also considered them as possessing the authority to reward good behavior and to punish rebellious behavior.

"Therefore he who resists authority has opposed the ordinance of God." Christianity is not a movement to improve government or to help society clean up a town. Its purpose is to preach a gospel that is the power of God unto salvation. When successful, this will bring into existence individuals who will seek to improve government and help society clean up the town. Obedience to the laws of the state is incumbent on the believer, in the same way that obedience to God's laws is incumbent in the spiritual realm.

At the great moments of crisis in history -- and that's where we are today - believers often have difficult decisions to make regarding the limits of obedience to civil authority. However, we must keep in mind *"... and they who have opposed will receive condemnation upon themselves."* The "condemnation" referred to here involves the possibility of both divine judgment and civil authority's reaction. We must not disobey conscience in submitting to civil government, but if disobedience is required, we must be willing to accept the consequences imposed by civil authority. Daniel and his friends never questioned the authority of the king to do what he decreed. They may have objected and even disobeyed him, but they did so recognizing and accepting the consequences that were to follow.

Verse 3* *For rulers are not a cause of fear for good behavior, but for evil. Do you want to have no fear of authority? Do what is good, and you will have praise from the same;

Paul is speaking of the legitimate design of government, not of the abuse of power by wicked men. ***"For rulers are not a cause of fear for good behavior… "*** The purpose of government is to maintain law and order. Authority deals with the deed; Christianity deals with the motive. ***"Do you want to have no fear of authority?"*** The person who obeys the laws of his state will have nothing to fear of the state's officials or law-enforcement agencies.

"… and you will have praise from the same;" This verse assigns an additional reason for magistrates to be obeyed. If you do well by them, you will receive their praise and be a positive influence to promote good. 1 Peter 2:14: *"… or to governors as sent by him for the punishment of evildoers and the praise of those who do right."*

Verse 4* *for it is a minister of God to you for good. But if you do what is evil, be afraid; for it does not bear the sword for nothing; for it is a minister of God, an avenger who brings wrath upon the one who practices evil.

The word in the Greek for "minister of God" is translated "deacon" as in 1 Timothy 3:10, 13: ***"… for it is a minister of God to you for good."*** Note that the state is intended to be a *servant* of God, not God. The design of civil government is not to promote the advantage of the rulers, but of the ruled. Paul states that civil authorities have the power to praise good works and punish evil actions. Paul describes the purpose of authority as to avenge evil, not protect the evil-doer. In these days, humanism has directed sympathy to the criminal instead of the victim,

"… be afraid;" The wrong-doer should fear of civil authority. ***"… for it does not bear the sword for nothing…"*** The sanctity of life validates the death penalty for the crime of murder. Part of the design of government is to protect the good, and the other is to punish the wicked: that 'right' is ordained by God to belong to the "authorities." ***"… an avenger who brings wrath upon the one who practices evil."***

Verse 5 Wherefore it is necessary to be in subjection, not only because of wrath, but also for conscience' sake.

"Wherefore it is necessary to be in subjection…" Subjection to the magistrates is not only a civil duty enforced by penal statutes, but is also part of our religious obedience to God. *"… but also for conscience' sake."* Paul adds that we should submit to authority out of regard to God, from conscientious motives. God has ordained civil government for the promotion of the physical welfare of men, as members of a civilized society, and the instruction and discipline of the Church, for their moral and religious improvement. 1 Peter 2:19: *"For this finds favor, if for the sake of conscience toward God a man bears up under sorrows when suffering unjustly."*

Verse 6 For because of this you also pay taxes, for rulers are servants of God, devoting themselves to this very thing.

Those who shed crocodile tears over paying their taxes remind me of Lewis Carroll's satire, *Alice in Wonderland* when the walrus and the carpenter in this story were walking along the seashore, weeping because there was so much sand and so few oysters. All along, they kept eating oysters, while weeping and weeping. In the Old Testament, taxes were included in the tithes, and when all the tithes were added up, they sometimes amounted to more half of an individual's income or possessions.

"For because of this you also pay taxes…" Taxes are to civil authority what the tithe is to the Church: an acknowledgment of a debt owed, and to allow others to be fulltime "ministers." Since civil government is constituted for the benefit of society, for the punishment of evil-doers, and for the praise of those who do well, it follows that we should expect to pay the taxes required for its support. The man in authority may be unjust in the collection of taxes, but the institution is not. *"… for rulers are servants of God…"* You may not have had a part in choosing your rulers, but whatever the circumstance of their obtaining their positions, God permitted it.

Verse 7 Render to all what is due them: tax to whom tax is due; custom to whom custom; fear to whom fear;

What is paid to the government in taxes presupposes a value received. ***"Render to all what is due them…"*** Matthew 22:21: *"They said to Him, 'Caesar's.' Then He said to them, 'Then render to Caesar the things that are Caesar's; and to God the things that are God's.'"* ***"… tax to whom tax is due; custom to whom custom…"*** The word "tax" is applied to land and income, while "custom" is applied to merchandise. Matthew 17:25: *"He said, 'Yes.' And when he came into the house, Jesus spoke to him first, saying, 'What do you think, Simon? From whom do the kings of the earth collect customs or poll-tax, from their sons or from strangers?'"*

"… fear to whom fear; honor to whom honor…" Fear is the natural accompaniment of wrongdoing. Since Paul exhorted the believer to render to the officials their due, the rendering "respect" would appear to be the best meaning of the word translated "honor" here.

Some Observations Regarding Verses 1 – 7

Christianity is not a movement to clean up society. Its purpose is to preach the gospel of Jesus Christ. If Christianity is successful, the result will be individuals in civil government and having a desire to improve that civil government, and to create a better society. Dr. Charles Swindoll said it best when, in one of his books, he wrote, "We are not called out to clean out the fish bowl, but to be fishers of men." Civil government is part of God's plan for mankind we need to think what life would be like without civil authority. Without civil authority, the alternative would be anarchy – the survival of the strongest. Notice, nations ruled by anarchist civil governments reject the need for religion and persecute those who may disagree with them. Or think of those nations controlled by "religions" that disavow Christianity. They invariably end up declaring Christianity an evil that must be eradicated. The reality is that Christians need the protection of civil government. We must be diligent, therefore, in our support of those civil governments that allow us to spread the gospel of Christ.

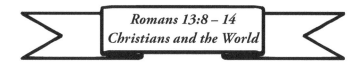

Romans 13:8 – 14
Christians and the World

Verse 8 Owe nothing to anyone except to love one another; for he who loves his neighbor has fulfilled the law.

Two thoughts are implied here:

- A condemnation of the practice of some, who are ever ready to borrow, but slow to repay the borrowed sum.
- Among all the debts a person may have incurred, there is one that can never be repaid in full: the debt of love, namely, the love "for one another."

"Owe nothing to anyone except to love one another;" A better translation might be "Do not keep on owing… " The prohibition includes the incurring of obligations when we have no certain prospect of repaying them. Few things bring greater reproach upon Christians than the accumulation of debts and the inability to pay them. You may ask, "Do you think we should turn in our credit cards?" No, but Christians are not to obligate themselves beyond their reasonable ability to pay their debts. If incurring any debt were contrary to God's will, the Lord would not have said in Matthew 5:42, *"Do not turn away from the one who wants to borrow from you."* Something that is often overlooked in this principle is that this should include any unfulfilled promises. Paul is also concerned about our personal testimony in the world, and making promises that we cannot, or are unwilling to, fulfill is very detrimental to our testimony.

Note that there is an implied debt mentioned here also -- to love one another. This is a debt that can never be completely paid. **"… for he who loves his neighbor has fulfilled the law."** If love is the fulfillment of God's law, then this means God's law cannot be fulfilled without involving love; fulfilling the law implies that we must love our neighbor. Matthew 22:39: *"The second is like it, 'You shall love your neighbor as yourself.'"* John 13:34, 35: *"A new commandment I give to you, that you love one another, even as I have loved you, that you also love one another. By this all men will know that* *you are My disciples, if you have love for one another."* Do you realize that contained in this last verse is the only standard Jesus gave to the world for identifying His disciples? How does your evidential love measure up?

Verse 9 For this, "You shall not commit adultery, You shall not murder, You shall not steal, You shall not covet," and if there is any other commandment, it is summed up in this saying, "You shall love your neighbor as yourself."

These verses are from Exodus 20:13-17, and they identify four areas in which we are to be above reproach: the sanctity of marriage; the sacredness of human life; the taking of another's possessions; and the coveting of that which we do not have, but think we need. All these commandments touch the believer's attitude towards his fellowman. Paul is saying that our love for our neighbor is revealed in what we do, rather than in what we say.

Verse 10 Love does no wrong to a neighbor; love therefore is the fulfillment of the law.

"Love does no wrong to a neighbor;" How often is Christian love brought into disrepute because those who are loud in their declarations of love, persist in actions that do not reflect an attitude of love towards their neighbors? If we possessed the same love of our neighbor as toward our family, it is clear that we would do "no wrong to a neighbor." **"… love therefore is the fulfillment of the law."** If love exemplifies the fulfillment of God's law, then it follows that God's law cannot be fulfilled without the expression of love. Fulfilling the law implies that we not only love our families, our neighbors, and ourselves as well. Remember Jesus said that He did not come to destroy the Law but to fulfill it. How did he do it? By showing his love for others was so great that He was willing to sacrifice His life, that others may personally experience God's love.

Verse 11 And this do, knowing the time, that it is already the hour for you to awaken from sleep; for now salvation is nearer to us than when we believed.

"… knowing the time… " God will not come until all He has chosen have been saved. 2 Peter 3:9: *"The Lord is not slow about His promise, as some count slowness, but is patient toward you, not wishing for any to perish but for all to come to repentance."*

"… for now salvation is nearer to us than when we believed." Our "salvation" is the evidence that the work of Christ in providing for our deliverance from this present world was successful and guarantees of our future presence in heaven. James 5:8: *"You too be patient; strengthen your hearts, for the coming of the Lord is at hand."* Every person who accepts Christ as his or her Savior brings us that much closer to His coming. Maranatha!!

Verse 12 **The night is almost gone, and the day is at hand. Let us therefore lay aside the deeds of darkness and put on the armor of light.**

One error we often commit is applying earth's concept of time to heaven's vision of eternity. Paul admonishes us not to be concerned about the exact time of His coming, but to live each day with the certain knowledge and anticipation that He *is* coming. Then darkness of the sins and sorrows of this life will be over; we will share an eternity in the light of His presence.

Verse 13 **Let us behave properly as in the day, not in carousing and drunkenness, not in sexual promiscuity and sensuality, not in strife and jealousy.**

The nearness of Christ's return should motivate us to live a life that is a credit to our Christian testimony. Luke 21:34: *"Be on guard, that your hearts may not be weighted down with dissipation and drunkenness and the worries of life, and that day come on you suddenly like a trap…"*

"Let us behave properly as in the day… " Paul is telling us we should live our life as if exposed for all to see. Paul goes on to identify six sins that show we may still be living in the darkness of our human nature.

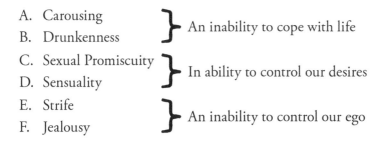

A. Carousing
B. Drunkenness
} An inability to cope with life

C. Sexual Promiscuity
D. Sensuality
} In ability to control our desires

E. Strife
F. Jealousy
} An inability to control our ego

Verse 14 *But put on the Lord Jesus Christ, and make no provision for the flesh in regard to its lusts.*

Galatians 3:27: *"For all of you who were baptized into Christ have clothed yourselves with Christ."* To be clothed with Christ means, that when others see us, they should see Jesus Christ living within us. Colossians 3:10: *"… and have put on the new self who is being renewed to a true knowledge according to the image of the One who created him."* Our success in doing this will show that we are living in the light of God's presence. In putting Christ first in our lives it follows that then there is no room for the things of this world.

Final Thoughts on Chapter 13

In this chapter, we are confronted with Paul's challenges to us as believers. If we claim a relationship with Christ, then it is necessary that our life reflects the example that Christ modeled for us while He was here on earth.

Jesus did not set Himself out to confront the civil authorities. In fact, He encouraged His followers to respect them. When confronted with the request for taxes, He paid them. When the soldier, who had accepted Him as his Savior, asked Jesus what he should do, Jesus did not tell him to stop being a soldier. Instead He simply told him to live a life where he did not take advantage of others. You see, Jesus knows we must live in a faulty world, but that does not mean we are to succumb to its attractions.

The last verses in this chapter present a special admonition to all believers. First, we are challenged to love our neighbors. Paul goes so far as to say that this attitude in our lives is the evidence of whether or not we are fulfilling God's Law in our lives. He warns us that we are to live as if the coming appearance of Christ is just around the corner. I am amused by the desire of so many wanting to know the exact date of His coming. To me, it raises this question: "Would you live differently if you knew Christ was coming next week or next month?" Obviously, we would! But that's the point. When Christ returns, He doesn't want to see us living an artificial life, but a normal lifestyle, where expecting His return is an everyday part of our life.

Finally, we are warned not to become victims to the evil that surrounds us. The final verse in this chapter says it all: We are to live so that others will see Christ in us. The question before us, then, is, "What does the world see when they look at our life?"

Chapter 14

Six Principles to Live By

Introduction:

In this chapter, Paul instructs believers about how they are to conduct their lives. Six great principles are presented: (1) We are not to judge fellow Christians based on *OUR* perception of their faith, verses 1 - 5; (2) Our personal relationship with God determines our spiritual maturity, verses 6 – 9; (3) We will all stand before God one day to give an account of our lives, verses 10 – 12; (4) You must live your life as a positive example to fellow Christians, verses 13 – 18; (5) let your desire be to build up the Body (i.e., Christ's Church) and fellow Christians, verses 19 – 21; and (6) Our personal beliefs do not have to be outwardly expressed to be appreciated.

Paul is concerned with the duties of church members towards each other, particularly in matters of conscience. The difference between the weak and the strong among the Jewish believers was that the strong recognize Jesus did not require literal obedience to the Old Testament ceremonial laws, while the weak felt that literal obedience to the ceremonial law was a necessary expression of their faith in Jesus Christ. Owing to ignorance, prejudices, weakness of faith, and other causes, there exists even today a diversity of opinion and practice among Christians regarding their understanding of doctrine. However, this diversity should not be a sufficient reason for rejecting fellow Christians from fellowshipping with the family of Christ.

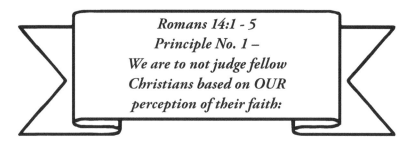

Romans 14:1 - 5
Principle No. 1 –
We are to not judge fellow
Christians based on OUR
perception of their faith:

Verse 1 *Now accept the one who is weak in faith, but not for the purpose of passing judgment on his opinions.**

Having condemned murder, adultery, stealing, bearing false witness, and coveting, Paul now warns against condemning things not expressly forbidden in Scripture. Paul is concerned that we accept immature believers and allow them to fully participate in the life of the church without judging them. Unfortunately, unnecessary judgments regarding non-essentials often destroy the unity of the Body.

"Now accept the one who is weak in faith… " The one "weak in faith" is the individual who is not fully confident in their beliefs. This results in their lacking an understanding of what their faith in Christ allows them to do. As a result, they do not fully have the freedom in their life that Christ's provision of salvation allows them.

"… but not for the purpose of passing judgment on his opinions." We must not commit the error of passing judgment upon those we perceive as "weak" in the faith. 1 Corinthians 9:22: *"To the weak I became weak, that I might win the weak; I have become all things to all men, that I may by all means save some."* The Church has no authority to decide questions of personal liberty in things not expressly forbidden in the Scriptures. One of the problems Christians often have is judging another's' faith by comparing them to the faith they think they themselves possess.

Verse 2 *One man has faith that he may eat all things, but he who is weak eats vegetables only.**

Many of the believers in Paul's time refused to eat meat purchased at the local markets because they did not know if it had been used as a sacrifice to local idols. This decision not to eat meat that might have been sacrificed to foreign gods was based on Old Testament regulations, which they assumed were required of all Jews, whether they were Christians or not.

"One man has faith that he may eat all things… " The mature Christian realizes the Jewish laws pertaining to food restrictions have been abolished under the gospel of grace. *"… but he who is weak eats vegetables only."* Adam and Eve were vegetarian, but God told Noah and his descendants that they were to eat meat.

Verse 3 **Let not him who eats regard with contempt him who does not eat, and let not him who does not eat judge him who eats, for God has accepted him.**

"Let not him who eats regard with contempt him who does not eat, and let not him who does not eat judge him who eats,' The problem was that both the weak and the strong were prone to adopt a censorious attitude toward each other regarding what they could eat. The weak felt the strong were not serious Christians, while the strong labeled the non-eaters as "legalistic" Christians.

The source of the problem was that the majority of the meat found in the public marketplace was from animals that had been sacrificed to one of the many pagan gods. This made it potentially "unclean" for two reasons: it was meat sacrificed to pagan idols; it had not been slaughtered in a kosher manner.

"… for God has accepted him." When God receives a person into His fellowship, He does not make eating or not eating certain foods a condition of acceptance. Christians must be willing to do likewise. With this admonition comes an implied warning, found in Colossians 2:16: *"Therefore let no one act as your judge in regard to food or drink or in respect to a festival or a new moon or a Sabbath day…"*

Verse 4 **Who are you to judge the servant of another? To his own master he stands or falls; and stand he will, for the Lord is able to make him stand.**

This beautifully expresses the position of the believer in the household of God -- a servant who lives with the family. It would be improper to intrude into the household affairs of another person and pass judgment upon their servants. Paul is saying, therefore, what right have we to sit in judgment on another Christian's conduct when he is not accountable to us? James 4:12: *"There is only one Lawgiver and Judge, the One who is able to save and to destroy; but who are you who judge your neighbor?"*

"To his own master he stands or falls... " It is the servant's own master who decides the value of his servant's services; no one else has the authority to do so. We are answerable only to our own master, namely, the Lord Jesus Christ, just as a servant or slave is answerable only to his own master." **"... for the Lord is able to make him stand."** To Him alone we stand or fall.

We often judge the value of another's beliefs by what church they attend. We seem to forget that when we stand before the judgment seat of Christ, He will not ask us what church we attended; instead, it will be *our* personal actions for which we will be held accountable.

Verse 5 One man regards one day above another, another regards every day alike. Let each man be fully convinced in his own mind.

"One man regards one day above another... " Observing Jewish festival days is not a doctrinal question and is irrelevant to the question of salvation. The weak in faith were convinced that they needed to observe all the feast days defined in the Old Testament, while the strong understood that such festivals belonged to the past.

"... another regards every day alike." The failure of a person to regard any day as having special significance is a matter of personal conviction..

"Let each man be fully convinced in his own mind." If someone is uncertain about the propriety of something they are doing, then for them it is wrong. Questionable activities are wrong for the believer if they are questionable to him. One person should not be forced to act according to another man's conscience, but everyone should act according to his own conscience, doing only what he is comfortable with in his mind.

The Christian's celebration of the Lord's Day is not the same as the Jewish celebration of the Sabbath. We observe the Lord's Day as our Sabbath to commemorate Christ's resurrection, not because it is necessarily a "sacred" day.

Some Observations Regarding Verses 1 – 5

These first five verses highlight problems Paul saw among the believers that were causing dissension among them.

The Weak	The Strong
Cannot eat meat	Can eat meat
Judges the strong as irresponsible	Regards the weak as legalistic
Regards all Old Testament festivals	Regards all days alike as required

These were special problems among believers during Paul's time. The reality is that many of today's churches and denominations have divided Christianity based on man-created doctrines. I grew up in a very conservative religious background in which the church said you could not play cards or go to movies. Clearly these were not biblical doctrines, but manmade rules perceived as necessary to avoid all appearance of sin. Many churches have their own lists of does and don'ts. Paul wants us to realize that we have to be careful not to judge another's relationship to God based on things not expressly identified in the Scriptures.

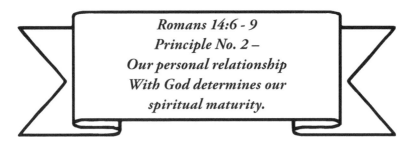

Romans 14:6 - 9
Principle No. 2 –
Our personal relationship
With God determines our
spiritual maturity.

Verse 6 **He who observes the day, observes it for the Lord, and he who**
eats, does so for the Lord, for he gives thanks to God; and he
who eats not, for the Lord he does not eat, and gives thanks
to God.

Thinking a certain day is especially holy, abstaining from certain foods, or eating certain foods does not make us better Christians in the sight of God. 1 Corinthians 8:8: *"But food will not commend us to God; we are neither the worse if we do not eat, nor the better if we do eat."* It is not what is on the table, but what is in the heart that is noted by God. 1 Corinthians 10:31: *"Whether, then, you eat or drink or whatever you do, do all to the glory of God."*

There is important subtle admonition in this verse that is often overlooked. Whatever we do, we should do it as if we are doing it for the Lord. This should apply to all our activities. I used to lead young people on missionary building projects. Many of the young people were not used to using building tools. When I inspected their work, I often saw bent nails and poor workmanship. When I commented on it, they would reply that it was the best they could do. At that point, I asked them if they felt their work was good enough that they would be proud to show it to Jesus. Usually they would get the idea and improve their work. I have dealt with many businesses and individuals who were quick to claim that they were Christians with the expectation that since we were Christians we should hire them. Unfortunately for many their work didn't reflect well on them. I used to have a part in hiring doctors and nurses for a Christian medical mission and we understood that for the positive reputation of our hospitals it was equally important that we hired individuals who were practiced good medicine and related in a positive way with the patients. Your Christian testimony is reflected in the quality of work you perform.

Verse 7 For not one of us lives for himself, and not one dies for himself;

As Paul said earlier, Christ lives in us therefore to those around us, what they see in us gives them an image of Christ. As was said in the previous verse it will be seen in the quality of our work. It will also be seen in our lifestyle. We cannot escape the fact that we are Christ's representatives here on earth and we will be judged by how others have seen Christ in us. Our whole life, even our death, is meaningful only in terms of our personal relationship with Christ. 2 Corinthians 5:15: *"… and He died for all, that they who live should no longer live for themselves, but for Him who died and rose again on their behalf."*

Verse 8 for if we live, we live for the Lord, or if we die, we die for the Lord; therefore whether we live or die, we are the Lord's.

Our life, including our death, must be viewed in the light of our eventual eternity with the Lord. If we understand that, many things that may otherwise occupy our minds and time should shrivel into trivialities.

Every Christian should endeavor to regulate his heart, his conscience, and his life as if he was in subjection to God's will. This is the most important thing that the created can render to his Creator. Revelation 14:13: *"And I heard a voice from heaven, saying, 'Write, "Blessed are the dead who die in the Lord from now on!"' 'Yes' says the Spirit, 'that they may rest from their labors, for their deeds follow with them.'"*

Verse 9 For to this end Christ died and lived again, that He might be Lord both of the dead and of the living.

The authenticity of Jesus Christ's identity was demonstrated by His overcoming death through His resurrection. Revelation 1:18: *"… and the living One; and I was dead, and behold, I am alive forevermore, and I have the keys of death and of Hades."* It verified Christ's claim to His deity by showing His power over death. In doing so, He freed us from the bonds of an eternal death. In this act of obedience to God Christ gives us the opportunity of spending an eternity with Him, rather than existing as nothing more than a dot on the pages of time.

Some Observations Regarding Verses 6 – 9

There is a particularly important principle illustrated in these verses. It is that the attitude and quality of our actions as seen by others and us, define our relationship with Christ. Whatever we do, we should be doing it as a service to, and for, Christ. It is only when we accept this realization that we will find our relationship with Christ growing more important in our life and its evidence as seen by others in our lives, that we will present a positive image of Christ in our lives.

Christ's power over death fully authenticated to mankind that He was indeed the Son of God. When we accept this reality, we cannot help but grow in our relationship with Him, as we now understand that whether we live or die, Christ is our Lord.

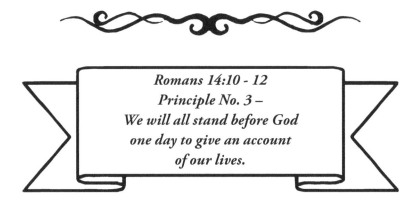

Romans 14:10 - 12
Principle No. 3 –
We will all stand before God
one day to give an account
of our lives.

***Verse 10 But you, why do you judge your brother? Or you again, why
do you regard your brother with contempt? For we shall all
stand before the judgment seat of God.***

As Paul stated earlier, both the weak and the strong are prone to judge others. The use of the word "brother" to refer to other Christians identifies the equality of their standing before God. The judgment in each case often ends with our view of with contempt at their perceived weaknesses. The problem here is that the individual doing the judging is assuming prerogatives that belong only to Christ and to God.

"For we shall all stand before the judgment seat of God." We are all to stand before the judgment seat of Christ, as He is our final judge. 2 Corinthians 5:10: *"For we must all appear before the judgment seat of Christ, that each one may be recompensed for his deeds in the body, according to what he has done, whether good or bad."*

Verse 11 For it is written, *"As I live, says the Lord, every knee shall bow to Me, And every tongue shall give praise to God."*

This verse emphasizes what will be our attitudes as we face the judgments of God. As believers, we will drop to our knees in joy at the knowledge that our sins have been forgiven. For unbelievers, they will drop to their knees at the realization of their coming judgment and what the future holds for them. Philippians 2:10: … *"that at the name of Jesus every knee should bow, of those who are in heaven, and on earth, and under the earth,"*

Verse 12 So then each one of us shall give account of himself to God.

We are to judge our life in view of the realization that ultimately we will have to account for it before God. The implication, then, is that rather than judging someone else's sin, we should be concerned with our own. That should be enough for us to worry about! Matthew 12:36: *"And I say to you, that every careless word that men shall speak, they shall render account for it in the day of judgment."* Matthew 16:27: *"For the Son of Man is going to come in the glory of His Father with His angels; and will then recompense every man according to his deeds."*

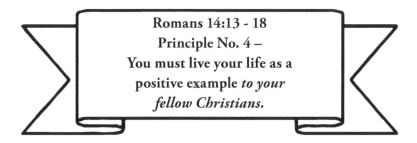

Romans 14:13 - 18
Principle No. 4 –
You must live your life as a
positive example *to your*
fellow Christians.

Verse 13 *Therefore let us not judge one another anymore, but rather determine this -- not to put an obstacle or a stumbling block in a brother's way.*

"*Therefore let us not judge one another anymore...*" Paul again urges us to stop criticizing and finding fault with one another. Matthew 7:1: *"Do not judge lest you be judged."* If we accept one another in love then we need to accept that we all will not have the same understanding of every doctrine of Christianity.

. "*... but rather determine this -- not to put an obstacle or a stumbling block in a brother's way.*" The Greek word "*skandalon,*" translated "obstacle," literally means a trap designed to ensnare a victim. The same word was used by Jesus in Matthew 16:23 in dismissing Peter's attempt to deter Him from going to the cross. We get our English word "scandal" from this Greek word. The Greek word "*proskomma,*" translated "stumbling block," literally means something against which one may strike his foot, causing him to stumble or even fall. The stumbling block Paul is talking about is something we may do that may cause a fellow Christian to do something that his conscience tells him is not right for him. Instead, we are to consider the advice of Paul. 1 Corinthians 8:13: *"Therefore, if food causes my brother to stumble, I will never eat meat again, that I might not cause my brother to stumble."*

Verse 14 *I know and am convinced in the Lord Jesus that nothing is unclean in itself; but to him who thinks anything to be unclean, to him it is unclean.*

In this verse, Paul accomplishes two things: A. He encourages the strong by telling them that he shares their position. B. He also reminds us the weak are right in refusing to do that which they may consider unclean.

"*... but to him who thinks anything to be unclean, to him it is unclean.*" A simple principle is evident here: it is wrong for a man to violate his own conscience. 1 Corinthians 8:7: *"However not all men have this knowledge; but some, being accustomed to the idol until now, eat food as if it were sacrificed to an idol; and their conscience being weak is defiled."*

Verse 15 For if because of food your brother is hurt, you are no longer walking according to love. Do not destroy with your food him for whom Christ died.

If Christ loved the weak to the extent of laying down His life for their salvation, than we must not jeopardizing this relationship by placing a stumbling block before others that may cause them to question their new Christian faith! Though a thing may be lawful, it is not always right to practice it. Why? Because ***"you are no longer walking according to love."*** To practice love may call for a measure of sacrifice of one's perceived liberty. We must be willing to limit our freedom because of our love for our fellow believer. Ephesians 5:2: *"… and walk in love, just as Christ also loved us, and gave Himself up for us, an offering and a sacrifice to God as a fragrant aroma."*

"Do not destroy with your food him for whom Christ died." Paul is particularly concerned that a dogmatic view of what foods are acceptable for us to eat may drive a person with a lesser view of what is acceptable to violate their conscience resulting in feelings of guilt causing them to question their faith. 1 Corinthians 8:11: *"For through your knowledge he who is weak is ruined, the brother for whose sake Christ died."* We may have the right to do what we believe is acceptable to God, yet we must consider relinquishing that right for the sake of offending others who may not feel as we do. One deed done in love is more valuable in God's eyes than a hundred correct opinions.

Verse 16 Therefore do not let what is for you a good thing be spoken of as evil;

Practicing something that we feel is acceptable, which the weaker in faith may see as unacceptable, may result in the weaker Christian questioning the validity of God's Word. In practice, Christian liberty must be exercised with Christian love, taking into account the possibility of the spiritual weakening of another.

Verse 17 for the kingdom of God is not eating and drinking, but righteousness and peace and joy in the Holy Spirit.

The Kingdom of God has nothing to do with eating or drinking, fasting, abstaining from meat on Friday, not eating pork, or observing a vegetarian diet. When questions of food and drink become our chief concern, then it is clear that our thinking and conduct have strayed from the interests of God's Kingdom. 1 Corinthians 8:8: *"But food will not commend us to God; we are neither the worse if we do not eat, nor the better if we do eat."*

The three attributes of righteousness, peace, and joy are some of the "fruits of the Spirit," described in Galatians 5:22, 23 and Ephesians 5:9. Righteousness is that which enables us to stand before God. Peace is the result of the agreement between our soul and God's will, and between reason and conscience. Joy is what we experience when we are in fellowship with the Holy Spirit. Galatians 5:22:*"But the fruit of the Spirit is love, joy, peace, patience, kindness, goodness, faithfulness, gentleness, and self-control."*

Verse 18 For he who in this way serves Christ is acceptable to God and approved by men.

To the Apostle Paul, Christ is God, and God is incarnate in Christ. Christians are to conduct themselves in a manner that will evoke the admiration of unbelievers, and so deprive them of the occasion for criticism. Negative judgments by those outside the body of believers are often to result of seeing inconsiderate conduct towards weaker Christians on the part of strong believers. A community of love and accord should always be evident within the church, so that adversaries may not find occasion to speak critically. "Approved of men" does not mean that men will get in your cheering section and applaud you because you are a believer. In fact, they may even persecute you. 2 Corinthians 8:21: *"... for we have regard for what is honorable, not only in the sight of the Lord, but also in the sight of men."* 1 Peter 2:12: *"Keep your behavior excellent among the Gentiles, so that in the thing in which they slander you as evildoers, they may on account of your good deeds, as they observe {them,} glorify God in the day of visitation."*

Some Observations Regarding Verses 13 - 18

1. We have the freedom to do what we are convinced in our minds is acceptable to God.
2. We must be willing to limit that freedom if our actions appear sinful in the eyes of fellow believers.
3. We will be judged by Christ, if our actions cause other believers to weaken in their personal relationship with Christ.

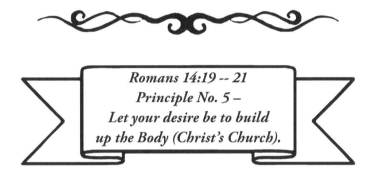

Romans 14:19 -- 21
Principle No. 5 –
Let your desire be to build
up the Body (Christ's Church).

Verse 19 *So then let us pursue the things which make for peace and the building up of one another.*

All the members of the Church are to be engaged in edifying their fellow believers in the Body. Before we argue with a brother about a matter of secondary religious significance, we need to ask ourselves: will this edify the brother or appear as a criticism? 1 Corinthians 10:23: *"All things are lawful, but not all things are profitable. All things are lawful, but not all things edify."* Ephesians 4:29: *"Let no unwholesome word proceed from your mouth, but only such a word as is good for edification according to the need of the moment, that it may give grace to those who hear."* Clearly, we are to encourage our fellow believers in their beliefs, as long as they are not contrary to God's Word.

Verse 20 Do not tear down the work of God for the sake of food. All things indeed are clean, but they are evil for the man who eats and gives offense.

The believer has the liberty to eat meat or abstain from it, but neither will commend him to God. 1 Corinthians 8:9-12: *"But take care lest this liberty of yours somehow become a stumbling block to the weak. For if someone sees you, who have knowledge, dining in an idol's temple, will not his conscience, if he is weak, be strengthened to eat things sacrificed to idols? For through your knowledge he who is weak is ruined, the brother for whose sake Christ died. And thus, by sinning against the brethren and wounding their conscience when it is weak, you sin against Christ."* Paul is warning us against letting our personal views come between fellow believers and their relationship with God.

The evil described is that of one strong in faith, using his liberty in such a way that it may cause a weaker brother to question their faith. 1 Corinthians 8:13: *"Therefore, if food causes my brother to stumble, I will never eat meat again, that I might not cause my brother to stumble."*

Verse 21 It is good not to eat meat or to drink wine, or to do anything by which your brother stumbles.

In this verse, Paul includes the drinking of wine as an example of the kind of things that a Christian is free to do, unless it offends others. Its use is not a violation of God's law; therefore, it is not a sin. Early Christians thought it necessary to abstain from wine because they feared they might use wine that had been previously offered to the gods, or end up overindulging, which would lead to drunkenness, which was forbidden by God. Because of this, the drinking of wine could be offensive to the one who may be weaker in faith and maturity.

We must be willing to forego the expression of our personal freedom if, by doing so, it leads to an action that may violate other believers' personal understanding of their freedom. If Christ was willing to suffer and endure the shame and pain on the cross in order to save us, we ought to be willing to give up anything questionable to the conscience of a weaker brother.

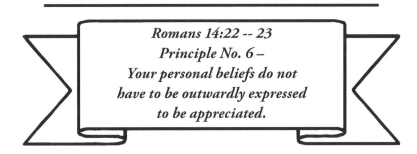

Romans 14:22 -- 23
Principle No. 6 --
Your personal beliefs do not
have to be outwardly expressed
to be appreciated.

Verse 22 The faith which you have, have as your own conviction before God. Happy is he who does not condemn himself in what he approves.

The freedom you have before God doesn't need to be visibly expressed to be appreciated. If a weak brother is going to be hurt by your expression of freedom, then be content with the inward knowledge of it.

Happy is the man who does not feel guilty in his actions. Is your conscience clear, or do you doubt the correctness of what you have done? Where believers are without a specific commandment to follow, they need to obey the dictates of their conscience. 1 John 3:21: *"Beloved, if our heart does not condemn us, we have confidence before God… "* Happy is he who has a clear conscience!

Verse 23 But he who doubts is condemned if he eats, because his eating is not from faith; and whatever is not from faith is sin.

If in our conscience we doubt the correctness of what we are doing, then it is wrong. If we are troubled by feelings of doubt as to whether or not it is right to do what we see other Christians doing, then to follow their actions will result in an inner condemnation, for it comes from a confident inner conviction.

"But he who doubts is condemned if he eats… " If any person is convinced in his own mind that a thing is contrary to God's law and yet practices it, he is guilty before God, even though it may ultimately be found to be lawful. *"… because his eating is not from faith… "* There is no question of saving faith, but only of the confident faith that we are free to use what God has set apart for man's good. *"… and whatever is*

not from faith is sin." A believer sins when he does what is not approved by his inner conviction and faith.

Final Thoughts on Chapter 14

One thing that is clear to Paul is that the greater our spiritual maturity, the greater is our responsibility toward others and towards ourselves. The true evidence of spiritual maturity is shown in how well we reflect God's love. Our guiding principle should be that our lifestyle should edify others. One of the principles of doctors is "First, do nothing that will harm the patient." This should also be one of the Christian's primary principles. It isn't what we know that is important; it is how something will affect the lives of our fellow believers that matters. When we stand before God on judgment day, we will have to answer for our own actions, not those of others.

The greater degree of maturity and faith
The greater degree of felt responsibility toward others
The greater love that will naturally be expressed
The greater chance that others will see Christ in us.

Chapter 15

Some Final Thoughts from Paul

Introduction:

The first verse of this chapter is the conclusion of the preceding chapter (14:22). Paul notes that proper Christian conduct must reflect an awareness of our convictions (what we personally understand that God expects of us) and conscience (what we can do without feeling guilty of displeasing God). In verse 2 in this chapter, Paul will add a third requirement, that of consideration (whether or not what we do will build up a weaker fellow believer). The apostle, in approaching the close of this epistle, assures the Romans of his confidence in them, and tells them that his motive in writing was not because of a deficiency in their knowledge, but rather as a reminder of those things they already knew. Paul uses the example of Christ, who did not live to please Himself but accepted whatever self-denial His mission required in His desire to please God, His Father.

Paul understood that many Christians might be divided by questions of convictions, conscience or consideration of others. These divisions often reflect the level of spiritual maturity of individual believers. Unfortunately, the result is often individual actions that, while not in themselves sinful, may be considered by others as unacceptable leading to feelings of resentment or insecurity in their faith.

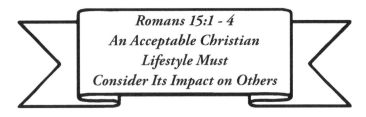

**Romans 15:1 - 4
An Acceptable Christian
Lifestyle Must
Consider Its Impact on Others**

***Verse 1 Now we who are strong ought to bear the weaknesses of those
without strength and not just please ourselves.***

The last guiding principle Paul gives, governing our conduct as
Christians, is the necessity of the strong being willing to help bear the
burdens of the weak.

When Paul says, "... ***we who are strong...***," he classes himself among
the strong. The strong hold the key to the solution of the problem. To them
belongs the responsibility of taking the initiative. The expression "***to bear
the weakness***" does not mean that the strong should merely "tolerate" the
weak, but that they must be willing to accept the weaknesses of fellow
believers in an effort to encourage them and ease their burden of guilt.
Galatians 6:2: *"Bear one another's burdens, and thus fulfill the law of Christ."*

"***... and not just please ourselves.***" The aim of strengthening the faith
of the weak must be a consideration by which the actions of the strong are
to be governed. The strong are not to support the weak with the idea that,
in doing so, they are showing the superiority of their faith.

Verse 2 Let each of us please his neighbor for his good, to his edification.

Scripture is silent on many things approved by our contemporary
society. Paul gives us three guidelines Christians are to use to guide their
actions. A. Conviction: are we convinced that it is acceptable to God
(Romans 14:22a)? B. Conscience; can we do it without having second
thoughts about its acceptability for us (Romans 14:22b)? C. Consideration;
will our actions offend or strengthen the faith of a weaker brother (Romans
15:2)? 1 Corinthians 9:22: *"To the weak I became weak, that I might win the
weak; I have become all things to all men, that I may by all means save some."*

"***Let each of us please his neighbor for his good,***" with a view to the
spiritual advantage of that neighbor. 1 Corinthians 10:33: *"... just as I also*

please all men in all things, not seeking my own profit, but the profit of the many, that they may be saved." The objective of all Christian conduct should be for the spiritual edification of our neighbor or ourselves. 1 Corinthians 10:23: *"All things are lawful, but not all things are profitable. All things are lawful, but not all things edify."* Ephesians 4:29: *"Let no unwholesome word proceed from your mouth, but only such a word as is good for edification according to the need of the moment, that it may give grace to those who hear."* This last verse is a warning to think about the impact of our actions on others before we act, recognizing that less mature Christians may be watching us.

Verse 3 For even Christ did not please Himself; but as it is written, "The reproaches of those who reproached Thee fell upon Me."

Christ identified Himself with the desire of His Father, which was to serve and to save mankind. He bore His reproaches because he was zealous of God's honor. To fervently espouse the cause of God will arouse the passions of sinful men and often cause them to ridicule those who are trying to live a life emulating that of Jesus. Psalms 69:9: *"For zeal for Thy house has consumed me, And the reproaches of those who reproach Thee have fallen on me."* Paul reminds his readers that those who bear Christ's name must be willing to follow Christ's example.

Verse 4 For whatever was written in earlier times was written for our instruction, that through perseverance and the encouragement of the Scriptures we might have hope.

The Word of God imparts the knowledge that should produce within us comfort and hope. One of the main purposes of the Scriptures is to sustain us in our present trials with the knowledge of our future "hope." In this verse, we are told that two specific things that are necessary to benefit from the Scriptures:

a. ***Patient endurance***: Those who diligently study Scripture will recognize their weaknesses as they become more aware of the distance between their own conduct and the ideal presented in God's Word.

b. ***The encouragement of the Scriptures***: Those who study of God's Word cannot fail to discover within these sacred writings, penned so long ago, the ability to encourage and heal their spirit.

Some Observations Regarding Verses 1 – 4

My wife and I were missionaries in Mexico for over forty years and lived in Cabo San Lucas, Mexico, for over twenty-five years. Cabo is a very tourist-centered city, and as we walked the streets, we always made an effort to engage the visitors in conversation. Quite often, they would express themselves and their experiences in a very "colorful" language. When they asked us what we were doing there, we would explain that we were missionaries. It was amazing how often the tenure of the conversation would change at that point; the language would become less colorful, and the people would often express how they were themselves church members and admired what we were doing. It is amazing how a little willingness to share our faith in God changes things.

As part of our personal testimony we decided not to drink any alcoholic beverages. We have been questioned many times about it and are often asked if we have a problem if a fellow believer drinks in front us at a meal. We usually say, no, and usually added that Paul even encouraged the use of drinking some wine and that we felt the Bible only warned against drunkenness. At the same time, we noticed how many reconsidered their drinking habits in front of us. Our decision hasn't hurt us in the least, but we are constantly reminded that accepting another's weakness without making an issue of it goes a long way towards allowing them to see Christ in us.

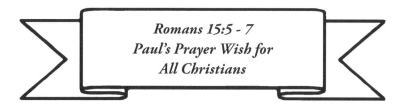

Romans 15:5 - 7
Paul's Prayer Wish for
All Christians

Verse 5 Now may the God who gives perseverance and encouragement grant you to be of the same mind with one another according to Christ Jesus;

Paul's prayer-wish was that believers live in harmony with one another according to the example of Jesus Christ. To accomplish this, he understood that we must be patient and seek to encourage our fellow believers. Unity on a horizontal level with our fellow man is a reflection of a vertical unity with Christ.

Verse 6 that with one accord you may with one voice glorify the God and Father of our Lord Jesus Christ.

Unity of belief leads to unity in praise. The order is significant because the latter can never be attained without the former. ALL Christians should be able to praise God together. A unity of praise is the external evidence of the working of Christ in us.

Verse 7 Wherefore, accept one another, just as Christ also accepted us to the glory of God.

Herein lies a fundamental issue: What did not matter to Christ should not matter to us. If Christ is able to receive all believers without distinction, then clearly we must not allow unimportant divisions within the Body limit our acceptance of one another. While Paul viewed the Church as composed of two groups, the strong and the weak, the gospel makes no such distinctions. All are adopted into God's family when we accept Christ as our Savior; therefore, we should accept one another, recognizing that in doing so, we are glorifying God.

Some Observations Regarding Verses 5 – 7:

In Christ's view, there is only one Church, composed of a Body of believers who have accepted Him as their Savior and are daily struggling to live their lives to please Him. However, today we have a proliferation of church denominations, each convinced that they have the inside track to God. Many are even convinced that, if you are not of their denomination, you do not have the correct understanding of God and His message. One of the great disappointments that Christ experiences when He looks down on us is the lack of unity among the followers of these denominations. In over forty years as a missionary in Mexico, I have worshiped in every imaginable church. I have been asked innumerable times what denomination I come from. I have always replied that I am a born-again evangelical Christian. If more of us were to think and act in this manner, I am convinced we would see a greater unity and harmony among the true Body of Christ.

Romans 15:8 -- 13
Paul Reminds the Jews that
Christ Is also the
Savior of the Gentiles

Verse 8 *For I say that Christ has become a servant to the circumcision on behalf of the truth of God to confirm the promises given to the fathers,*

In these verses, notice the element of progression in the marshaling of quotations from the Old Testament. In this verse, Paul reaffirms his commitment to God's chosen people, the Jews and the promise that God made to their ancestors that *all* men might be blessed who accepted and obeyed Him.

Verse 9 and for the Gentiles to glorify God for His mercy; as it is written, "Therefore I will give praise to Thee among the Gentiles, And I will sing to Thy name."

The Gentiles cannot lay claim to God on the basis of a "covenant" relationship, as the Jews can. No promise was ever made to their fathers, as was made to Abraham, Isaac, and Jacob. The inclusion of the Gentiles is based on the provision of God's mercy. Christ came to confirm the truth of the promises made to the ancestors of the Jews; He also came that the Gentiles might experience God's blessings as well.

"As it is written" introduces the first of four quotations from the Old Testament. The first quotation is found in Psalm 18:49: *"Therefore I will give thanks to Thee among the nations, O Lord, And I will sing praises to Thy name."* In this quotation, David promises to celebrate his victories by confessing and praising the Name of God in the midst of the Gentile nations, which surrounded him that he had defeated. Clearly the Gentiles can praise God for the mercy shown to them.

Verse 10 And again he says, "Rejoice, O Gentiles, with His people."

The second quotation is from Deuteronomy 32:43 where the Gentiles are encouraged to praise God WITH the Jews. The Gentile nations are to praise **the God of Israel**, not **Israel**. In those days, the defeat of any nation by another nation was considered evidence that the god of the victorious nation was greater than the god of the defeated nation.

Verse 11 And again, "Praise the Lord all you Gentiles, And let all the peoples praise Him."

This third quotation is from Psalm 117:1: *"Praise the Lord, all nations; Laud Him, all peoples!"* Note the occurrence of the word **all** twice in this brief quotation. First, the Gentiles are independently called upon to praise God; second is the reminder that the entire world is to praise the Lord. This is intended to include the Jews.

Verse 12 ***And again Isaiah says, "There shall come the root of Jesse, And He who arises to rule over the Gentiles, In Him shall the Gentiles hope."***

This fourth quotation is found in Isaiah 11:10: *"Then it will come about in that day That the nations will resort to the root of Jesse, Who will stand as a signal for the peoples; And His resting place will be glorious."* Here the attention is fixed upon the Root of Jesse. To the Jews, the "root of Jesse" was a reference to the Messiah. The Gentiles, then, are being encouraged to recognize that Jesus, the Messiah of the Jews, is also the provision for their salvation. This is an explicit prediction of the dominion of the Messiah over all nations. In Christ shall the Gentiles find their hope, the "confident expectation of an eternal future with Him."

Verse 13 ***Now may the God of hope fill you with all joy and peace in believing, that you may abound in hope by the power of the Holy Spirit.***

Paul concludes with a brief prayer for his readers in Rome. The prayer begins and ends with the accent upon hope, a hope that was based on Paul's confident trust in the promises of Christ.

"Now may the God of hope fill you with all joy and peace in believing…" The "God of hope" generates within us the peace and joy that arises from the confidence we receive in the knowledge that we will share eternity with Him.

The phrase ***"by the power of the Holy Spirit"*** indicates that the existence of hope is not possible except through the intervention of the Holy Spirit. 1 Thessalonians 1:5: *"… for our gospel did not come to you in word only, but also in power and in the Holy Spirit and with full conviction; just as you know what kind of men we proved to be among you for your sake."*

Some Observations Regarding Verses 8 – 13

Notice the logical legal progression of Paul's argument that Jesus, the Jewish Messiah, is the God of hope for the Gentiles also.

- The ministry of Jesus and His message fulfilled the promises of the Scriptures.
- The ministry of Jesus was a reflection of God's mercy for both Jews and Gentiles.
- Jesus is both the Messiah of the Jews and the salvation of the Gentiles.
- Therefore, both the Jews and the Gentiles are praising the same God.
- Therefore, through this God we all receive our confident hope of an eternity with Christ.

Romans 15:14 -- 15
Paul Shares His Purpose
in Writing to the Romans

Verse 14 And concerning you, my brethren, I myself also am convinced that you yourselves are full of goodness, filled with all knowledge, and able also to admonish one another.

Here Paul offers a gentle apology for his frankness and boldness in speaking to the Romans in the previous sections. The apostle had pointed out certain weaknesses characterizing members of the Roman church, but now he is quick to compliment them on their virtues.

"I myself also am convinced that you yourselves are full of goodness" implies that he has seen trustworthy evidence of this by them. In this instance, Paul uses goodness as the quality they possess that constrains them from actions that will discourage the weak. **"… filled with all knowledge…"** In other words, he is expressing that they have an understanding of what God expects of them. 1 Corinthians 1:5: *"… that in everything you were enriched in Him, in all speech and all knowledge,"* The apostle concludes this verse with the statement that there exists in them a mutual openness to the counseling of one another.

Verse 15 But I have written very boldly to you on some points, so as to remind you again, because of the grace that was given me from God,

On the basis of his God-appointed office as an apostle, Paul feels he must write as he does. He tactfully points out that the design of his letter is not to introduce them to new doctrine, but rather to remind them of the truth they already possess. Paul has written, not because of any particular weaknesses on their part, but because of his special interest in them. Since he was an apostle to the Gentiles, he naturally had upon his heart a concern for the Christians who were living in Rome, the greatest imperial capital of the Gentile world.

Some Observations Regarding Verses 14 – 15

Paul, knowing that he was chosen by God to be His ambassador to the Gentiles as well as the Jews, felt a deep concern regarding the spiritual condition of those God had given him a responsibility for. Recognizing the importance of the testimony of Christians in Rome, it was his duty to warn them against potential spiritual weaknesses, yet a be quick to admire their spiritual strengths. To him, this was just Christian courtesy. Perhaps if we had more of that diplomacy displayed in the Church today, we would have a better image in the world.

Romans 15:16 -- 22
Paul Shares His Special
Calling to the Gentiles

Verse 16 to be a minister of Christ Jesus to the Gentiles, ministering as a priest the gospel of God, that my offering of the Gentiles might become acceptable, sanctified by the Holy Spirit.

In verses 16 – 19, Paul identifies the distinctive relationships and functions of the three persons of the Trinity.

In this verse, Paul reiterates the emphasis of his ministry: *"… to be a minister of Christ Jesus to the Gentiles…"* Acts 9:15: *"But the Lord said to him, 'Go, for he is a chosen instrument of Mine, to bear My name before the Gentiles and kings and the sons of Israel.'"*

"… ministering as a priest the gospel of God… " The purpose of the Levite priests in the temple was to insure that the sacrifices offered were acceptable to God (i.e., clean, without blemish etc.). Thus, Paul says he acts the part of a priest in this ministry to the Gentiles to insure *"that my offering of the Gentiles might become acceptable"* to God. There were some who maintained that Paul's converts were "unclean" because they were not circumcised. Paul's reply was that his converts were "clean" because the same Holy Spirit sanctified (i.e., made them acceptable to God) both the Jews and the Gentiles.

Verse 17 Therefore in Christ Jesus I have found reason for boasting in things pertaining to God.

Paul could rejoice in the success of his ministry to the Gentiles, because the same Holy Spirit sanctified and empowered both the Jews and Gentiles. This "boasting" was not about himself but because of this sanctification of both the Jews and Gentiles.

Verse 18 For I will not presume to speak of anything except what Christ has accomplished through me, resulting in the obedience of the Gentiles by word and deed,

The apostle affirms that he is merely an instrument in the hands of Christ. The "***Resulting in the obedience of the Gentiles by word and deed…*** " The Gentiles' evidential obedience "by word and deed" was evidence of their faith and acceptance of the gospel of grace. As a result Paul was convinced that Christ working through him.

Verse 19 *in the power of signs and wonders, in the power of the Spirit; so that from Jerusalem and round about as far as Illyricum I have fully preached the gospel of Christ.*

Signs and wonders refer to the same events, viewed from different aspects. "Signs" point to the evidence of God's power being displayed. "Wonders" produce awe and amazement in the minds of viewers. Both serve to authenticate the authority of the messenger and validate the truth of his message. These were necessary to establish the validity of Christ's messengers at a time before the written Word was available. John 4:48: *"Jesus therefore said to him, 'Unless you people see signs and wonders, you simply will not believe.'"* In spite of fierce opposition from some of the Jews and pagans, even they had to admit that Paul and his companions were, *in my words,* "turning the world upside down."

Paul again reminds his readers that the success of his ministry was because of the inward working of the Holy Spirit in the minds of those to whom he ministered. Paul stated in 1 Corinthians 2:4, *"And my message and my preaching were not in persuasive words of wisdom, but in demonstration of the Spirit and of power."*

Paul draws a great arc, reaching from Jerusalem to Illyricum, to mark the course of his travels and labors. In an age when travel was very difficult and slow, the area identified is amazing in its extent. Illyricum was on the eastern shore of the Adriatic, comprising roughly what is now Yugoslavia and Albania. In this wide circuit, the apostle preached and founded churches in a way that would leave no doubt that he was a divinely appointed minister of Christ.

Verse 20 *And thus I aspired to preach the gospel, not where Christ was already named, that I might not build upon another man's foundation;*

Paul considered himself a pioneering missionary. It was a point of honor with Paul not to preach the gospel where someone else had preached it before him. This reflected his desire to be a trailblazer for the gospel. 1 Corinthians 3:10: *"According to the grace of God which was given to me, as a wise master builder I laid a foundation, and another is building upon it. But let each man be careful how he builds upon it.*" Paul is also quick to recognize that the man who reaps the harvest is not always the one who sowed the seed.

Verse 21 but as it is written, *"They who had no news of Him shall see, And they who have not heard shall understand."*

Isaiah 52:15: *"Thus He will sprinkle many nations, Kings will shut their mouths on account of Him; For what had not been told them they will see, And what they had not heard they will understand."* Paul saw the prophecy of Isaiah 52:15 as being fulfilled in his day; and was being realized through him as "the apostle to the Gentiles." It was also because of this prophecy that Paul felt compelled Paul to preached where Christ was not previously known.

Verse 22 For this reason I have often been hindered from coming to you;

Because of Paul's to preach Christ where He had not been previously been known, he felt that it was not a priority yet to make a journey to Rome, where he knew the gospel had already been preached. For Paul, the demands of his ministry in support of Isaiah's prophecy had thus far kept him from fulfilling a desire to visit Rome.

Some Observations Regarding Verses 16 – 22

Paul took his calling to preach to the Gentiles seriously, and he wanted his readers to understand why he felt that way. He begins by pointing out to Jews that they needed to realize that the same Holy Spirit worked within both the Jews and the Gentiles. As a result, God had confirmed the validity of Paul's ministry by the many Gentile believers who were living lives in obedience to God because of Paul's preaching. As further confirmation of God's blessings on his ministry he had been a part of experiencing both signs and wonders. He goes on to say that because of the success of his ministry he had been reluctant to visit the Roman church earlier.

In today's world, the success of a minister is often defined by the size of the church he leads, rather than by the success of the production of people who are living in obedience to Christ. Paul clearly felt that the success of his ministry was the production of individuals living in obedience to God's will.

Romans 15:23 -- 29
Paul Shares His Future Plans

Verse 23 but now, with no further place for me in these regions, and since I have had for many years a longing to come to you

Here we see Paul's thinking regarding his motivations for writing this letter to the church in Rome. Paul felt that his pioneer work of evangelism in the regions where he had labored was complete. Paul decided it was time to visit Rome on his way to a new area of ministry.

Verse 24 whenever I go to Spain -- for I hope to see you in passing, and to be helped on my way there by you, when I have first enjoyed your company for a while --

Paul planned to minister in Spain next. In the course of this journey, he wanted to visit the Roman Christians. While in Rome, he hopes to receive help towards his proposed ministry to Spain. In other words, he hoped to receive an offering and encouragement from them in support of his planned ministry in Spain.

Did Paul ever get to Spain? In 2 Timothy 4:7, Paul states, *"I have fought a good fight, I have finished my course, I have kept the faith."* It is probable he would not have said that if he had not been to Spain because he specifically had mentioned Spain as his next destination. Also, extra-biblical writings from that time period seem to confirm his visit to Spain.

Verse 25 but now, I am going to Jerusalem serving the saints.

Beginning his journey to Rome and on to Spain, he wanted to visit Jerusalem first. It was probably in Paul's heart to help make up for his persecution of the believers in Jerusalem by bringing a gift from the churches where he had been ministering.

Verse 26 For Macedonia and Achaia have been pleased to make a contribution for the poor among the saints in Jerusalem.

The contribution was intended to reflect visible evidence of the loving concern of the believers in Asia for their Jewish fellow believers, who were currently suffering from a famine in Jerusalem. Paul hoped that this contribution, fro the Gentile churches in Asia, would result in mutual feelings of unity with their fellow Jewish believers in Jerusalem.

Verse 27 Yes, they were pleased to do so, and they are indebted to them. For if the Gentiles have shared in their spiritual things, they are indebted to minister to them also in material things.

The contribution had two purposes: First, as a love gift from the Gentiles (***they were pleased to do so***); and Secondly, as a felt spiritual obligation to help fellow believers in need (***they are indebted to them***). The Gentile Christians had received the gospel message of the works and words of Jesus, with the approval and support of the mother church in Jerusalem, and they felt an obligation to provide what material help they could to the needy members of the Jerusalem church. 1 Corinthians 9:11: *"If we sowed spiritual things in you, is it too much if we should reap material things from you?"* If Jewish Christians from Jerusalem had not preached the gospel to the Gentiles in Asia, the Gentiles would have continued in their lost condition.

Verse 28 Therefore, when I have finished this, and have put my seal on this fruit of theirs, I will go on by way of you to Spain.

"*This fruit of theirs*" reflects Paul's desire that the church in Jerusalem see this gift as tangible fruit from his missionary efforts among the Gentiles. Paul had a deep desire that this would encourage the uniting of the Jewish and Gentile believers into one body. As we will read later Paul was also concerned about whether the Jewish believers in Jerusalem would accept this gift in the right spirit. Finally, he reminds the recipients of this letter that, after he had delivered this gift, he would visit them on his way to Spain.

Verse 29 *And I know that when I come to you, I will come in the fullness of the blessing of Christ.*

Paul was convinced that God, who had blessed his labors, would also bless his visit to Rome with the same abundant blessings from Christ. Acts 19:21: *"Now after these things were finished, Paul purposed in the spirit to go to Jerusalem after he had passed through Macedonia and Achaia, saying, 'After I have been there, I must also see Rome.'"*

Some Observations Regarding Verses 23 – 29

In these verses, Paul identifies his plans for the future. He feels he has accomplished mission in his present area of ministry and plans to go to Spain next. Before he goes there, he wants to take an offering, from the churches he has established in Asia, to the "mother" church in Jerusalem. Israel is in the midst of severe drought and the people were desperate for help. Clearly, Paul had previously communicated his intent to the churches in Asia that he would be collecting an offering from them to take to the mother church in Jerusalem. Paul was also hoping that this offering would help bring the Jews and Gentiles into a closer spiritual unity. There were probably still many Jews resentful of Paul's sharing of "their" gospel to the Gentiles.

Finally, Paul gives the church in Rome notice that, after he delivers this gift, he will visit them and anticipates that they will provide him help and encouragement in his journey on to Spain.

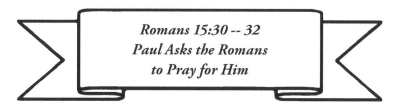

Romans 15:30 -- 32
Paul Asks the Romans
to Pray for Him

Verse 30 Now I urge you, brethren, by our Lord Jesus Christ and by the love of the Spirit, to strive together with me in your prayers to God for me,

Paul is conscious of his need of the prayers of his fellow believers. Paul knows that he is still the object of fierce hostility on the part of some of the believing Jews in Jerusalem, and that he will probably encounter hostility from them while he is in Judea and Jerusalem.

"… to strive together with me in your prayers to God for me… " The Greek word here translated "strive" is the same root word we use for the English word "agonize." Paul is literally saying, "Agonize with me." You and I need people who know how to agonize and pray for us!

Verse 31 that I may be delivered from those who are disobedient in Judea, and that my service for Jerusalem may prove acceptable to the saints;

Paul identifies those who may still oppose him and cannot accept the validity of his ministry to the Gentiles.

It would be a terrible blow to the unity of the "body of Christ" if the love-gift from the Gentile congregations were spurned or accepted ungratefully. What would your attitude be towards someone giving you a gift and saying it was fellow believers who you may have doubted as to the their being "fellow" believers? Paul knew all too well that, in spite of the decision of the Jerusalem Council, opposition to himself and his gospel of freedom in Christ never entirely ceased. All the time, Paul sincerely desired that the Christians in Jerusalem would accept the gift as an expression of love from fellow believers.

Verse 32 so that I may come to you in joy by the will of God and find refreshing rest in your company.

Paul clearly hoped that the response of the church in Jerusalem would be positive and allow him to arrive in Rome feeling that God had blessed his endeavors. Paul also seemed to look forward to his visit to Rome as a time of relief from conflict and labor. He looked upon Rome as a resting-place, rather than a field of labor, and hoped to gather strength for his apostolic labors in still more distant lands. The rest he hopes for is not that of leisure, but the spiritual encouragement this fellowship would impart.

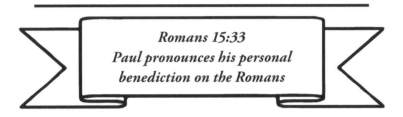

Romans 15:33
Paul pronounces his personal
benediction on the Romans

Verse 33 Now the God of peace be with you all. Amen.

The expression "the God of peace" literally means "the God who is the Author of peace." How wonderful and comforting it is to have peace with God!

Final Thoughts on Chapter 15

In this chapter, Paul reveals some of his innermost concerns and motivations. He began by explaining his view of a proper Christian lifestyle. He expresses that our actions must be motivated by our convictions, conscience, and a consideration of others, not centered on us. When we live for Christ, we must, at the same time, be willing to accept others we may perceive as not as "mature" as we are, and be willing to love them.

Paul next reminds the Jews that the same Holy Spirit sanctifies both the Jews and the gentiles. Paul shares his feelings that his ministry to the Gentiles called him to go to areas with the gospel where no man had gone before him. He explains that he feels he has accomplished his purpose in his area of ministry in Asia, and it is time to move on. He shares that his future plans involve beginning a ministry in Spain. He will visit the Christians in Rome on his way to Spain. He anticipates the church in Rome will support and encourage him in his plans to travel to Spain. However, first he plans to visit Jerusalem with a gift from the churches he started in Asia. He expresses concern about how the Christian Jews in Jerusalem might accept a gift from Gentile "*believers*" and asks for the prayers of the Roman Christians for a positive response of the Jewish believers in Jerusalem. He closes with a benediction upon his readers in Rome.

Chapter 16

Final Words of Encouragement to the Romans

Introduction:

In this chapter, we see the results of Paul's diplomacy. Paul sends his personal greetings to the friends he has met elsewhere in the course of his labors, and he salutes the leaders of the five groups in whose "houses" the church in Rome is currently meeting t for worship (see verses 5, 10, 14, 15). There are thirty-five persons mentioned in this chapter. This list of names gives an aspect of reality and deep human interest to the whole epistle. Paul sends greetings to twenty-six Christians in Rome, eight of whom are women, and only five or six are Jews (Aquila, Prisca, Andronicus, Junias, Herodian, and possibly Mary). The remaining nine persons were believers of Paul in Corinth who are now in Rome. A special feature in list is the prominence of women in the life of the Church in Paul's time. From the beginning, women had taken an active and important part in the promotion of the gospel.

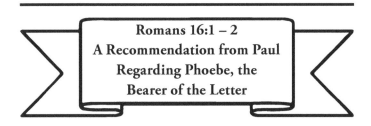

Romans 16:1 – 2
A Recommendation from Paul
Regarding Phoebe, the
Bearer of the Letter

Verse 1 I commend to you our sister Phoebe, who is a servant of the church which is at Cenchrea;

Letters of introduction were a necessity when a believer traveled from one community to another, in which they were unknown.

Phoebe, a Greek name, which means "bright or radiant," was a Gentile Christian. She apparently was the bearer of this epistle. Phoebe was very likely a deaconess in the church. (Remember, deacons were considered servants of the church.) This is the first time that the word "church" has occurred in Romans. Cenchrea was the eastern seaport of Corinth, nine miles east of that city.

Verse 2 that you receive her in the Lord in a manner worthy of the saints, and that you help her in whatever matter she may have need of you; for she herself has also been a

helper of many, and of myself as well.

The words "in the Lord" indicate Phoebe is to be received as a fellow believer. She was apparently traveling to Rome on some other matter. Her help could be construed in terms of both hospitality and finances. This suggests that she possessed some wealth and independence, as she had frequently aided others, including Paul himself. Therefore, it was reasonable for Paul to expect that she would be welcomed into the Christian fellowship in Rome.

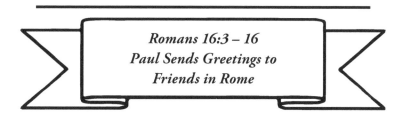

Romans 16:3 – 16
Paul Sends Greetings to
Friends in Rome

Verse 3 Greet Prisca and Aquila, my fellow workers in Christ Jesus,

Prisca (i.e., Priscilla) and Aquila were a Jewish couple. Aquila is a Latin name meaning "eagle." They were tentmakers, whom Paul first met in Corinth (see Acts 18:1 - 3). Acts 18:2: *"And he found a certain Jew named Aquila, a native of Pontus, having recently come from Italy with his wife Priscilla, because Claudius had commanded all the Jews to leave Rome. He came to them."* Paul made his home with them while in Corinth. They subsequently traveled with Paul to Ephesus (see Acts 18:18). When Paul left Ephesus for Jerusalem, they remained in Ephesus and helped lay the groundwork for Paul's subsequent ministry there (see Acts 18:19). There they were also used of God to guide the spiritual development of Apollos (see Acts 18:24-28). Priscilla and Aquila represent a fine example of Christian married life. Neither Luke, in Acts 18:2, 18, 26, nor Paul, in Romans 16:3, 1 Corinthians 16:19; and 2 Timothy 4:9, ever mentions one without mentioning the other. When we first meet them, it is "Aquila and Priscilla." Now, here, it is "Priscilla and Aquila."

Verse 4 who for my life risked their own necks, to whom not only do I give thanks, but also all the churches of the Gentiles;

Somewhere in their relationship with Paul, they had apparently risked their lives for him. It is possible that this was in Ephesus, when Paul was dragged before the crowd and then saved through the intervention of fellow believers. In any case, the reputation of Prisca and Aquila was so widespread that Paul included thanks from all the churches of the Gentiles. Now, apparently, they were back in Rome.

Verse 5 also greet the church that is in their house. Greet Epaenetus, my beloved, who is the first convert to Christ from Asia.

The most natural interpretation of the beginning of this verse is "the church which is accustomed to assemble in their house." . There is no decisive evidence, until the third century, of the existence of special buildings used for churches. According to 1 Corinthians 16:19, Prisca and Aquila were a couple whose house was apparently always at the disposal of the Lord, so it is not surprising to find that this was also true when they had returned to Rome. It is interesting to note that, in our present environment, the practice of "house" churches is again considered as a means of the successful propagation of the gospel.

"Greet Epaenetus, my beloved, who is the first convert to Christ from Asia." Epaenetus is a Greek name meaning "praised" or "praiseworthy." His name makes it likely he was a Gentile. Epaenetus, as Paul's first convert to Christ in Asia, must have occupied a special place in his heart. It is easy to imagine that, whenever he or any of his fellow workers looked back upon the success of Paul's ministry in and around the Roman provinces of Asia, they must have said, "And it all began with Epenetus; he was the first-fruit."

Verse 6 Greet Mary, who has worked hard for you.

Mary is a relatively common Jewish name (Miriam) meaning "rebelliousness." *"… has worked hard…"* suggests that Mary was an early member of the church at Rome, and she probably had an influential part in its establishment.

Verse 7 Greet Andronicus and Junias, my kinsmen, and my fellow prisoners, who are outstanding among the apostles, who also were in Christ before me.

It is apparent that these individuals were well known to the apostles for their faith and service.

Andronicus is a Greek name. Junias is a Roman name. Probably, Andronicus and Junia were husband and wife, or possibly sister and brother. *"My kinsmen…"* Since they were not Paul's kinsman in the physical sense, it is likely he felt a close spiritual family relationship with them. That Paul should include a woman among the apostles and describe her as outstanding is significant evidence (along with the importance he accords others in these verses) of the falsity of the notion that Paul had a low view of women.

These were fellow prisoners with Paul. This should be taken literally. *"… who also were in Christ before me."* Evidently, their conversion to the faith occurred in the early years of the history of the Church, possibly at Pentecost; at any rate, it was before Paul's conversion on the Damascus road. Quite possibly, their faithful testimony, while in prison with Paul, was the source of Paul's special feelings towards them.

Verse 8 Greet Ampliatus, my beloved in the Lord.

Ampliatus is Latin name meaning "elegant or polite" (from which we derive "urbane"). The use of "***my beloved***" would seem to indicate that he occupied a special place in Paul's heart.

Verse 9 Greet Urbanus, our fellow worker in Christ, and Stachys my beloved.

Urbanus was usually a name for a slave, and meant "city-bred." The name Urbanus was Roman and would suggest that he was a Roman who had worked together with Paul.

"… and Stachys, my beloved." Stachys is a Greek masculine name that literally means "ear of corn." Again the use of "***my beloved***" would seem to indicate that he also had a special spiritual relationship with Paul, whether it was because of shared experiences or their Christian testimony is unclear. However, Paul's making note of them in this way certainly indicates that he thought very highly of them.

Verse 10 Greet Apelles, the approved in Christ. Greet those who are of the household of Aristobulus.

Church tradition identifies Apelles as bishop of either Smyrna or Heracleia. Apelles had an uncommon recommendation as one who was "approved in Christ." To be approved in Christ would indicate that his life and testimony were considered to be pleasing to Christ. Consider James 1:12 for a picture of what it means to be "approved in Christ": "*Blessed is a man who perseveres under trial; for once he has been approved, he will receive the crown of life which the Lord has promised to those who love Him.*"

"Greet those who are of the household of Aristobulus." Aristobulus has been identified as the grandson of Herod the Great. Aristobulus apparently lived in Rome as a private person and was a friend of the Emperor Claudius. History indicates it is possible Aristobulus had died before this letter was written, in which case members of his household continued to meet together as Christians.

***Verse 11 Greet Herodion, my kinsman. Greet those of the household
of Narcissus, who are in the Lord.***

Herodian's name suggests that he was a Jew. It is probable that he was
part of the household of Aristobulus, and should have been part of the
previous verse.

"Greet those of the household of Narcissus, who are in the Lord."
Narcissus can mean one of three different things: A. a bulb plant with
smooth leaves in clusters of orange, white, and yellow; B. a mythological
youth who pined away for love of his own reflection in a spring; C. any
person characterized by excessive self-love. Some commentaries conclude
that this Narcissus was extremely wealthy and had unlimited influence
with Claudius, the Roman emperor, but had been forced to commit suicide
after that emperor's death. In any case, there were Christians among the
members of his household. Apparently, not all those who belonged to
the household were believers, as Paul sends his greetings to those of this
household who were "in the Lord."

***Verse 12 Greet Tryphaena and Tryphosa, workers in the Lord. Greet
Persis the beloved, who has worked hard in the Lord.***

Here three more women are greeted. The first and second, Tryphaena
and Tryphosa, possibly twin sisters, are names that mean "delicate or
dainty." The third, to judge from her name, was probably a slave or freed
woman. Persis literally means a lady from Persia. Again, notice the use
of "beloved." The distinction in tense Paul uses when talking about their
labors is interesting: Tryphena and Tryphosa were "workers in the Lord,"
while Persis "has worked in the Lord." Whatever the case, Paul takes care
that her past labors are not forgotten.

***Verse 13 Greet Rufus, a choice man in the Lord, also his mother and
mine.***

Rufus means "red." His father was most likely Simon the Cyrenian,
spoken about in Mark 15:21: *"And they pressed into service a passer-by coming
from the country, Simon of Cyrene (the father of Alexander and Rufus), to bear
His cross."* The book of Mark was thought to have been written in Rome.

Apparently, Rufus also carried a good reputation regarding his spiritual nature. Perhaps the use of the word "choice" indicates that he might even have been a pastor, a man chosen by God.

"*... also his mother and mine... *" Apparently, Rufus either was in contact with, or was possibly even taking care of, both his mother and Paul's. Another possibility was that Paul thought of Rufus' mother as his own. It is likely that by this time, Paul's mother had passed away.

Verse 14 Greet Asyncritus, Phlegon, Hermes, Patrobas, Hermas and the brethren with them.

This verse and the one that follows are apparently greetings to two different groups of Christians, meeting to worship together. Although nothing is known of these five men, their names suggest that they are slaves, and it is likely that they were the members of a Christian fellowship within some nobleman's house. The names listed in this verse and the brethren with them indicate a certain community of believers in a particular location or even vocation, all of the male sex. The expression "and the brethren with them" refers to the other members of the same house-church.

Verse 15 Greet Philologus and Julia, Nereus and his sister, and Olympas, and all the saints who are with them.

Philologus and Julia were probably a married couple and part of a large group of believers who met for worship in their home. Nereus, his sister, and Olympas were likely a part of the church meeting in the same house-church.

Verse 16 Greet one another with a holy kiss. All the churches of Christ greet you.

This salutation was expressive of mutual affection and equality before God. 1 Corinthians 16:20: *"All the brethren greet you. Greet one another with a holy kiss."* A "holy kiss" implies three parties: God, and the two people who are kissing. It betrays an unnecessary reserve, or loss of ardor, of the church's first love, when the holy kiss is conspicuous by its absence in the Church.

Some Observations Regarding Verses 3 – 16

Several things are interesting in this list of names. First, it seems to identify five house-churches in Rome. In verse five, there is one at the home of Prisca and Aquila. Then in verse ten, there seems to be one that involves the household of Aristobulus. Next, in verse eleven, there are those of the household of Narcissus. Next, in verse fourteen, five individuals are identified by name as meeting together, plus other fellow Christians not mentioned by name. Finally, in verse fifteen, Paul mentions five other individuals by name, as well as other fellow Christians, meeting together. These groupings are clearly intentional, and reflect people meeting together to worship. In that time, there were no "church buildings," as worship was held in private homes by small groups of individuals. The "Church," was understood to mean a Body of believers in Jesus Christ, not some building.

Second, of the twenty-six individuals that Paul specifically names, eight are women. Clearly, Paul felt the women were an important part of the early Church. Remember, this was at a time when much of the world, including the Romans, felt women were nothing more than chattel to be owned. They had few "rights," and even among the Jews were not counted as the equal of men. Finally, notice that of the twenty-six by names mentioned, only five or possibly six were Jews. Paul's ministry was focused on the Gentiles, and he made no excuses for it.

Romans 16:17 – 20
Paul's Warning to the "Church"

Verse 17 Now I urge you, brethren, keep your eye on those who cause dissensions and hindrances contrary to the teaching which you learned, and turn away from them.

Those whom Paul is referencing were probably outsiders, possibly traveling self-chosen teachers who were propagandists of error. There were probably two evils in the apostle's mind when he wrote this passage: the divisions occasioned by erroneous doctrines, and the dissensions caused by the immoral conduct of the false teachers. The Roman Christians were not only to mark such people, in the sense of recognizing them for the danger that they were, but they were also to avoid them, to keep out of their way. Paul does not say to oppose them, but to avoid them totally.

Verse 18 ***For such men are slaves, not of our Lord Christ but of their own appetites; and by their smooth and flattering speech they deceive the hearts of the unsuspecting. "For such men are slaves, not of our Lord Christ but of their own appetites;"***

The idea behind "***their own appetites***" denotes those who are the slaves of their own ego. A person zealous for doctrines that God has not commanded, often set more importance to their own messages than those of God. Philippians 3:19: *"… whose end is destruction, whose god is their appetite, and whose glory is in their shame, who set their minds on earthly things."* In some cases, the people were merely attempting to raise money for themselves. Paul also may be alluding to Judaizers, whose purpose was to enslave the Gentile believers to the Mosaic Law, such as their insistence that the Gentile believers must observance all of the Jewish traditions and food laws.

"***… by their smooth and flattering speech they deceive the hearts of the unsuspecting.***" The probability is that there were in the early Church, as in the Church today, people who cause divisions among their fellow believers, simply out of a desire to demonstrate their own self-importance. The word "unsuspecting" signifies not merely those who may be innocent, but also those who are susceptible to deception.

Verse 19 ***For the report of your obedience has reached to all; therefore I am rejoicing over you, but I want you to be wise in what is good, and innocent in what is evil.***

"For the report of your obedience has reached to all… " Paul does not want to insinuate that these false teachers had entered the church at Rome, but was concerned that that their spiritual development would not be affected by these teachings. Believers must be experts in discerning that which was "good" and avoiding that which was "evil." Today, sadly, some act offended by the doctrines of the true Church, while embracing false doctrines, they are proud of.

Verse 20 And the God of peace will soon crush Satan under your feet. The grace of our Lord Jesus be with you.

Remember, behind the work of those who cause divisions and false doctrines stands Satan, the father of lies. God's "peace" is not obtained through compromise or negotiation. Paul assures us in this verse is that God will crush Satan; He will crush him under the feet of the faithful, and He will do it speedily. Paul closes with a consolatory declaration that his readers always experience the grace of our Lord.

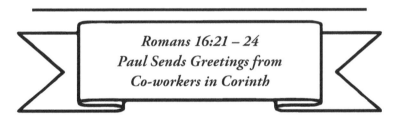

Romans 16:21 – 24
Paul Sends Greetings from
Co-workers in Corinth

Verse 21 Timothy my fellow worker greets you, and so do Lucius and Jason and Sosipater, my kinsmen.

Timothy was a fellow worker, but to Paul he was far more than that. Lucius, Jason, and Sosipater were fellow Jewish Christians whom Paul recognized would be known to the Roman believers.

Verse 22 I, Tertius, who write this letter, greet you in the Lord.

Tertius was Paul's *amanuensis* (his secretary). It is the Lord alone who knows how greatly indebted we, and the authors of the Bible, are to their faithful and competent Christian secretaries.

Verse 23 Gaius, host to me and to the whole church, greets you. Erastus, the city treasurer greets you, and Quartus, the brother.

"Gaius, host to me and to the whole church, greets you." Paul had himself baptized Gaius (see 1 Cor. 1:14). It was in his house that the church in Corinth was meeting.

"Erastus, the city treasurer greets you…" Erastus was the treasurer of the city. ***"… and Quartus, the brother."*** By "the brother" Paul simply meant a fellow Christian. Probably Quartus had acquaintances in Rome and, accordingly, asked Paul to include his greetings.

Verse 24 The grace of our Lord Jesus Christ be with you all. Amen.

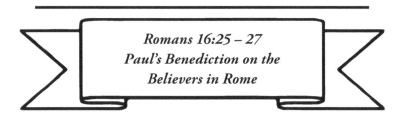

Romans 16:25 – 27
Paul's Benediction on the
Believers in Rome

Verse 25 Now to Him who is able to establish you according to my gospel and the preaching of Jesus Christ, according to the revelation of the mystery which has been kept secret for long ages past,

In these last few verses, Paul summarizes his view of the gospel, essentially repeating the opening verses of this epistle.

"Now to Him who is able to establish you according to my gospel and the preaching of Jesus Christ…" "To Him who is able" applies to God and the Holy Spirit. The gospel is essentially the preaching of Christ and His message. The word "mystery" in scripture does not mean something obscure or incomprehensible, but simply something previously unknown and undiscoverable by human reason, which can only be known by a revelation from God. In this sense, the gospel is called a mystery. The "mystery" here was that the Gentiles should be brought into full relationship with God on the same basis as the Jews. Paul says three things about this "mystery" here and in the following verse: A. … *which has been* *kept secret for long ages past...; B. ... now is manifested... C. ... has been made known to all the nations, leading to obedience of faith.*

Verse 26 **but now is manifested, and by the Scriptures of the prophets, according to the commandment of the eternal God, has been made known to all the nations, leading to obedience of faith;**

With the advent of Pentecost, it was revealed that the Scriptures became everyone's property. The features of this revelation are: 1. The Scriptures were to be made known to **all** nations; 2. The availability of salvation was available to **all** who accepted it through the obedience of faith. The message of the gospel, so long concealed yet partly revealed by the ancient prophets, was now, by the command of God, to be made known among all people.

Verse 27 **to the only wise God, through Jesus Christ, be the glory forever. Amen.**

The simplest construction of this verse is "To the only wise God, through Jesus Christ, to Him, I say, be glory forever." To God all reverence and submission is due.

Final Thoughts on Chapter 16

As we come to the end of Romans, it was time for Paul to say his farewells to his readers. But, as he does, he adds farewells of a personal nature to those in Rome.

He began the chapter by recommending the bearer of this letter to the believers in Rome.

He was concerned that they show her Christian hospitality as she had apparently shared with many in Corinth. He then sends personal greetings to all the people in Rome who had worked with him, as well as individuals whose reputation as Christians had come to his attention, and those whom he knew personally in Rome. He makes a special effort to greet several of the house-churches that he was aware of. This is a diplomatic side of Paul that is sometimes overlooked. He was always careful to encourage those he knew were in the service of the Lord. This is a characteristic that we would do well to emulate today.

Paul next warns them against those who cause dissention by preaching a different gospel. In Paul's experience, most of these were doing this for monetary gain or to satisfy their ego.

Paul ends this chapter by including greetings from those directly involved with helping him with his ministry in Corinth. Finally, he closes with a benediction that is also intended to show the natural progression of the gospel. First is the preaching of the words of Jesus Christ. Second is a proper understanding of the gospel (specifically that it reveals Christ and His offer of salvation to all mankind). Third, the gospel is for everyone. Finally, he says to his readers that it is their obedience to this gospel that is the true indicator of the depth of our faith.

Bibliography

BAXTER, J. Sidlow
"Explore The Book"
Zondervan Publishing House; Grand Rapids, Michigan; 1978

CRANFIELD, C. E. B.
"Romans A Shorter Commentary"
William B. Eerdman's Publishing Co.; Grand Rapids, Mich.; 1985

ERDMAN, Charles R.
"The Epistle of Paul to the Romans"
Baker Book House: Grand Rapids, Michigan; 1983

GAEBELEIN, Frank E.
"The Expositors Bible Commentary" - Volume 10
"Romans" - Everett F. Harrison
Zondervan Corp.; Grand Rapids, Michigan; 1976

HENDRIKSEN, William R.
"New Testament Commentary - Romans"
Baker Book House: Grand Rapids, Michigan; 1981

HODGE, Charles
"Commentary on the Epistle of Romans"
William B. Eerdmans Publishing Co.; Grand Rapids, Mich.; 1994

McGEE, J. Vernon
"Through The Bible With J. Vernon McGee"
Thomas Nelson Inc.; Nashville, Tennessee; 1983

MILLS, Stanford C.
"A Hebrew Christian Looks At Romans"
American Board of Missions to The Jews; New York, NY; 1971

MURRAY, John

"The Epistle To The Romans"

WM. B. Eerdmans Publishing Co.: Grand Rapids, Michigan; 1968

WILSON, Geoffrey Wilson

"Romans"

The Banner Of Truth Trust; Carlisle, Pennsylvania; 1984